ANDY GRAY, who began his professional career in 1973, is the only footballer to be named PFA Player and Young Player of the Year in the same season and was at one time the most expensive footballer in Britain. Having won almost every domestic honour, he joined Sky Sports in 1991 where, among other accolades, he has been named the Royal Television Society's Sports Presenter of the Year.

ANDY

GRAY MATTERS

GRAY

PAN BOOKS

First published 2004 by Macmillan

This edition published 2005 by Pan Books
an imprint of Pan Macmillan Ltd
Pan Macmillan, 20 New Wharf Road, London N1 9RR
Basingstoke and Oxford
Associated companies throughout the world
www.panmacmillan.com

ISBN 0 330 43199 4

Picture Credits
© Tony Duffy / Allsport – 12; © 2002 Getty Images – 33;
© Fiona Hanson / PA Photos – 32; © Paul Lewis / North West Counties Press – 22;
© Mirrorpix – 1, 4; © PA Photos – 10, 17; © Michael Stephens / PA Photos – 34;
© Bob Thomas – 5, 8, 9, 13, 14, 15, 16, 19, 23, 24, 25; © Terry Weir – 11

1 3 5 7 9 8 6 4 2

A CIP catalogue record for this book is available from
the British Library.

Typeset by SetSystems Ltd, Saffron Walden, Essex
Printed and bound in Great Britain by
Mackays of Chatham plc, Chatham, Kent

All Pan Macmillan titles are available from
www.panmacmillan.com
or from Bookpost by telephoning +44 (0)1624 677237

PREFACE

A little while ago my thirteen-year-old daughter Sophie came into my study. She stood for a moment looking at some of the photos and plaques that decorate the walls and asked, a little surprised, 'So were you a footballer then, Daddy?'

I had to smile. I'd retired from playing a few years before Sophie was born, so her question was understandable. It's one I get asked all the time by kids who know me only as Andy Gray off Sky. I told Sophie that yes, I had been a footballer. She said, 'What, like David Beckham?'

I said that I wasn't sure I was quite like David Beckham – I was never much good at taking free kicks and nobody ever offered me a modelling contract – but that I had played in many of the grounds he had and won some of the same things.

There were other similarities, too. The fact that I was transferred from a club whose manager felt that fame had gone to my head (it hadn't) and that I jeopardized my international career by getting sent off in a World Cup match for lashing out at an opponent (though I made considerably better contact with the chin of Anton Ondrus than Becks did with Diego Simeone's leg), but I thought I'd better keep those facts to myself.

What came to mind more, though, were the massive changes the game has gone through since I'd travelled up on the train from Glasgow as a nervous seventeen-year-old to sign schoolboy forms with Dundee United.

In the three decades since then I've seen football transformed dramatically. Rule changes such as the abolition of the tackle from behind and the pass back to the goalkeeper have made the game faster and far less physical. The Premiership arrived along with the Champions' League. Foreign players and coaches, once unheard of in England unless they were Scots, Welsh or Irish, have become fixtures of the domestic game. Money from Sky television has flooded in. I've seen ramshackle grounds that hadn't altered for half a century quickly turned into state-of-the-art stadiums and players assume the wealth and lifestyles of film stars. And I've been lucky enough to see it all happening from the inside.

As a centre forward with Dundee United, Aston Villa, Wolverhampton Wanderers, Everton, West Bromwich Albion and Glasgow Rangers I experienced most of the ups and quite a few of the downs football has to offer. At twenty-one I became the only lad in history to be voted PFA Young Player of the Year and Player of the Year in the same season and for a while when I was twenty-four I was Britain's most expensive footballer. I even came within a whisker of signing for Manchester United.

I've turned out alongside some of the best players, and at least one of the oddest, served some of the greatest managers and a few of the worst. I won League championships in England and Scotland, domestic and European cups and international caps, and got to wear the jersey of my boyhood idols. I almost became the first British player to move to Europe for over a decade and very nearly ended up as manager of Everton. I also suffered a career-threatening knee injury, signed for a club that went bankrupt and, when my playing days ended, faced what, for a while, looked a bleak and uncertain future.

In the summer of 1989 I was sitting at home and starting to wonder if another job offer would ever come my way when the telephone rang. It was the head of sport at a new satellite broadcasting company. He assured me cheerfully that so far they had no football, no studios and no viewers. Would I like to join them as a commentator? How could I say no?

Since then I've enjoyed a second career in the game and come to be a familiar face to a generation who never saw me play. I've enjoyed the camaraderie and teamwork that goes into putting together Sky's football coverage and got to know the current generation of star players. I've watched over a thousand live matches and hundreds more on television, but I've never ever lost my enthusiasm for the game that's been my livelihood since I gave up my milk round in Drumchapel in 1973.

Like David Beckham? I'll let you decide.

ANDY GRAY

When Jim McLean told you to sit down you didn't look around for the chair. The Dundee United manager wasn't anybody's idea of a hard man. He was five feet five inches tall, slightly overweight and had been balding from an early age. But there was a fierce intensity about him. At home he was one of the kindest and most mild-mannered people you could meet, but when it came to football he suffered a total character transformation. He became an ogre. I've seen him reduce hardened pros to tears at half-time with the kind of harangue that would leave the paint peeling off the walls.

For all of that I had huge respect for Jim, a manager who transformed his club in much the same way Brian Clough and Don Revie did theirs. The fact is that his ferocious attitude stemmed from one thing – his desire to be the best. I shared that desire and I believe Jim knew it.

Certainly he must have seen something in me because my first game in front of him was nothing short of a disaster. On the recommendation of a scout, Maurice Friel, who'd been watching me play for the juvenile side Clydebank Strollers, I'd been called up to Tannadice for a trial in December 1972, a few weeks after my seventeenth birthday.

Nowadays a promising youngster would have been picked up at fourteen and played his way up through a club's youth academy system. He'd have got used to the feel of the place before the selection process turned serious. Back then, though, things were a lot more haphazard. It was a case of plunging in and seeing if you'd sink or swim.

That resulted in some bizarre incidents. My Sky colleague Alan Shearer, for example, had been a ball boy at St James' Park. Al desperately wanted to play for Newcastle. But at his trial for United the future England centre forward was stuck in goal the entire time. Sure enough he failed to impress and ended up at Southampton instead. Eventually Newcastle had to pay £15 million to get him back.

I wasn't put between the sticks at Tannadice, but I might as well have been. Having travelled up alone and nervous on the train from Glasgow, I took a taxi to the ground and straightaway found myself pitched into a full-blooded game between the reserves and the first team. With only schools and juvenile league experience I was way out of my depth. Any thoughts I had of creating a big impression quickly went out of the window. As the game flashed by around me my only hope after the first few minutes was that somehow I'd disappear. Jim would later tell me that he could sum up my performance in one word, 'pathetic'.

I went back to Glasgow sure that any chance I had in the professional game had gone. I still loved football, though, and I went on turning out in schools matches and for the Strollers. I kept finding the net, too. And luckily Maurice Friel kept on watching me and sending positive reports back to Jim McLean.

In the New Year of 1973 I was chosen to play for the Scottish Professional Youth side. All the other players came from top clubs like Rangers, Celtic and Hibernian. For a player to be picked from a tiny little club such as Clydebank Strollers was almost unheard of. The match was against England at Clyde's Shawfield Stadium. I went off to the game on the number nine bus with my Strollers' kit bag over my shoulder. We won 3–2. I scored two of the goals and created the other. The next day one of the newspapers reported the game under the headline 'It's a Gray Night for England'. It was the first time the sub-editors had made a pun on my surname. Believe me it would not be the last.

A short while later I found myself travelling up to Dundee again. The performance against the Old Enemy had persuaded Jim McLean that I was worth another look. This time I was more confident. In the game that followed I got a goal and did enough to convince the boss to offer me schoolboy terms with a view to turning professional at the start of the following season.

Player's contracts are complex things, as we've seen over the past few years with the protracted negotiations of Patrick Vieira, Roy Keane and Michael Owen. Top agents safeguarded those boys' interests, and I was fortunate that day to have my own representative in the shape of my older brother Willie. Willie had insisted on accompanying me to Dundee, where he promised to 'look after you, kid and make sure you get a fair deal'. As it turned out he was more Eric Morecambe than Eric Hall.

Jim McLean offered me a signing on fee of £20 and £16 a week, of which £6 would go on paying for my accommodation. He then left us alone in his office to consider the deal. Personally I wasn't so sure about it. I'd read all sorts of stories in the papers about the signing on fees paid by other clubs and this didn't sound so great. Did Willie think £20 was enough? My brother mulled it over, 'Aye,' he said, after a few seconds, 'It seems fair enough. It'll be a tenner for you and a tenner for me.'

Willie might not have known much about sell-on clauses or image rights, but he'd mastered one aspect of the agent's job – calculating his commission – right enough.

When I arrived in Dundee to begin my new life as a professional footballer I was under no romantic illusions. My first trial had shown me the massive gap that existed between the level of football I was used to and the professional game. As I lay on my bed in my new digs in the suburb of Broughty Ferry I set myself a deadline – I'd work as hard as I could and if I hadn't become a first-team player by the age of twenty-one I'd pack in football altogether.

Up until then I'd never considered any other career. I'd wanted to be a footballer all my life. But I'd done OK at school. I wasn't a dunce. I'd got seven O-levels. I decided that if Dundee United didn't work out I'd emigrate to Canada like my brother James had done and get a job working with a new piece of hi-tech machinery called the computer.

Whether I'd have become another Bill Gates we'll never know, because my football career took off faster than I could ever have imagined. Much of the credit for that must go to Jim McLean.

As I've said, Jim wasn't an easy man. He was permanently on his guard, wary of everyone. He drove himself hard and he drove his players hard. He was uncompromising in his pursuit of success and he expected everyone involved with the club to be the same. Jim couldn't bear the thought of being short-changed either financially or in terms of effort. If he thought anybody was putting one over on him in the office or on the training ground he would be furious.

It's reported that Jim once took Duncan Ferguson – who like me led the line at Tannadice – to one side and told him 'I know I care too much about football, son, but the trouble is you care eff all.' If that's true, then for Jim that would have been the worst insult he could think of. To not care about football – to him that was sacrilegious.

It wasn't an accusation that could be levelled at me and Jim knew it. For every other player at the club training ended at midday with a hot bath. Meanwhile I was called back in at one o'clock for extra work. At Tannadice on most afternoons you'd find Jim and me practising headers and shots at goal in front of the empty terraces. Jim would hammer in crosses, hit through balls, work on my control. He would have me take high clearances on the chest and turn to the right, on the thigh and spin to the left. We'd spend a lot of time on my movement, too – Jim, who'd been a decent footballer in his day, explaining how if you want the ball on your right side you should move to the left first, then back to the right to shake off the defender.

It was Jim who taught me the value of having a picture in your head – to look up when you don't have the ball and make a mental note of where your teammates are, so that you can find them with a first-time pass as soon as you receive it. Jim saw that as the basis for the kind of instinctive, fast-flowing football he liked his teams to play. Years later at Everton I'd use it whenever we had a throw-in on the right. I'd stand with my stronger side to the touchline and my back to goal and when I received the ball instantly hook it over my left shoulder to the opposite wing, where I knew Kevin Sheedy was waiting.

Hour after hour, day after day, week after week for a year

and a half we did that. At first I thought Jim was picking on me, forcing me to do overtime when my mates lounged around town. Later I came to see that the reason Jim put me through it was because he had seen something in me, an appetite for the game that came close to matching his own, a willingness to graft to make myself a better player. The extra training wasn't a criticism or a punishment – it was a reward.

I wasn't a skilful player, but the hard work Jim put in undoubtedly made me a better one. As a result of it I was able to earn a good living from the game. I'm grateful for that. Of course, you could argue that it benefited the manager, too, because it made me a more valuable asset to the club. But I honestly don't believe Jim did it for the advantage of himself or of Dundee United. He did it simply because making footballers into better players was what he loved doing.

Later, at Aston Villa, I was lucky enough to find another guy as dedicated as Jim, Ron Saunders' assistant Roy McLaren. I spent nearly every afternoon working with Roy practising my ball control and concentrating on my weaker right foot. Football isn't just about talent. It's about willingness to learn and working hard at perfecting what you've learned. Not all players are prepared to do that. Some are happy to coast.

When I was coaching at Villa myself I remember a kid there who was very quick, but awkward in the way he collected the ball. I got him to stay behind a few times to help iron out his problems, but I could tell he wasn't really bothered. He was only there because I'd told him to be. One day I said, 'I tell you what, son. If you don't feel like doing extra work you don't have to.' He never stayed behind again. His name was Bryan Small. Ever heard of him? No, I thought not. Believe me, the great players are always the first ones on the training field and the last ones off it.

When I arrived at Tannadice the process of building Dundee United into a team that would one day take on the cream of Europe, and beat them more often than not, too, had just begun. Dundee United were still overshadowed by their neighbours at Dens Park, Dundee. The clubs are literally neighbours, too. The grounds stand practically next to one another. Dundee had won the Scottish league title in 1962 and produced players like Ian Ure, Charlie Cooke and Alan Gilzean. But even though they'd won the League Cup the year following my arrival, it was plain the balance of power was shifting. Jim was assembling a powerful squad that over the next few seasons would come to include Iain McDonald, Paul Sturrock, Paul Hegarty and Dave Narey, scorer of that incredible goal for Scotland against Brazil in the World Cup of 1982.

Apart from those star names there were a lot of good senior pros at the club, men like the centre back Dougie Smith, Pat Gardner and Jacky Copland. Hamish McAlpine, the goalkeeper, also deserves a mention. Hamish was a wonderfully accurate striker of goal kicks and generally had fantastic distribution, easily the best of any keeper I've played with. It's part of goalkeeping that's often ignored and while it's not as important as shot stopping, a keeper who can pick out teammates with his kicks and throws is a real bonus. Just look at how many successful Manchester United counter-attacks started with Peter Schmeichel bowling the ball out.

Walter Smith, who I'd later work under at Rangers, was another teammate. So was Archie Knox, who went on to be Fergie's assistant at Old Trafford. Walter was a jobbing midfielder who was sometimes drafted in to partner me up front. He was a decent footballer, a bit one-paced, but an absolute champion at head tennis. He would have played head tennis in the gym until he'd worn his skin away. I've been flabbergasted that some of the people I played alongside have gone into coaching. Walter wasn't one of those. He was always thoughtful about the game.

The other player who had a big influence was Pat Gardner. Pat was a classy front man. He was coming to the end of his career, but he still had all the moves and just watching him at work was an education.

As a player you learn a lot from watching others. You see a guy do a little trick or piece of business and you go away and work out how he does it, then practise it yourself on the training ground. I'm not just talking about the obvious things here like ball skills, but less noticeable ones such as the angle certain players take up to receive the ball and the way that allows them to move it on. If you watch Zinedine Zidane you get a masterclass in that. The guy is just superb when it comes to letting the ball do the work for him.

My earliest hero was Rangers' Colin Stein. Colin was a robust no-frills centre forward who lead the line superbly. That was my own style and I copied a lot from the Ibrox number nine. Another player I admired when my own professional career was beginning was the German forward Gerd Muller, who I'd seen on TV during the 1970 World Cup. For a man of his height Muller had incredible power in the air – an inspiration to me because I'm not the tallest. The Bayern Munich star was a past master at finding space in a crowded area and I also took on board the way he manoeuvred his body so that whatever position he was in when he received the ball he could always work a shot on goal.

I learned a lot from men like Pat Gardner and Jackie Copland. Not just about how to play the game but how to look after myself. That was important because when you signed for a club as a teenager in those days you were put into digs and pretty much left to fend for yourself. There's no wonder some youngsters – George Best and Graeme Souness amongst them – got homesick and made a run for it. The only time you got what you might call guidance from your employers was if you got into trouble with the police.

The senior pros at Tannadice helped me a lot with coming to terms with my new life. These were guys who knew the importance of training hard, of getting enough sleep before matches. Admittedly not everything they did would have met with the approval of today's managers. The favourite pre-match meal was still steak and chips, for instance, and pay night on Thursdays generally lasted until the early hours of Friday morning. Then again the game wasn't quite as fast as it is now and there weren't the same demands on us. We could allow ourselves a few beers.

I'd only been at the club for a few weeks and played just four games, three for the reserves and one in a practice game at an army camp, when I was moved up to train with the first team. I got my first goal coming off the bench in a 5–2 win over East Fife. Andy Rolland – always known as 'the Major' for reasons I never discovered – whipped in the cross from about forty yards out and I met it on the edge of the penalty box. It was a long way from goal but I got such good contact that my header went into the top corner like a bullet.

A few weeks later I made my first start against Dumbarton and got the winning goal in a 2–1 win. Just after Christmas I scored four in a 6–0 gubbing of the same opposition. It should have been five. We got a penalty late on and the rest of the lads insisted I take it. I slid it past the left-hand post. I never liked taking spot kicks.

My performances hadn't gone unnoticed. Already there was talk of Willie Ormond calling me up to the Scotland squad for the 1974 World Cup finals. I found myself compared with everyone from Tommy Lawton to Scots legend Willie Bauld, and the newspapers were full of rumours about a big money transfer to England. According to the press Newcastle, Spurs, Liverpool and Leeds were watching me, and the *Scottish Daily Express* reported that Everton had made United an offer of £150,000 to take me to Goodison Park. All this came just a few weeks after my eighteenth birthday.

Over the past decade the way young players are handled has altered dramatically. At Old Trafford Alex Ferguson has shielded his junior stars from the media and David Moyes has taken a similar approach with Wayne Rooney at Everton.

David has made a point of resting Rooney from time to time for fear that he might suffer injuries from playing too often. I'm not sure about that. I often wonder if Wayne's disciplinary record doesn't stem in part from frustration because he's not getting on the field as often as he'd like. He's sitting on the bench and all that emotion is building up in him. Then he gets on for twenty minutes and it comes boiling out. I know when I was his age the only thing I wanted to do was play football. Even an old bruiser like Jim McLean would have struggled to stop me.

My game was all about energy and physical commitment. I

was brave, sometimes foolishly so. My Everton teammate Kevin Ratcliffe would later claim that my true vocation in life was as a kamikaze pilot. As a result I know there was an opinion around at the time that I wouldn't be able to sustain it, that I'd self-destruct. When I moved to England I recall the manager of Norwich City at the time, John Bond, saying, 'There's no need for other teams to worry about Andy Gray. The kid will burn himself out in eighteen months.' I wasn't listening. I was still a teenager and I thought I was invincible.

One morning in a practice match I discovered how wrong I was about that. The injury had nothing to do with tiredness, though. I simply went into a challenge on another young player, a big mate of mine Allan Forsyth, and suddenly felt my right knee give way. I didn't know what was wrong and for a few days tried to run it off, but the team doctor had no doubt – I had a serious cartilage problem and needed surgery.

An operation on the knee was something all players in those days feared. The techniques of keyhole surgery hadn't yet been developed and to reach the cartilage the surgeon had to make a six–inch incision around the knee, lift up the kneecap and prod around in the joint. It was crude stuff and it had ended hundreds of careers down the years. I was paralysed with worry. I'd never so much as missed two games back to back and now I was looking at hospital and wondering if I'd ever play again.

Fortunately the operation went off without any problems and incredibly within three weeks I was back in training. Admittedly I wasn't capable of doing much more than hobbling around the touchline, but that didn't stop Jim McLean yelling at me.

If the extra training had been the positive side of the

manager's obsession with the game his attitude now was the negative aspect. Jim was desperate to get me fit in time for the quarter-final of the Scottish Cup, when we were due to play Dunfermline Athletic. His view was that seeing my name on the team sheet would give us a psychological advantage over our opponents.

On the Friday before the game Jim called me aside after training. 'How is it?' he asked. I said, 'Well, to be honest, boss, it's pretty sore.'

It wasn't the answer the manager was looking for. 'Do you want to effing play Dunfermline?' he bellowed.

'Aye, I do, but . . .'

'But nothing. Do you want to effing play tomorrow, or not?'

I told him I did but that I was worried about the long-term effect on my knee. 'Right,' Jim snarled, 'You wait here.' And off he stormed.

Ten minutes later back he came, still fuming, 'The medical staff tell me it will do you no lasting harm if you play tomorrow,' he barked. 'So can I take it you will?'

So I played. My knee was still so sore I could barely put any weight on it without wincing, but we won 4–0.

In the semi-finals we beat Hearts 4–2 in a replay with me scoring with one of the best goals of my career, bringing the ball down with my thigh twenty yards out and volleying it into the net.

Unfortunately the final against a Celtic side that included Kenny Dalglish, Jimmy Johnstone and Billy McNeill proved a massive disappointment. McLean's ploy of bringing me back early against Dunfermline had worked brilliantly, but in this game he decided to tamper with our tactics. Jim felt that Billy

McNeill, the Celtic captain and centre back, would know too much for me and keep me out of the game. To stop that from happening I would start on the left wing and drift into the middle, evading McNeill's attentions.

Celtic's manager that day, Jock Stein, once said that football is a simple game: you need eleven men, one who can catch, four who can tackle, four who can pass and two who can score. I agree with that. No matter what some coaches might like you to believe football isn't rocket science. The successful teams are usually those that *don't* change things. They just play their way and let the opposition worry about it. You see that today with Manchester United and Arsenal. And it seems to me that the current Real Madrid side's only tactic is to score more goals than their opponents. Sometimes when you watch them it's hard even to tell what formation they are playing. Everyone knows how these teams are going to play. Stopping them doing it is another matter.

Jim McLean was usually pretty much of the same opinion. In fact, I'd have to say this was the first and only time he made a tactical switch while I was with him. It proved a total waste of thought and effort. We were 2–0 down at half-time and I hardly touched the ball.

I was pushed back into my usual position in the centre for the second period. The move might have, should have, paid off. About ten minutes in the ball was crossed over from the left and I met it six yards out with a great header. Since then I've watched the incident dozens of times on TV and I still can't figure out how Dennis Connaghan in the Celtic goal saved it. But he did and we ended up going down 3–0.

I collected my losers' medal with the rest of the boys, but in the dressing room I tossed it into the corner and left it there.

I only have it today because the kit man found it and gave it back to me.

Coming second didn't interest me then and it still doesn't. If we lost on Saturday all social engagements that night were cancelled. Whatever I do I want to be the best at it – whether it's football, golf, snooker or TV presenting. I'm not sure where that competitive streak comes from, but it's a fact that I can't even play tiddlywinks without wanting to win.

I think all top sportspeople have that attitude. It's the old 'show me a good loser and I'll show you a loser' thing. People might point to somebody like Jack Nicklaus and say that he is a man who, whether he won or lost, always behaved like a gentleman. But to me that's different. Just because losing hurts doesn't mean you can't be magnanimous in defeat. Nicklaus is one of the sportsmen I really admire. I think if you look at sporting legends he's right up there with Muhammad Ali.

In respect of the way he prepared for tournaments, the practice he put in, Jack changed the face of golf. People say that Tiger Woods will beat Nicklaus' records but I don't think he will. Eighteen majors takes a bit of doing. He won his last, the Masters, at forty-six, so he was at the top of his profession for twenty years. That's amazing and believe me you don't achieve a fraction of what Jack did in a sport as difficult as golf unless you are a real competitor.

Where my own attitude had come from I can't say, but I remember the first time I noticed it – at Lochgoin Primary School in Glasgow. Our school team was coached by one of the women teachers, Mrs McArthur, and we battled our way to the final of the Glasgow Cup, a competition entered by hundreds of local schools. We won it 1–0 with a scruffy goal. I can't recall much about the match or what the trophy looked like, but I remember how good winning it felt. And that feeling became my motivation. During my playing days you couldn't make millions from the game. That never bothered me. Winning things was always more important to me than money. When I retired I knew I wanted to be able to look at my medals not my bank balance. I know it's easy for somebody to say that, but I can prove it, too.

Shortly after our defeat by Celtic the first team contracts came up for renewal. In those days players didn't negotiate individually like they would now. It was a blanket contract for the whole of the first team. Everybody got the same money regardless of whether they were a star or not.

I was the club's top goal scorer and I'd been voted United's Player of the Year. I was Dundee United's most valuable asset and the other players felt I'd have more leverage with Jim McLean than anybody else. So they told me to go in and sort out a bigger salary for us all. 'This is what we want, Andy. You go and wheedle it out of him,' they said.

Jim, as I've noted, was constantly watching out for people fiddling him over cash. He was paranoid about it. Any sort of pay talks invariably ended in blows. So I went into his office quaking with terror. 'What do you want?' Jim snapped.

'I've come to see about the playing contract, Boss,' I said, trying to keep the squeak out of my voice.

'Here it is,' Jim said, handing me a document. By now I was so nervous I snatched it off him and signed it straightaway without even looking at it.

'What the hell do you think you're up to?' Jim barked when he saw what I was doing, 'I haven't filled in the figures yet.'

'Oh, that's all right, Boss,' I replied, 'You put in whatever you think we deserve,' and I legged it straight out of the door.

The other lads were waiting for me outside. 'That was quick,' they said, 'Did it go OK? What did you get for us?'

'To be honest,' I replied, 'I don't know.'

'What do you mean, you don't know?'

'Well . . .'

I don't think my teammates were too impressed. And I guess it's why I'm not head of the PFA. Still, it makes my point. After all, you don't sign a blank contract if it's money you're after, do you?

My second season at Tannadice was even better than the first. United rarely dropped out of the top four and we won a place in Europe. My own form was exceptional. I hit twenty-six goals in forty-two matches and I was called up for the Scotland U-23 side to play upfront alongside the legendary Motherwell striker Willie Pettigrew.

At Dundee I was a young star in a small town, but I can't say I ever felt any pressure. Life for players today is very different from the way it was back then. With United I was earning around £2,500 a year, whereas Wayne Rooney is picking up that sort of cash practically every day. Sums of money like that bring complications. A lot of them are good ones, admittedly, but not all of them. Wayne lives in the media spotlight in the way I never did. Even though I was grabbing the headlines on Tayside I could still live a normal ordinary life. Not that it always worked out best that way.

One Wednesday night me and a few of the boys went out for the evening and ended up at Tiffany's nightclub in the city centre. I was in the gents washing my hands when a group of three or four blokes – Dundee supporters clearly – walked in and without warning waded into me. They gave me a right hiding, but after they'd left I staggered back into the club, rounded up my pals and went after them. This time I ended up getting a pint pot smashed over my head. With blood gushing from a cut I ended my evening having stitches in the local accident and emergency.

Jim McLean was not a happy man. Luckily I succeeded in persuading him that none of it was my fault. After that Jim's main concern was that no one should find out about the incident. Clearly if I was left out of the team there was a chance that local reporters would start asking why and the story would get around. As a consequence, stitches or not, I played on the Saturday and nobody was any the wiser. I don't think there'd be much chance of that these days.

Midway through that second season Jim came to me and said that Nottingham Forest had offered £75,000 for me but that United had turned them down. I had just finished top scorer in the Scottish First Division and been voted United's Player of the Season for the second year running and my departure was now pretty much inevitable, but the club were holding out for a bigger fee. Jim was realistic. He knew that United, with small attendances, were a selling club and the tradition in those days was that Scottish players who were talented – even those at the Old Firm – eventually ended up in England.

There was another aspect to it as well. In the summer of 1975 as we prepared for the new season Jim took me aside, 'I'm going to have to sell you this season, son,' he said, 'If I don't I'm going to hold you back.' A lot of people will maybe think that he was just saying that to soften me up. But I genuinely believe he meant it.

After I'd moved south, Jim lifted Dundee United to the heights. They won the Scottish title in 1983 and reached the semi-final of the Champions' Cup the following year, losing out narrowly to Italian giants Roma in a game quite a few people suspect might not have been entirely straight. On top of that there were two Scottish League Cups and an appearance in the final of the UEFA Cup in 1987. It was an incredible record for a provincial Scottish club with average home gates that rarely rose above the 15,000 mark.

The other remarkable thing is that McLean's teams had been built almost entirely out of raw talent discovered by the manager. It's an achievement that would be very, very hard to replicate today. One of the saddest things, to me – and I'd guess a lot of football fans would agree with this – is that teams made up in the main of local lads who cared passionately for the club and the town or the area it represented have, to some extent, become a thing of the past. In the age of cheap foreign imports and high wages, the idea that a team like Dundee United could gather together a group of kids and a few older pros and over time forge them into a side good enough to win the Scottish title is almost impossible to believe. And the same applies in England, too.

But Jim did it back then and there's little wonder that for a time he was ranked alongside another up-and-coming provincial Scottish manager, Aberdeen's Alex Ferguson, as one of the best in Britain.

Jim has a lot of similarities to Alex. They both have short fuses and they share a habit of doing the unexpected, which keeps players on their toes. There's a famous bit of footage of Fergie being interviewed after Aberdeen had won the Scottish Cup and instead of celebrating he launches into this furious tirade about how badly the team played and how they have let down the club and its supporters. Jim was always likely to act that way, too. You'd come off the pitch at the end of the game feeling pretty pleased with yourself and seconds later you'd be pinned up against the dressing-room wall with the boss yelling in your face about what a disgrace you were.

Not surprisingly given their records in Scotland, both Alex and Jim were linked with moves to larger, more prestigious clubs. But while Fergie always seemed to have his eye on the bigger prize, Jim seemed content to stay where he was.

Sadly it all turned sour and the boss's belligerence ended up landing him in big trouble. The notorious incident with BBC reporter John Barnes occurred in the autumn of 2000. I wasn't there, but knowing Jim as I do I could understand how it happened. By now he'd bought up a 40 per cent holding in United and was chairman of the club.

Dundee United were going through a rocky patch. They'd had three poor seasons on the bounce. There'd been protests from fans eager to see the back of McLean and his brother Tommy. After United had lost 4–0 at home to Hearts, taking their points tally for the season to two out of a possible thirty-three, about four hundred supporters demonstrated outside the ground calling for Jim to resign.

At this point Jim was interviewed by Barnes. The BBC man persisted in questioning him about the future of manager Alex Smith despite the fact that Jim had asked him not to. Now, the way Jim McLean is, if he tells you not to do something and you do it he's going to see that as a challenge. And if you challenge Jim he is only going to react one way. Which is precisely what he did. He subjected Barnes to a torrent of abuse that must have given the BBC censor cramp in his bleeper finger and then allegedly assaulted the reporter off camera.

That was typical Jim. A lot of people have no time for the

man. In many ways I can see why. He was demanding, awkward, irascible and suspicious. But he was also knowledgeable, dedicated, generous with his time and never asked anybody to do anything he wasn't prepared to do himself. The fact is that I owe Jim McLean a massive debt and so do dozens of other players he worked with at Tannadice.

David Beckham's move to Real Madrid was one of the biggest stories British football has known. David is a world-class player. He's a leader, a worker, a great crosser of the ball, and he has tremendous determination. Leaving United was a huge risk. I admire him for taking it. Because if David wants to improve as a player there can certainly be no better place to be than the Santiago Bernabeu. Watching Zinedine Zidane, Raul and Ronaldo in training will be the best education he can get.

David's chance to play abroad came when he was twenty-seven years old and at his peak. The offers I received weren't so well timed.

In September 1974 I'd returned from a UEFA Cup tie in Iceland with Dundee United. Mrs McAlman, my landlady, told me that while I'd been away a Mr Neef had been trying to get in touch with me. It turned out to be Gerry Neef, a former goalkeeper with Glasgow Rangers. When I phoned him Gerry told me that he was scouting for the West German side Schalke 04. On his recommendation the club from Gelsenkirchen were prepared to make an offer of up to £150,000 for me.

At that time British players, with the notable exception of the Welshman John Charles, had not fared that well on the

Continent. Denis Law was the idol of practically every Scottish football fan of my generation. Everywhere that kids played you'd find at least one running about with his shirt cuffs held in his fist in imitation of the great man. My own early goal celebrations were copied from those of Denis.

Yet the Law's £100,000 move from Huddersfield Town to Torino in Italy had been a disaster. Denis had found it impossible to cope with the intense media scrutiny that came with being a star abroad and the monastic existence of the Italian pro. Denis and his teammate, the England centre forward Joe Baker, ended up getting into a series of silly incidents that culminated in a fight with a paparazzo and the totalling of an Alfa Romeo.

Another British goal scorer, Jimmy Greaves, did well on the field for Milan, but likened his life in Italy to being locked in a prison cell and came back the first chance he got. That had all gone on in the early 1960s. Since then no British players had moved anywhere abroad apart from the North American Soccer League.

I was thinking about my future, though. I was hoping for a move to England. That was where I saw my career progressing. Top clubs south of the border were said to be tracking me but, as yet, apart from Forest no firm offer had been made. And so I agreed to meet Gerry Neef along with Schalke's manager and coach.

The arrangements were all carried out in cloak-and-dagger style because the Germans were worried about alerting the interest of other clubs. In fact, our initial meeting place – the Albany Hotel in Glasgow – was declared unsuitable at the last minute because some Celtic players were drinking at the bar. We ended up in a tiny Italian restaurant instead.

Once again Willie came along to handle the financial side of things. This time, though, we were talking about really serious cash. The Germans offered me a signing on fee of £100,000 and a contract worth around £70,000 a season. These were amazing sums of money in those days. Possibly too amazing – I remember Willie and I left the meeting with a feeling that it was all too good to be true.

I had other doubts as well. I was still only nineteen and I'd hardly been out of Scotland. There were no other British players at Schalke, or in the rest of the Bundesliga for that matter. I was worried about being isolated and homesick in a foreign country. I thought of what had happened to Denis Law and the rest. This was in the days before jet travel was as common as it is today. Holidays abroad were still a rarity. Europe seemed a lot further away and lot more mysterious than it does now. So, incredible though the Germans' offer was, I turned it down.

It would have been different had the chance come a little later. Two years afterwards Kevin Keegan left Liverpool for SV Hamburg. He led them to the Bundesliga title and the Champions' Cup Final and he was twice named European Footballer of the Year. His success led a number of British players to try their luck abroad, including my Scotland teammates Joe Jordan and Graeme Souness.

Unfortunately when I finally did get another opportunity to move abroad I had turned thirty. I was on my way out of Goodison when an impressive offer came in from PSV Eindhoven, then the dominant force in Dutch football. The directors of the club actually flew out to Portugal, where I was holidaying, in a private jet to discuss it with me. I was flattered and tempted, but by then I had a wife and young daughter and moving to the Continent seemed impractical.

On both occasions when I rejected moves to Europe my eventual destination was the same – Villa Park.

Having turned down Schalke's offer I spent the next few weeks worrying if I'd done the right thing. There'd been lots of paper talk about clubs watching me but nothing had happened. What if no other offer was made? What if I got injured and couldn't get back into the Dundee United side? I knew from the knee operation how close disaster could be for a footballer.

The season was six weeks old. We were playing Celtic on the Saturday and I planned to travel down in the afternoon after Friday training and spend the night with my mum in Drumchapel. That morning I had my first and only clash with Jim McLean. From the minute I arrived at Tannadice he was on my top. He wasn't shouting and bawling in his usual style, but kept chipping at me and moaning. I couldn't help thinking that maybe somehow he'd found out about the Germans' secret approach. As I walked off the pitch at the end of the session he bellowed, 'Gray! Where can I get in touch with you this afternoon?' By now I'd had enough. I yelled 'Drumchapel. Where do you think?' and stormed out.

I drove down with my teammate Jacky Copland. Jacky had noticed the way Jim had been treating me. 'What was all that about?' he asked. 'I'm not sure,' I said, 'but I reckon I won't be playing tomorrow.'

Jacky said I was talking nonsense, but the minute I arrived home I got a message to phone Tannadice. I was convinced that McLean was calling to tell me he was dropping me. It was something that had never happened to me before and I was terrified by the prospect. When I eventually summoned up the courage to speak to him my fears seemed to be confirmed by his opening words, 'You won't be in the team against Celtic.'

His next words came completely out of the blue, though. 'We've agreed a fee with Aston Villa. The deal has got to go through tonight. They want to meet you this evening. You'll have to fly down for a medical.'

I hopped in the taxi to Glasgow Airport with just one thought in my mind – where on earth was Aston Villa? I knew the club's name, of course, but was it in London or Manchester? I had no idea. It may sound stupid, but I'd guess an Englishman might have similar trouble with Partick Thistle or St Johnstone. And let's not forget the BBC radio commentator who told listeners that fans would be 'dancing in the streets of Raith tonight', clearly unaware that Raith Rovers FC is in Kirkcaldy. Luckily I discovered the flight was booked to take me to Elmdon Airport, Birmingham, which gave me a bit of a clue.

Aston Villa boss Ron Saunders and the club's chief scout Neville Briggs were waiting for me at Elmdon. Briggs had obviously been watching me up in Scotland but my appearance took him by surprise. 'You're much taller than I thought,' he remarked. The 1970s fashion for platform shoes plainly hadn't caught on with Neville.

The deal went through that evening with Villa paying £110,000 for me. It was a record for both clubs. Still, it was a lot less than Dundee United might have expected. The reason for that is interesting. Around that time there was talk of players being granted the sort of freedom of contract they enjoy today. Ron Saunders played on Jim McLean's fear that if the law changed I'd be able to walk away on a free transfer when my contract ran out at the end of the season – what we'd now call a 'Bosman'. Always worried by the thought of having one put over on him, Jim had panicked and taken the first offer that came along. Typically he made sure it wouldn't happen again. After my departure outstanding young players at Tannadice were put on ten-year deals.

Although my new boss Ron Saunders would later say that he'd inquired about me twelve months before the transfer, the fact was that he had never actually seen me play. He'd based his decision to buy entirely on Neville Briggs' report. I think Saunders' claim that he had been tracking me for a year was an attempt to show the world how smart he was. The truth was, however, that he'd snapped me up quickly only because he needed a replacement for Keith Leonard, a big strapping centre forward who'd been sidelined early in the season with cartilage trouble.

Ron Saunders prided himself on being rugged. I guess he must have been. After all he'd once spent a summer working as the games organizer in a Butlin's holiday camp. He came from Birkenhead and he'd played, briefly, for Everton before moving on to Portsmouth, Watford and then Charlton. As a manager he'd had spells with Yeovil, Norwich and Manchester City before pitching up at Villa in June 1974.

Saunders had an image of being a bit sergeant-majorish. What he wanted most from his players was effort. I'm pretty sure it was Saunders who invented the phrase 'giving 110 per cent'. He certainly used it so often that the press called him 'Mr 110 per cent'. He was very proud of that nickname.

Pre-season training with Saunders was brutally hard, easily the toughest I ever experienced in my career. There was loads and loads of running and exercises to build strength. We spent as much time with a medicine ball as a football. He put huge emphasis on being physically strong and he was particularly keen that all his players had powerful stomach muscles. The Villa boss believed that because the stomach was at the centre of the body it controlled the rest of it. This may be what led to a peculiar restriction he imposed. Diet wasn't usually high on the agenda of football clubs in those days, but Villa players were forbidden to eat seafood. The manager thought it was bad for us.

Liverpool boss Bill Shankly, for one, was not impressed with Saunders' methods. I spoke to Shanks a few times when I was considering the move to Wolves and he made it plain he didn't approve of this style of coaching, 'I can't understand why he makes you run up and down hills,' he said, 'I've never seen a football field with a one-in-four gradient.'

The training didn't bother me, though, and I felt initially that I learned a lot under Saunders. He was an old-style centre forward himself and he knew his way around. At Dundee United I'd been very much a back-stick player. I'd waited for the ball to come to me. Saunders got me to be less static, to attack the near post as often as I could, and that brought me a lot of goals. He was also good on how to go about looking after myself physically on the pitch. I'd already developed a way of jumping with my arms sticking out to protect myself from people clobbering me and we worked on aspects of self-preservation like that. The First Division was tough and combative and if defenders thought they could frighten you, believe me they would.

Early on in my career at Villa I was playing in a local derby at St Andrews against Birmingham City. I was standing on the halfway line, the ball was miles away and suddenly I felt a tap on my shoulder. I turned around and – *bang!* – the Blues centre half Joe Gallagher landed one on the point of my chin, knocking me flying. That was Joe's subtle way of introducing himself.

That sort of thing didn't happen every week, thank God,

but there was plenty of it about. Even the least likely people could dish it out. Denis Law, for example, was notorious. You'd often see a defender lying on the deck and Denis standing innocently thirty yards away on the left touchline looking like butter wouldn't melt in his mouth. Nowadays, with the TV cameras everywhere, you wouldn't get away with it, but there wasn't the same amount of scrutiny then.

Rule changes have made football less physical, too. There's less tackling than there was, for instance. If you look at United in 2003 they won the Premiership with Rio Ferdinand at centre back. Rio has never been booked since he moved to Old Trafford. In the past, that would have been more or less unthinkable for the centre half of a title-winning side. When I was playing there were managers around who literally demanded that their centre backs got booked half a dozen times in a season. And if they weren't they wanted to know the reason why.

When I was playing as a forward you knew that the first time you received the ball with your back to goal the centre half would go straight through you. It was known as the 'welcome to the game' tackle. It wasn't pleasant, but it was a fact of life and you just had to learn to live with it.

Saunders was in the process of strengthening the Villa team, which had won promotion back to the top flight and the League Cup the previous season. I was his second major signing in the space of three days. The other was goalkeeper John Burridge, who he'd bought for £100,000 from Blackpool. As it happened Budgie was the first Villa player I met. He was to leave an indelible mark on my life.

Keepers are supposed to be crazy and John Burridge certainly worked overtime to prove it. This was a guy who dressed like a bin man and whose idea of a romantic night out was to take his wife Janet to watch Peter Shilton play. Poor Janet, as if she didn't have enough to put up with, what with the Budge leaping and diving about in his sleep and waking her up on Saturday nights to explain how he'd just seen some keeper on *Match of the Day* who hadn't narrowed the angles properly.

Budgie was the biggest joker I ever met in football or any other walk of life. One of his greatest moments came at Birmingham Airport when we were returning from a European trip with Villa. He got off the plane before the rest of the team and unbeknown to the rest of us, managed to get hold of a customs officer's uniform and station himself at an unmanned passport-control desk. God knows how he did it. After we'd collected our luggage we found ourselves confronted by Budge looking very official in his cap. He waved the whole lot of us through, but then started stopping the other passengers on the flight, quizzing them about where they'd been and where they were going, searching their baggage and confiscating their duty-frees. When the real customs officers turned up there was hell on. But Budgie gave them some of his usual mad patter and a big grin and somehow talked his way out of it.

Unfortunately Budgie didn't stay long at Villa Park and part of that may have been down to some fun he had, this time at Ron Saunders' expense. As I say Saunders cultivated this rugged public image. He wasn't quite so hard when it came to aeroplanes, though. He tried to disguise it, but it quickly became plain to the lads in the team that when we flew anywhere the manager was petrified. One day when we were coming in to land at Birmingham, Budge sneaked up behind the Villa boss, blew up a sick bag and then, just as the landing gear came down, burst it. When he heard the bang Saunders jumped so high he almost smacked his head on the luggage rack. He was not amused. And that marked Budgie's card.

Apart from meeting John Burridge the other major highlight of my first few days in the Midlands was being taken to Villa Park. The day after I'd flown down from Glasgow I was led out onto the pitch in front of a crowd of 53,000 fans. Villa were up against local rivals Birmingham City and the atmosphere was staggering. The wall of noise as I came out of the players' tunnel practically knocked me over. I walked along to the dugout looking up at the Holte End and the hairs on the back of my neck stood up. I'd been happy in Dundee, playing in front of 10,000 or 12,000, but this was something else. I'd hardly had a chance to think about the move, but that moment convinced me I'd done the right thing. I heard that great wave of sound and saw the packed stands of claret and blue and thought, 'This is it!'

I made my debut the following Saturday at Ayresome Park, Middlesbrough. In the next match against Manchester United in the League Cup I got my first goal. There were 41,000 fans packed into the ground and as the ball hit the back of the net I ran to celebrate with the Witton Lane End. It was something I made a point of doing wherever I played. I wanted to show the supporters that I shared their joy, because basically I am one of them. I'm a fan in a football shirt. It's just that I'm lucky enough to be wearing mine on the field. I think that attitude came across. It helped me form a bond with the supporters at all the clubs I played for. It saddens me when players don't show their delight at scoring. When somebody like Darius Vassell gets a goal and doesn't even crack a smile, I wonder what the supporters make of it.

In total that season I played in thirty League games and

scored ten times. Villa finished in mid-table. It was very respect-
able. What was really exciting, though, was the fact that Saunders had continued to spend. He'd broken the club record he'd
set buying me to bring midfielder Dennis Mortimer in from
Coventry, and he'd also added two young Scots to the squad,
forward Gordon Smith and the midfielder Alex Cropley, a really
talented lad who, as the old football expression had it, could
open a can of peas with his left foot.

Up front I'd forged a great partnership with Brian Little. We
complimented each other perfectly. I was hard running, bois-
terous and powerful, a real handful. Brian was smaller, subtler,
with terrific skill and amazing vision. He was a fantastic crosser
of the ball. If I got a yard of space in the box he could almost
always pick me out, usually without even looking up to see
where I was.

The tradition in those days was for a forward partnership
built around a big, bustling target man and a smaller, quicker
and maybe more creative guy: Toshack and Keegan at Liverpool,
Brian Little and me at Villa. I guess the equivalent today would
be Shearer and Bellamy at Newcastle. These days that type of
partnership is becoming more unusual, though. The change has
been gradual. Leeds won the title with a very traditional front
two of Lee Chapman and Rod Wallace, and there was a similar
style about United when Sheringham and Cole were there. But
then Dwight Yorke replaced Teddy and the character of the
partnership changed. Now we've got a different type of forward in the Premiership, men like Thierry Henry and Ruud van
Nistelrooy, who tend to play upfront on their own with runners
coming from midfield to join them.

In our first full season together Little and I scored fifty-five
goals between us. Brian had joined Villa as a fifteen-year-old

and like me he'd made his professional debut at seventeen. He was unfortunate to only win a single cap for England and even unluckier that a serious knee injury forced him to give up the game before he'd turned thirty. I played upfront with other fine players, but few, if any, were better than Brian.

Sadly, while my relationship with Brian had blossomed, the one I had with the manager had deteriorated badly. I first began to clash with Saunders during my second season over his policy of playing me no matter what kind of physical shape I was in. At Dundee United I'd suffered a career-threatening knee injury and once in a while it still gave me problems. I was young and enthusiastic, and as I've said I wanted to play at every opportunity whether I was fully fit or not. Often that ended with me in considerable pain. Nowadays I'm sure the club I was playing for would force me to rest until I was fully recovered. At that time, however, I played whenever it was practicable and sometimes even when it wasn't. Saunders was convinced that even when I was 60 per cent fit my presence unsettled the opposition and created opportunities for others. He was particularly keen on having me turn out in every League Cup tie and that was to lead to our first major confrontation.

We'd made it through to the final against Everton at Wembley. We'd already beaten the Blues twice that season and we were so confident that even the usually tight-lipped Saunders was predicting a 3–1 win. The opposition had other ideas. They knew we were the better side and that if they let us play football we'd paralyse them, so instead they strangled the game. If anybody ever wonders why the rule abolishing the pass back to the goalkeeper came in they should watch a video of that match. I think in total Everton played the ball back to the keeper over forty times. I don't blame them for that. If we'd been in their position we'd have done the same. It worked, too. The game was all stops and starts and we couldn't build up any rhythm. I was suffering from an ankle injury. I'd had it heavily strapped up before the game and it severely hampered my movement. Ken McNaught was marking me and he had an easier afternoon than he might have expected. If I'd been 100 per cent fit I don't think he'd have been so comfortable. The funny thing was though that Saunders was so impressed with the way Ken handled me that he went out and bought him the following season.

The game finished in a goalless stalemate and the replay was scheduled for the Wednesday night at Hillsborough.

The day after the League Cup Final the Professional Footballers' Association, the players' trade union, were holding their annual awards dinner in London. Along with a number of Villa lads I had been planning to attend, but my ankle problem had flared up again and so on Saturday night rather than stay over in the capital I travelled back to Birmingham for treatment.

On Sunday morning I was sitting at home when the phone rang. It was Derek Dougan, chairman of the PFA. I'd been voted Player of the Year and Young Player of the Year by my fellow pros. To be recognized by your peers in that way is an incredible thing and to win both awards, well, it is something that had never happened before and has never happened since. In fact, it will never happen again, because shortly afterwards the voting rules were changed so that it couldn't. My double is unique and will remain so.

It wasn't all good news from the Doog, however. Because of the replay Derek had already phoned Ron Saunders to ask the manager's permission for me to attend the dinner. Saunders in typical style had refused to give it. He'd told Dougan that I was injured and he didn't want me to travel in case it aggravated the problem. Now the PFA were in a panic because the awards ceremony – which had only been introduced in 1974 – was being shown live on ITV and suddenly it seemed that the principal attraction wasn't going to be there.

Derek Dougan was an Ulsterman and a truly forceful character, as I'd later learn during my spell at Wolves, but even he couldn't make any progress against the stone-faced Saunders. The Doog had offered to send a car to Birmingham to collect me and return me straight after the ceremony. He'd even proposed flying me there and back. It made no difference to the manager.

Derek was desperate to get me down to London and was now proposing that I ignore Saunders and go anyway. If it happened today, believe me I wouldn't need to be asked twice. But then I was still a young player and did what I was told. If Saunders said I couldn't go, I wouldn't.

A while later Derek was back on the phone again. He had another proposal to make. Once again I said no, but this time I have no regrets about it. What the Doog asked was if I would surrender one of the awards so they could give it to somebody who was actually at the dinner. I was staggered. I couldn't believe he'd ask me that. I told him that the PFA's members had voted for me and that what he was proposing was a fix purely for the benefit of the TV cameras. It stank and I wanted no part of it.

Another half-hour went by and Dougan was back on the line again. Could a TV camera crew come up to my house and film me receiving the award on a live relay link? I didn't see any objection to that. So the trophies were sent up from

London and I was presented with them in my own living room by Chris Nicholl, the Villa captain.

The whole thing was really downbeat and awkward, certainly not the way a player should remember one of the real highlights of his career. I've been to the PFA dinner many times since then. It's a genuinely fantastic occasion. I was forced to miss it in 1977 purely because of Ron Saunders. And I find it hard to forgive him for that.

Why had he done it? I don't honestly believe it was to help me recover from injury. What harm would it have done to my ankle if I'd gone? No, Saunders had other reasons for preventing me from going to London. He was trying to teach me a lesson.

In his previous job at Manchester City Saunders had made a point of taunting two Maine Road legends, Denis Law and Francis Lee, by calling them 'The Old Man' and 'Fatty' in front of the other players. In the end the team had revolted and he'd been booted out of his job.

Manchester City were a powerful club. They'd won the League not that long before and the players, like Law and Lee, were top guys with the medals to prove it. When Saunders came to Villa, on the other hand, they were down in the Second Division and struggling. Unlike City this was a club the manager could really get a grip on and control, and he bought players he could control, too. Looking back on it I'm sure that's why he brought me in. I was a fresh-faced nineteen-year-old and he thought he'd be able to manipulate me.

The Villa manager's view was that good teams make good players not the other way around. He couldn't stand any individual drawing the limelight. He made out that this was because he felt it might disrupt the team, or create resentment amongst the other players. To me that was nonsense. Footballers are realistic. If you're a centre back you know you are not going to get the same attention as the strikers. The guy who scores the goals, or runs at defences beating people with the ball, will always get the adulation of the fans and the attention of the media.

Saunders wouldn't have it, though. At first he tried to make a joke of it, sarcastically telling reporters, 'Andy Gray is this club. All this club's about is Andy Gray.' When that failed to have an impact he turned belligerent. After games he'd get angry with the pressmen. 'Why do you always want to talk to effing Andy Gray? It's Andy this and Andy that. What about Frank Carrodus? This is a team game and he's just as important a part of the team as Andy effing Gray.'

That's true, right enough. But, as I say, the fact is that there are some players who make headlines and some who don't. I'm sure that, for example, Nicky Butt doesn't expect to get the same number of interview requests as Ruud van Nistelrooy or Ryan Giggs. It's just the way it is. And footballers accept that.

In my view what Saunders really resented was not that star players took the focus off the team, but that they took the spotlight off him. Villa was his side. He had created it. And he wanted all the praise for it. That's how it seemed to me.

Saunders of course told things differently. According to him fame had come too quickly for me. It had gone to my head. I was unable to handle it. As evidence he cited a couple of incidents on the field that had occurred earlier that season. I admit both were really stupid. The first came in a Scotland international in Prague when I was sent off for fighting with an opponent, Anton Ondrus, who'd whacked me in the face when the referee wasn't looking.

The incident that followed was in many ways even dafter. It happened during Villa's home game with Manchester United. Then as now United had a massive travelling support and they occupied the old Witton Lane End where they amused themselves for most of the game by taunting me with obscene chants. It was incessant, it was loud and I soon got pretty sick of it. We were trailing for much of the game but came back to win 3–2. When Dennis Mortimer got the equalizer it was at their end of the ground, so I celebrated instinctively by hoisting a double V-sign at them and standing there proudly.

It was a stupid thing to do, but since they'd been showering me with all kinds of abuse and filth throughout the afternoon I can't imagine they were exactly shocked. Unfortunately one of the press photographers captured the gesture and the next day it was all over the *Sun*. I'll never forget the headline, 'Andy You Are a Super Player – Don't Become a Yob'. The Football Association were forced into action and fined me the princely sum of £110, or £27.50 per finger.

To be honest, even in those days that kind of figure wasn't much of a deterrent. But then the FA never seems to have caught up since the abolition of the maximum wage. The fact that they carry on fining players nowadays is ridiculous. When Roy Keane was hauled over the coals because of what he wrote in his autobiography about the foul on Alf-Inge Haaland they fined him £150,000. To an average working person that is a huge sum of money, but it's hardly going to worry somebody as wealthy as Keane. The FA would be better off dropping the fines altogether and increasing the length of match bans. That hurts the players and the teams.

Giving the inverted victory salute to the Man United fans was a silly thing to do, I admit. The best response was not two fingers, but the two goals I scored after that. Later I came to realize that when opposition fans picked me out as a target for their barracking it was a kind of back-handed compliment. It meant that I was the one they feared. I don't think it was worth splashing across the sports pages either. People may think that nowadays if I saw a player do something similar I would highlight it on Sky. I don't believe I would. A dangerous tackle, something that might end a player's career – I'd pick up on that. A gesture to the crowd or an opponent is a different matter, especially in a game like that, one that was already packed with incident and good football. Unless I thought it was serious or that it maybe had an impact on something that happened later in the game, I'd leave it alone. Football is a passionate game and sometimes people get carried away. We should never lose sight of that.

The V-sign came shortly after the sending off in Prague, and put together the two were seen in some quarters as proving that I was becoming an undisciplined hooligan.

Was I? I don't honestly think so. I enjoyed myself but didn't live a wild life. If we were playing on a Saturday my last night out of the week was always on a Wednesday. I was always aware of what the priority was and that was to play football. I never lost that and if anything had threatened it then that would have gone.

This is because as soon as you take your sport for granted and think you've cracked it, that is the moment you're likely to fall. Despite the problems he suffered off the field this year David Beckham remains an example as a player. He is the first into training every day and the last out. He's never lost track of the fact that what has given him everything he has is the ability to kick a football. You have to be like that. And I was.

Certainly I'd started to become famous in a way I hadn't known before. People now recognized me in the street and when I was out for the evening I'd constantly find myself being approached by fans wanting to chat. I'd even had to move house after the PFA awards because the sight of all the TV vans outside my house had alerted the whole neighbourhood to my presence and people had started turning up on my doorstep at all hours asking for autographs. I can't say I felt any pressure from it, though. The fact that the two incidents had occurred so close together at a time when I was getting a lot of public and media attention was simply a coincidence. Unfortunately some people thought they were connected and it is plain that one of those people was my boss Ron Saunders.

The manager never said anything to me about it at the time. He waited until after I'd left Villa Park to start telling everyone that fame had come too quickly for me and turned my head. If he'd talked to me about it while I was still at Villa you can rest assured I'd have put him straight on that score. It was absolute nonsense. And frankly I find it staggering that anybody should make that accusation about me, then or now.

I've never at any time in my life courted fame or celebrity. But if you're a forward and you're scoring goals fame is thrust upon you. That is inevitable. The idea that it somehow changed me is rubbish. And I object to anyone saying it did, because it suggests that there is an arrogance about me, which is not the case. Throughout my career I worked at my game. I knew I wasn't the most talented player, so I couldn't afford to ease off in training. Every game I played I had to give everything I had; I never ever got casual or dismissive.

My lifestyle changed during my time at Villa. Of course it did. It was hardly a film-star existence, though. I bought a three-bedroom semi-detached on an estate and a Ford, and I opened the occasional church fete.

I earned more money, certainly. But that honestly did not affect me. I still have the same set of pals from Scotland that I've had for thirty years. If you get arrogant and let fame go to your head you lose those people. They see a change in you. Plain and simple: if Saunders thought I'd come over all dizzy with celebrity he was totally and utterly wrong.

However, as the 1976–7 season drew to a close what the manager was thinking didn't seem all that important. We drew the replay of the League Cup final with Everton at Hillsborough 2–2 and had to play for a third time at Old Trafford. Villa eventually won that one 3–2, but I didn't feature. My leg was in plaster yet again. I'd suffered serious ligament damage in a game against Derby County three days before. As usual I was rushed back into action and played out the rest of the season. Villa finished fourth, their best league position for forty-four years, and I was equal top scorer in the top division with Arsenal's Malcolm Macdonald.

We'd done well. We had a great side packed with really good pros. Villa would win the title four years later, but I don't believe the championship team was any stronger than the one we had then.

Some people complain that there is too much football on television these days. It seems to me that's something people have been saying since I first signed for Dundee United. What I would say is that from a player's point of view one of the great things about the blanket coverage is that there is always TV footage of what they've done. When I was playing, the terrestrial channels between them generally covered half a dozen games on a Saturday at most and in midweek sometimes they didn't do any at all. That was true of one of the greatest team displays I was ever part of.

During that season Villa played Liverpool on a Wednesday night. The Reds had just been crowned champions and we absolutely tore them apart. There was Brian, John Deehan and me up front and we ripped into them right from the kick-off. I scored early from a John Robson cross, Brian got a peach with a curling shot from the edge of the area and I got a second with a header after a neat free kick from Dennis Mortimer. By half-time we were winning 5–1. It was fantastic stuff, but because the game wasn't televised only the people who were in the ground saw it and the only record I have of it is in my head.

The 1977–8 season promised to be fantastic. Unfortunately, for me at least, it didn't work out that way. The reason can be summed up in two words: Ron Saunders. Ironically, he might not have been there at all if it hadn't been for me. After our League Cup win the manager was offered a lucrative deal to go and coach in the Middle East. Don Revie had just left the England manager's job to go out to the Arabian Gulf. There was a big demand for British coaches out there and Ron had been targeted to follow him. In pre-season he called us all together, told us about it and asked us to have a get-together and then tell him what we thought. Given the season we'd just had it was natural that none of the boys wanted the manager to leave.

Along with three other players I formed the party that went to his office and told him we would like him to stay. Looking back now it seems to me that he was probably just using the team as leverage against the board. With the backing of the players his power was increased. And whatever he asked the directors for they obviously gave him because by the time the season kicked off the move to the Middle East had been totally forgotten.

I suffered from injuries off and on throughout 1977–8. As usual this brought me into confrontation with Saunders. By March we had reached the quarter-finals of the UEFA Cup. We'd beaten Fenerbahce, Gornik and Athletic Bilbao along the way. A Barcelona side featuring the Dutch greats Johan Cruyff and Johan Neeskens stood between us and a place in the last four. I missed the first leg at Villa Park with a thigh injury. The boys did well in my absence and we finished with a 2–2 draw. Even with away goals counting double the feeling was that we could still win it over there in the Camp Nou.

The return leg was two weeks later. I was desperate to be fit, but the muscle strain was one of those niggling ones that take time to heal. We were flying out to Spain on the Monday and on the Sunday afternoon Saunders came to see me and asked if I would be fit to play on the Wednesday night. I told him I wasn't sure, but I hoped that, with three days to go, I would be.

He said, 'That's not good enough. I need to know now.' I couldn't understand why. So I repeated that I wanted to play, but I wasn't certain I'd be able to. He said, 'Right, if that's your attitude, you're not going.' Just like that.

So I didn't make the trip and we lost narrowly 2–1. On the flight back from Barcelona a journalist I'd become friendly with, Peter White, asked Saunders whether he thought it might have been a different result if I'd been able to make the trip. The manager said, 'Let me tell you something about Andy Gray – he has not only cheated this club, he has cheated its fans and he's also cheated himself.' Peter was stunned and so was I when he told me about it.

There were a lot of things people accused me of when I was

a player that maybe, if I'm honest, I'd have to put my hands up and confess too. But one thing I can say for sure is that I never cheated anyone, and certainly not Ron Saunders or Aston Villa.

Time and again I'd played for him against medical advice. Once I was suffering from a back injury and had spent a week lying in traction in a clinic, yet I checked myself out despite the protests of the doctors and played in a derby match against Birmingham twenty-four hours later.

There were dozens of such examples. A lot of the time I could only play for Villa because I'd had painkilling injections. The doctor would pump them into me half an hour before kick off. Sometimes when the opening whistle blew I literally couldn't feel my legs. On top of that I had hydrocortisone banged into me from all angles and I spent more time on ice than Torvill and Dean. Was that the action of somebody out to defraud the club and the fans? I don't think so. The actions of an idiot more like. God alone knows what long-term damage I could have done to myself. And now the man I'd taken those risks for was going round telling people I was a cheat. It made me furious.

The following season was the worst of my career so far. Injury problems dogged me from the start. I got another thigh strain when we'd barely started and when I came back in a League Cup tie at Luton I took a hefty whack from a defender and knew immediately I hit the deck that my knee had gone again. I had another cartilage operation. I came back and scored a few goals only for the stiffness in the joint to return and it was into hospital for more surgery. In total I managed just eighteen games. I got more stitches than goals. My final match for Villa was a 4–0 defeat to Nottingham Forest. It was a fitting way to end my relationship with Ron Saunders.

As a way of investing my earnings I'd opened a nightclub in the centre of Birmingham called Holy City Zoo. It was here that I became good friends with Tony Iommi from Black Sabbath. I think Tony and I hit it off because he didn't have any interest in football and I didn't have any in heavy metal, so neither of us had to talk about our work.

Tony's fellow band member Geezer Butler was a massive Villa fan and on the strength of that I was invited to spend a couple of weeks with the band over in Los Angeles, where they were recording a new album. I was recovering from the knee operation and everybody reckoned the warm weather would help me recover, so when the season finished off I went.

The band's mansion in LA was extraordinary, a real Hollywood palace. Nowadays top players have a much more glamorous lifestyle than we did back then. They'd be used to it. But to me it was a real shock even to be allowed into such a place. It shows how naive I was that when I first arrived I asked Tony which bit of the house they had rented. 'All of it,' he said.

My housemates didn't generally get up before noon, but I was up early each morning to go running in the hills to try and get my knee back into shape. It was during these lonely sessions jogging around the roads of Bel Air that I decided it was time for me to leave Villa Park.

In July when we reported back for pre-season training I went to see the manager and asked for a transfer. Despite having accused me of everything from arrogance to cowardice, Saunders said that he wouldn't let me go. I was adamant about leaving, however. I told the board and I even told the press. In all I put in three separate transfer requests.

To spare myself having to go through that any more I went to see the manager again. I said, 'I want to leave and I won't be happy until I do. That's the situation. You know it and I know it. I'm telling you now so I don't have to come banging on your door every day asking for a move.' The next day Saunders was quoted in the newspapers saying that 'Andy Gray has now withdrawn his transfer request.' Unbelievable.

I wasn't the only player having problems with Saunders. Brian Little didn't exactly see eye to eye with the manager and John Gidman had also fallen out with him in a big way. Giddy was a big, flamboyant character, popular in the dressing room and on the terraces. In other words just the sort of player the manager hated. Like me John had put in a transfer request.

Around this time there was a bit of a power struggle going on at Villa Park between Doug Ellis, who'd resigned as chairman in 1975, and a group of other directors including the chairman Harry Kartz and Ron Bendall who, unlike Doug, were supportive of the manager. The board had been split over the decision to sell Giddy and me, and now a battle was raging between pro- and anti-Saunders factions fuelled by protests from the fans who didn't want either of us to leave.

One day John and I were training when we got a message to get changed and go to Villa Park. When we got there we were invited into the boardroom, where the directors were holding a meeting. John and I were told that we were not to discuss what we were about to hear with anybody. It quickly became obvious why when the directors began to quiz us about our reasons for wanting to leave. At one point one of the directors asked, 'If we sack Ron Saunders will you stay?'

Giddy, who was happy to stick the boot into the manager any chance he got, said, 'Definitely.' I was more cautious. No matter how much I disliked Saunders I wasn't keen to start plotting behind his back, so I said that I wouldn't. I wanted to leave and that was it. It seemed to me an extraordinary question, though, and it just goes to show the kind of in-fighting that can go on behind the scenes at a football club.

Saunders rode out that particular crisis and eventually agreed to sell Gidman and myself. He wasn't prepared to give us up easily, though. The figures he was talking about – £750,000 for Giddy and £1 million for me – were immense sums in those days. Especially since I'd just had two knee operations and had effectively been out of the game for five months.

In my view the manager felt that by asking for so much he'd put off potential buyers and I'd end up staying at Villa Park no matter what I wanted. Unfortunately for him he'd miscalculated. The transfer market was about to go through one of its periodic explosions.

After I left Saunders criticized me publicly for disloyalty and for failing to honour my contract with the club. But oddly enough he walked away himself in 1981, a few months after leading Villa to the League title. He went because the directors refused to give him a three-year rollover contract. He wanted to wake up every morning with the next thirty-six months wages guaranteed and the board wouldn't give him the chance.

Saunders' destination was St Andrews. He had left the Champions, a team that would win the European Cup eight months after he'd gone, and a group of players he'd forged into an excellent side, for their bitterest rivals Birmingham City. It was an extraordinary decision. Totally incredible. In my view it could have been governed by only one thing – money. And in many ways that tells you everything you need to know about Ron Saunders.

Looking back now, if I'm honest, I'd have to say it was bad timing. On 8 September 1979 at the age of twenty-three I became the most expensive player in British football history when I signed for Wolverhampton Wanderers for £1,469,000. It nearly didn't happen. I was due to sign my new contract on the pitch at Molineux before the kick-off of Wolves' game against Crystal Palace. I got to the ground early and I was in a cheerful mood, not least because I was getting away from Ron Saunders at last.

I know that at the time there were lots of rumours going around the Midlands that I needed the cash. It was no secret that Holy City Zoo was in financial trouble. I wasn't the first sports person to get caught out in that way, nor was I the last. But there was not a scrap of truth in the gossip. Despite the size of the transfer there was little extra money in the deal for me. In fact, when I sat down with Barny to discuss personal terms the talks lasted less than five minutes. Saunders was my sole reason for leaving Villa Park.

My feeling is that Ron Saunders had not really wanted to sell me at all, despite our frequent disagreements. He'd put a massive price tag on me thinking it would deter everybody. It worked, too, until Wolves' boss John Barnwell somehow managed to persuade Malcolm Allison at Manchester City to part with £1.2 million for midfielder Steve Daley.

The most important thing that Saturday at Molineux was to prove my fitness. I hadn't played for months and I was still recovering from a third operation on my right knee. After arriving at the ground I was taken off to see a specialist for an extra medical. Following the usual round of X-rays the doctor spent a good fifteen minutes prodding at the offending joint. It was now so criss-crossed with scar tissue it looked like a plan of Spaghetti Junction. It was plain to see he wasn't happy about it. He asked me if I was in pain from the knee. I told him it was fine, there was just a bit of stiffness and that cleared up when I ran about, which was true, more or less.

After that I went off to have lunch and meet a couple of Wolves' directors. At half past two I was due to be led out onto the pitch to sign the transfer forms in front of the fans. That was John Barnwell's idea. The TV people had wanted to film it in his office, but the manager insisted it was done out on the field. He wanted the Wolves supporters to be part of it. He said I was their player and he wanted them to savour the moment. That said something about the type of man he was.

I'd got on really well with Barny – who these days is head of the League Managers Association – right from the start. The Wolves manager was a north-easterner who'd played for Arsenal and Forest as an inside forward and he impressed me with his ambition for the club. More than that he was a total contrast to Saunders – a bouncy, bubbly character.

When Barny greeted me that Saturday, though, he was a lot more sombre. He took me through into his office. It was under the main stand at Molineux. It must have been one of the smallest in the football league. There was only room in it for a desk and a couple of chairs. The ceiling sloped because of the banking for the seats and that meant that anybody over about five foot six had to crouch to get in. By now the ground was filling up and you could hear the rumble of the supporters feet as they made their way to the seats above us. The noise was deafening. 'I'm afraid we've got a problem,' Barnwell shouted above the racket. 'It's your knee. The specialist has studied the X-rays and he says he's not happy with it. He wants the deal calling off.'

I was stunned. But before I could say anything John was talking again. He told me not to worry, that he was going to sort something out. He said he knew that I was fit, but that with all the money involved the doctor and the board were acting more cautiously than usual. 'They're worried about the insurance,' he said, and then disappeared out of the door.

Failing a medical doesn't mean a player is finished. You only have to look at somebody like John Hartson to see that. The Welshman had transfers to Spurs and Chelsea collapse because of doubts about his knee and ended up playing for Coventry on a match-by-match contract, but since then he's hit getting on for a century of goals for Celtic in the SPL and captained his country. Paul McGrath was another. Macca was written off by the doctors when he was twenty-six but ended up playing until he was in his mid-thirties. The insurance angle makes the whole thing a big risk for the buying club, though. Especially when you're talking about a British record transfer.

It was half an hour before Barnwell came back. That was enough time for me to convince myself that my career was over, or worse yet that I'd be going back to play for Saunders. But when John returned he was his usual cheerful self again and I knew straightaway that the signing was back on. Barny had gone to the directors and told them that if they didn't sign me he'd walk out. The thought of losing not only a new centre forward but also their manager in front of a capacity crowd was too much for the board and they caved in. That was a measure of the confidence the manager had in my ability and my long-term future. It was a big lift to my self-belief – something that had been gradually worn away by what had been going on at Villa Park.

I signed on the pitch in front of the Wolves supporters as planned, and I was convinced that this was the right move for me. Wanderers had a good squad. There were a lot of excellent old pros. Guys like Kenny Hibbitt, Willie Carr, John Richards and Emlyn Hughes.

Admittedly, Emlyn was on his last legs, or maybe that should be leg because he only had one good one left. In spite of that he was a top-class professional: hard-working, dedicated, good trainer. The ex-Liverpool captain was one of the reasons I'd signed for Wolves in the first place. Bill Shankly had got to know the club through his old skipper. Shanks rated John Barnwell highly and thought little of Saunders, so when I'd telephoned him to ask for advice about the move the great man had been enthusiastic.

I know a lot of people in football have had a problem with Emlyn over the years. Certainly some of his teammates in those great Anfield sides he captained didn't exactly get along with him. It was an open secret that Tommy Smith, for one, couldn't stand Hughes. I always found him fine, though. In fact I'd have to say that I've got on OK with almost everybody I've played alongside. Just about the only exception to that was Martin Keown. I was in my second spell at Villa and Martin was a youngster just breaking through into the first team. I can't put my finger on exactly what it was but there was definitely something about Martin that rubbed me up the wrong way. I think it was his attitude. He had a lot of self-confidence and that sometimes meant he didn't listen.

I remember one time in particular when we played Chelsea. Martin was at centre back and detailed to mark David Speedie. The Scot was very mobile, very quick and basically knew too much for an inexperienced defender. All through the first half Speedie was drifting out to the wings with Martin trailing after him leaving a great chasm in the centre of our defence, which the Blues midfield runners could pour into. We were a couple of goals down inside thirty minutes.

As we came off I collared Martin. I said, 'You've got to watch your positioning or you're going to cost us the game.' Martin looked at me as if I was the biggest idiot on the planet. 'What are you talking about?' he snapped back, 'The man I'm marking hasn't scored has he?' In recent seasons I've come to admire Martin. He's a terrific defender and he's had a brilliant career. But replies like that didn't exactly endear him to me when we played together.

I was the most expensive player in Britain, one of the costliest in the world (that title belonged to the Italian striker Paolo Rossi, who'd just moved to Juventus for £1.75 million) but the transfer fee didn't bother me. I wasn't frightened by it. I was still the same player. I was just doing my job playing football. I can say I felt no more pressure then than when I went to Everton for a hundred grand five years later. In fact in many ways less.

Besides, if there was pressure then it was the sort I'd always wanted, the type that comes with being the best. To my mind I was still the player I'd been at Dundee United and Aston Villa. The price was something other people had decided, not me. It didn't enter my head to worry about it. I was just relieved to have finally torn myself free from Saunders. And for the first time in a year I felt fully fit again.

My career at Molineux couldn't have started better. I scored on my debut against Everton at Goodison, a game we won 3–2. Next we thrashed League leaders Manchester United 3–1 at home and then travelled to Highbury and won 3–2 again. The results kept rolling our way and we ended up finishing fourth in the League and qualifying for the UEFA Cup. The highlight of the season, though, was the League Cup Final against Nottingham Forest. It was a game I almost missed because of suspension.

I was only sent off three times in my career: once for Scotland and twice for Wolves. One of the latter was for mouthing off at the ref and the other came in a game a few seasons later against Villa, when I had a wild hack at Dennis Mortimer. For a physical player who was allegedly badly disciplined, that's not too bad a record in seventeen years. I did get booked a lot, though, mainly for dissent, but I was rarely suspended. When I got up close to the maximum number of bookings you were allowed in those days before you were forced to miss games, I always managed to rein myself in a bit. I also knew the referees – which ones I could push a bit and which ones I shouldn't say a word to, and I adjusted my behaviour accordingly.

And despite all the talk about how match officials these days are all robots being controlled by Sepp Blatter, it's still true that refs are all different. The players know who is tough and who isn't; what they will tolerate and what they won't. I know for a fact that there was a game last season where Sam Allardyce at Bolton spent half of his pre-match team talk speaking about the referee because he was so worried about him.

As a result of this approach I usually managed to avoid suspensions by totting up the points and then staying out of trouble. On this occasion, however, I must have got my sums badly wrong because I'd reached the twenty penalty-point limit and earned a one-match ban. The ban was due to be served in a League fixture with Aston Villa. The only problem was that Villa had an FA Cup tie with West Ham on the Saturday. If they drew it would mean a replay, our League encounter would be postponed to accommodate it and I'd miss my day at Wembley.

With minutes remaining of the match Hammers and Villa were drawing 0–0 and I had begun to wonder if Ron Saunders was doing it on purpose just to spite me. Fortunately another former Dundee United player, Ray Stewart, popped up and scored in the eighty-ninth minute to give the Londoners victory and ensure I had my day at Wembley. Amazingly all these years later, Ray still reminds me of it whenever we bump into each other and there's a bar handy.

If luck seemed to be on my side there it was still working for me the following Saturday in the final. Player for player Forest were a much better side than us. Frank Gray, John Robertson, Viv Anderson and Trevor Francis were all there. Cloughie's team played great football and they were on the way to winning that season's European Cup. We weren't exactly Rag-arsed Rovers, but we were a mixed bunch and there's no doubt we were massive underdogs on the day.

As a result there was no pressure on us. John Barnwell used that to get us relaxed. Did a first-class job, too. Telling stories, laughing and joking, making sure we didn't tense up. On top of that we had plenty of experience. A lot of us had been there before – I had with Villa and Kenny and Willie had with Wolves. But the odd thing was that the League Cup was the one trophy that Emlyn Hughes hadn't won when he'd been at Liverpool. His knees had gone. So this was his last shot and he was determined to give it everything and lead by example.

The game wasn't a pretty one to watch, of that I'm certain. We didn't believe we were at Wembley to provide entertainment. If Forest wanted to do that, then so be it. All we were looking to do was walk up the steps as winners. The way we were going to do that was by making the game as scruffy as possible, which we did.

The Forest keeper Peter Shilton was unbelievably good, one of the best in the world, but I always liked to try and rough him up a little. In the first five minutes of the game I'd get the boys to try and hang a ball up in the box, so I could challenge him. I'd give him a real bang. Then I'd noise him up, as the expression is in Glasgow. I'd say, 'Enjoyed that, did you, Shilts? Well, don't worry, you'll get another one in a minute.' He hated it. And he watched out for it. It unsettled him.

That showed in the first half. A cross came over, I headed it more or less straight up into the air, Shilton came to claim it, made a right hash of it under a fairly polite challenge from John Richards and the ball ended up bobbling into the net. The goal was disallowed, but perhaps it was still on the keeper's mind in the sixty-sixth minute when another high centre was slung towards him.

A Forest attack broke down and Peter Daniel got the ball in the inside right position around the halfway line. Peter had a terrific right foot on him, really accurate, and generally what he'd do when he was in that area and he had time and space was fire a long ball down into the inside-left channel, where he knew I'd be waiting. We'd used that diagonal pass a lot that season and it had worked well for us.

Peter controlled the ball, looked up to check I was making the run and pinged it down the field towards me. The Forest defender David Needham had read the situation perfectly, though, and he'd got himself in front of me. Normally I'd have bustled into him and in all likelihood given a free kick away, but as the ball came towards us I noticed that for some reason Shilton had come racing off his line. I've no idea why he did it. I'm not sure he had either. Maybe he was worried about giving me the chance to clatter into him.

I knew Needham hadn't seen him and I guessed that might cause problems, so instead of challenging the defender I ran off past him. Sure enough, David went to chest the ball back to Shilts in the Forest goal only to realize at the last moment that not only was the keeper not in the goal, but also he was just about to crash into him. Which he did a split second later. My run, meanwhile, carried me around them both. The goal was empty in front of me and the ball was running towards it. I had only one thought in my mind, 'Whatever the hell you do now, Andy, don't fall over.'

I got to the ball about two yards from the line. I should have struck it with my right foot, but such was my confidence in my weaker side that instead of doing that I ran around it a bit and hit it with the outside of my left. A simple goal.

After that we hung on for grim death with me filling in as a third centre back. Forest attacked and attacked. Emlyn was gigantic. We blocked them with everything we had, we hacked the ball clear every time we got it and we rode our luck – at one point Martin O'Neill had a shot and our keeper Paul Bradshaw stopped it by sitting on it, which just about sums it up. That's what happens in finals, though. Sometimes it goes your way. And it certainly did for us that day.

That proved to be the high point of my career with Wolverhampton. In many ways I wish I'd gone to Molineux sooner, so that I could have had a longer spell playing alongside the likes of Emlyn, Willie, Derek Parkin and Richo. They were terrific performers, big characters and great lads. But sadly I only caught them right at the tail ends of their careers.

Richo in particular was superb. John was in his thirties then, handicapped with injury, but the talent was still plain to see. He was quick, intelligent and a tremendous finisher. Even though he had a bad knee and was struggling at times I struck up a good partnership with John, one that Barny felt would terrorize the division. On occasions early on we did, too. We took Everton apart at Goodison and did the same to Arsenal at Highbury. I'd loved to have played alongside him when he was in his pomp, I really would.

The trouble was that the best elements of the Wolves team had grown old together. The squad needed a major overhaul. As it turned out there wasn't even a remote chance of that happening. And after that first season things went very rapidly downhill at Molineux.

In the 1950s Wolves had been a major force in the English game. Under Stan Cullis, 'the iron manager', they'd won three League titles and two FA Cups and established themselves as one of the best sides in Europe. Since then every Wolves side had lived in their shadow.

I believe that while you should never forget your history, you must never dwell in the past. Despite John Barnwell's efforts to revive the club I felt that was a lesson that hadn't been absorbed at Wolves. It's said that when Howard Wilkinson took over at Elland Road one of the first things he did was remove all the pictures of the great Leeds side of the 1970s. He didn't do it out of disrespect for Don Revie, but so the present team could come out from under their shadow. They could have done with something similar happening at Wolves, where a lot of the time it seemed as if the Stan Cullis and Billy Wright era was still in progress.

The club's most pressing problem, however, was less psychological than economic. The truth was that from the day I signed they were caught in the grip of an ever-mounting financial crisis. John Barnwell had initiated a pay policy designed to bring Wolves into line with other top English clubs. He'd also spent heavily in the transfer market. Or at least he had on me. I was his only big money buy and he'd only got me because of the extraordinary sum Man City had paid for Daley. The size of that deal had totally floored everyone. Not least Steve Daley. Barny said that when he told Steve how much Malcolm Allison had offered for him the midfielder went white in the face with shock. I'm not sure he ever recovered. Before that had happened the Wolves boss had been convinced I was out of his price range and been looking at an older, less expensive option like Everton's Bob Latchford. He thought I'd end up at Forest or Liverpool.

The real problem wasn't the money spent on players but the vast new stand in Molineux Street that had been built just before I arrived. It was a white elephant that had cost £2.5 million. It was supposed to be the first phase of a redevelopment that would bring capacity up to 40,000 when it was complete. I'm not sure why anyone thought that was necessary, because average gates at the time were more like 20,000. Having this massive stand – always half empty – looming over the pitch totally destroyed the atmosphere in the ground. So much so, in fact, that most of the team preferred playing away from home and generally we did better on other teams' pitches than on our own.

More damaging in the long run was the effect the stand was having on the club's bank balance. The Wolves board had arranged to let out some of the space under the stand to the local polytechnic at a rent of £50,000 a year. That sounded impressive until you heard that the interest payments on the debt the club had amassed building the stand were running at around £4,000 per week. You don't need to be a business genius to see where those figures were leading.

Bill Shankly once said that if you built a good team fans would come and watch it even if it was playing on a roped off pitch in the local park. Supporters are probably fussier about their surroundings now than they were back when Shanks was speaking, but it's still true that most fans are more interested in players than architecture.

The best grounds in Britain now are light years ahead of anything that was on offer in those days, but the fact is that the supporters who flood in to Old Trafford or the City of Manchester Stadium do it to watch football not to sit and admire the roof. Recently we've seen that proved conclusively by Darlington. They built a spectacular ground, the Reynolds Arena, but never even came close to filling it. As far as fans are concerned, marble sinks in the toilets are no substitute for success on the field.

In fairness to Wolves it has to be said they weren't the only team that were struggling. Those were difficult times for the game. Hooliganism was on the rise, crowds were dropping and most stadiums were in dire need of renovation if only for safety's sake. Yet despite the gloom and the falling gate receipts some clubs were still spending crazily in the transfer market. It's hardly surprising that there were people in the game, including the PFA chairman and former Wolves stalwart Derek Dougan, who predicted that the League in England would collapse by the end of the eighties if nothing was done to change things.

As it turned out the situation would get far worse before it got better. More clubs would face ruin and the game had to endure the disasters at Bradford, Heysel and Hillsborough before it finally pulled out from the nosedive. Within ten years England's fourth place at Italia 90, the Taylor Report, the formation of the Premiership and the massive injection of cash from Sky would transform the game.

That doesn't mean that some clubs aren't still teetering on the brink of insolvency. We've seen both Leicester and Leeds facing administration in the last couple of seasons and Manchester City getting massively in debt. It doesn't matter how much money is coming in, if you spend more than you earn the results are the same.

The situation lower down the League is even worse. I've always been amazed that this country has sustained a fully professional League of ninety-two clubs. I don't think there's anywhere else in the world that could or has done that. It maybe that part-time football, which we all thought was a thing of the past, will become the thing of the future. People have talked about regionalizing the League but I don't really see how that would help financially. I just don't think the money is there to sustain a lot of the clubs as full-time professional outfits. But then as Barny was fond of saying, 'Football is a great sport but it is a bad business.'

At Wolves things deteriorated as rapidly as they would later at Elland Road. With money increasingly tight John Barnwell found himself in an impossible situation. The age of the players meant that a massive rebuilding programme was needed, but finances didn't allow it. That became plain during my second season when we were on the verge of signing Peter Reid from Bolton, only for the fee to prove beyond the club's pocket. And when Barny did scrape together sufficient funds to buy someone, things never seemed to work out. The winger Dave Thomas, for example, was brought in to supply crosses for me. Dave had been brilliant at Burnley and QPR but he never came off at Molineux. I'll come to why in a moment.

Barny was a great guy and I had a lot of time for him. He was a manager who stuck up for his players. One Saturday we were playing at Southampton at the Dell. We got a penalty and for one of the only times in my career I took it. Peter Shilton was in goal, he guessed right and tipped it round the post.

As you can imagine the Saints' fans behind the goal thought this was very amusing and they started yelling abuse at me. All the usual stuff about my sexual habits and those of the Scots in general. I had the last laugh, though. The corner resulting from Shilt's save was swung in and I met it perfectly, thumping it into the net. I celebrated by running behind the goal and letting fly with a good old-fashioned mouthful.

At half-time Barny's team talk was interrupted by a knock at the door and when he opened it there was a police officer saying, 'We wish to speak to Mr Andy Gray about a reported use of foul and abusive language.' One of the fans had complained. Barny said, 'I'll tell you what, officer. I'm issuing a complaint now about the foul and abusive language that was directed at my players from behind the goal. So when you've been and arrested the entire home end you can come back and I'll hand Mr Gray over to you. Until then, piss off, because I've got a job to do.' And that was the end of that.

So Barny was an excellent man. Unfortunately he'd been badly injured in a car crash shortly before I signed and he was still recovering. It was clear the strain of the situation was leaving him drained. Although he talked in the papers about taking the team on to win the European Cup we were never really certain how long he intended to stay. Even around the time of the League Cup Final there was talk of him retiring.

That uncertainty may have played a part in the slight niggle between him and his assistant Richie Barker. When John had been in hospital after his accident Richie had run the club for several months and I'm not sure if he ever really came to terms with going back to being number two again, especially since no one was sure about Barny's intentions. Eventually Richie left to take charge of Stoke City.

From a professional point of view I wasn't that sorry to see him go. Richie was a great guy socially. Really good company. I'd go for a drink with him any time. But as a coach he was too black and white for me. He had a set way of doing things and that was it. We didn't always see eye to eye about that. When I first arrived from Villa he started telling me that he wanted me to get to the back post more. I said, 'Have you ever watched me play? My game's about aggression and movement. I'm five feet eleven. I'm not going to win towering headers. I get goals by getting to the near post ahead of defenders.' But he still went on at me about it.

Richie's blinkered approach had a particularly bad effect on Dave Thomas. Dave could beat people and he could cross. He was well known in the game because he played in boots with rubber soles, never wore shin-pads and always had his socks rolled right down around his ankles. Everyone knew that about him. It was his trademark. But the minute Dave arrived at Molineux Richie insisted that he wore boots with studs in, put shin-guards on and, literally, pulled his socks up. It totally ruined the guy. Here was a player whose ability to get past the full back and whip the ball in would have guaranteed me twenty-five goals a season, and the coach had destroyed him more or less because he didn't like the way he dressed. It made no sense.

We started the 1980–81 season disastrously, losing five of our first eight matches and getting bundled out of the League Cup in humiliating style by Cambridge United. Our European campaign, meanwhile, ended at the first hurdle with defeat to PSV Eindhoven.

We recovered well enough in the League to finish in mid-table, and had a great run in the FA Cup, too. We reached the semi-finals and met Spurs at Hillsborough. In many ways that was the turning point for Wolves. Tottenham had a good side – Glenn Hoddle, Ossie Ardiles, Ricardo Villa – but it was a tight game and we could easily have won it. We'd gone one up early but Spurs had come back and taken a 2–1 lead. There was about ten minutes to go when Kenny Hibbitt burst into the Spurs penalty area. Glenn Hoddle tried to tackle him, caught him a bit and the referee, Clive Thomas, awarded us a penalty. It was a soft one, no doubt about it, but Kenny picked himself up and slotted it home. The incident deflated Spurs and from then on we were all over them.

Very late in the game I had a chance, a really good chance, to win it for us. A cross came into the box about seven or eight yards from goal, I stooped to get it and I was just ahead of the Spurs defender Paul Miller. As I went to head it Paul stretched out his leg and caught me straight in the face with his boot. The contact was enough to put me off. The header flew over the bar. I was really gutted. I knew that was the moment. Spurs hung on. I missed the replay with a thigh strain. They beat us 3–0 and won the Cup.

If we could have made it through that tie and into the final maybe things would have turned out differently for Wolves. It's possible. But as Sir Bobby Robson said recently, ' "If" is the biggest word in football.'

The following season the financial position was even worse and the one on the field was not much better. My own situation was unsettled. There was talk of Arsenal wanting to buy me and I almost moved to Elland Road for £900,000. Barny was keen to accept the offer, not because he wanted to get rid of me, but because he knew it was the only way he could raise money to strengthen the other areas of the team that desperately needed it. The Molineux chairman Harry Marshall refused to budge on their £1 million valuation, though, and eventually Leeds got tired of haggling. Incensed by the directors' failure to back his judgement, Barnwell agreed a £175,000 severance package with them and resigned. Sadly, because of subsequent events he never saw a penny of the money.

The man who replaced Barny was Ian Greaves. As a player Ian had won a League Championship with Man United and as a manager he'd taken the old Second Division title with both Huddersfield Town and Bolton Wanderers. He was a capable manager and very tough guy – just about the only person I've come across who could rival Jim McLean when it came to handing out a verbal battering. He gave me a particularly nasty time after I'd been sent off for dissent in the relegation battle with Stoke City. 'You've cost us the First Division,' was the gist of what he bawled at me, though it was padded out with several dozen choice bits and pieces. The tirade that followed went on for several minutes, during which Greavesie must have used every swear word in the English dictionary and quite a few that aren't. Unfortunately, no amount of shouting and cursing could have saved us that season and we were relegated.

As if that were not bad enough Wolves also went into receivership with a debt of £2 million. Doug Ellis, who'd temporarily severed his connections with Villa after a prolonged boardroom battle with Ron Bendall, had come in briefly at the end of the season in an attempt to save the club, but it couldn't be done and we slid into bankruptcy.

For a player that's an incredibly unsettling situation, because you know that you are just one phone call away from moving. To the administrator you are simply a saleable asset like a photocopier or filing cabinet and you can go at any time. At Wolves, by that stage, I was about the most valuable single item the club owned. And given the way my transfer value had dropped that's a fair indication of how bad things were. Every match when the final whistle went you wondered if that was your last game for the club, or even the club's last game in the League. In that scenario it's very hard to concentrate on football. But that's what you have to do.

Ironically the financial crisis almost resulted in me becoming a Manchester United player. Ron Atkinson, the manager at Old Trafford, had approached the liquidator with a £50,000 offer for me. It was a typically cheeky Ron move and it came very close to succeeding. A deal had been struck and a medical arranged for me in Manchester. I was hanging about at home waiting for a call to say when I was to go up and take it. But when the phone rang it was Derek Dougan to say he'd taken over at Molineux and was turning down United's bid.

I knew Doog from the PFA awards business and I respected him. Derek was a high-profile figure back then. He was larger than life, brimming with confidence, never slow to voice an opinion, and he was forever on TV or sounding off in the newspapers. The Northern Irishman was a football man. He loved Wolves, was a legend at Molineux and undoubtedly had the kind of energy needed to run a football club. To me he was the right man at the right time. His presence lifted the club, inspired the fans and briefly put us back on the right track.

Unfortunately, Derek's financial backers, the Bhatti brothers, didn't share his passion for the game. They were pleasant enough the few times we met them at the club, but it seemed to me that they only saw Molineux as development land with a football team on it. They had saved the club with the sole idea of demolishing the ground and building a supermarket on the site. When they found that the town planners in Wolverhampton wouldn't let them do that the investment they put in was minimal. Within a few seasons of me leaving Wolves were back in the mire again. Consecutive relegations left the proud old club in the bottom division, three sides of the stadium were condemned and the Bhattis slipped off back to Saudi Arabia, never to be heard of again. The local council stepped in to stop Wanderers disappearing altogether and then they at last found a genuine saviour in Sir Jack Hayward.

Ian Greaves and the Doog had some long-standing disagreement and the fact that Ian had only won five games in six months didn't help his cause, so he was quickly out of the door. Graham Hawkins replaced him.

Graham was a nice lad and a lifelong Wolves fan who'd played at centre half a few times for the club when Doog was the rampaging frontman. His management experience was strictly limited. He'd had a spell as assistant at Shrewsbury and that was it. Because he was a relative unknown a lot of people thought he was just a puppet with Dougan pulling the strings. That was unfair to both men. As far as I can recall Derek only ever interfered in team matters once and that was over the signing of a winger called Tony Towner from Rotherham. The Doog had watched Tony play while he was working as a pundit for Yorkshire TV and he went out and bought him without even consulting the manager.

The deal might have worked out, but poor Tony quickly fell foul of one of the maddest guys I've ever shared a dressing room with, Billy Kellock. Billy was a Glaswegian, an attacking midfielder, who'd wandered around English football for a decade without ever stopping anywhere long enough for the dust to settle. Before he'd arrived at Molineux he'd been with Villa, Cardiff, Norwich, Millwall, Chelmsford, Kettering, Peterborough and Luton. That's an impressive list, but then Billy had an unfortunate habit of upsetting people. It was strange, really, because he was a big-hearted lad and a real trier. He wasn't malicious in any way. He was just accident prone. He was one of those people who never goes looking for trouble but seems to stumble across it wherever he goes.

We were on a pre-season tour of Sweden shortly after Tony Towner had signed. I was sharing a room with Kenny Hibbitt. At about 2 a.m. there's this frantic banging on the door. Kenny opens it and in steps Billy white as a sheet. 'It's Tony,' he said, 'I think I might have killed him.'

'Don't be stupid,' we said. 'It's true,' Billy said, 'I've smashed him in the face. There's blood everywhere.'

We rushed next door to the room Billy was sharing with Tony, and sure enough there was his victim lying spark out on the bed with blood pouring from a gash over his eye. He turned out to be more shocked than anything else, but for a moment it was possible to believe that Billy had murdered him.

We got Tony sorted out and then asked Billy for an explanation. It turned out he'd returned to the room late that night feeling a bit the worse for wear. The room was dark and he'd blundered about for a while until finally he got it into his head to chuck a chair through the window. Unfortunately for Tony, at this point he'd woken up and popped his head out from under the covers. The chair had caught him right across the forehead. I'm not sure if Tony ever really recovered.

On another occasion Billy somehow got involved in a hamburger-eating contest with Alan Dodd, who used to play for Stoke. They set off with about a dozen hamburgers each and they were ramming them into their mouths as fast as they could. It was an absolutely extraordinary exhibition of scoffing, which, if I remember correctly, Billy won.

With crazy Billy Kellock in the team Graham Hawkins led Wolves straight back into the top flight. We got off to a great start with an unbeaten run of ten matches without conceding a single goal and practically had promotion wrapped up by Christmas. I helped by knocking in ten goals playing up front with Mel Eves and Wayne Clarke.

Despite our success I can't say I enjoyed the experience of

playing in the Second Division much. The ability of the players was poorer, the game was more physical and the surroundings you played in were often depressing. Even when we made certain of promotion with a 3–3 draw with Charlton at the Valley I came off the field feeling like somebody who'd put in a shift at a job they don't much like. The move to Wolves had promised a lot, but all it had delivered was this. The effects of failure creep up on you in football. They gradually wear away at your self-belief. That season for the first time in my life I started to doubt myself as a player, to wonder if I could still do it.

Given our resources the First Division was never going to be easy and it proved even tougher than we could have imagined. Graham Hawkins had done well in the Second Division, but I think he found the step up pretty hard. The money situation didn't help. Graham had gone to the board in the summer asking for cash to buy Paul Bracewell and Mick McCarthy but they wouldn't let him have any, so the only new players we got in were poor Tony Towner and my old pal John Burridge.

Budge had nowhere to stay when he arrived in the Midlands so he moved in with me until he could sort out some accommodation for himself. Budge was completely dedicated to his job. He was a training fanatic and he had his own unique way of sharpening his reflexes. On Friday nights he'd come down into the lounge with his gloves on and lie on the sofa watching TV. My job was to test him out by throwing bits of fruit at him without warning. There'd be apples and bananas whizzing around and all the while Budgie would apparently be concentrating all his attention on Bruce Forsyth's *Play Your Cards Right*.

'Keep me sharp, Andy. Keep me sharp,' he'd shout, diving

across the cushions to grab a flying satsuma, 'Oh c'mon. You'll have to do better than that to catch the Budge out.'

After he retired from playing and was managing Blyth Spartans, Budgie got a slot on a Tyne Tees TV football show on which he fronted a rock band. I think I caught an early rehearsal for that programme because one night when I came back from an evening out I found him standing in the sitting room, stripped to the waist and miming along to a record using a snooker cue as a microphone. That was the only time I've ever seen him blush.

Despite his eccentricities in many ways Budgie was ahead of his time, particularly when it came to looking after himself. He didn't drink or gamble, and his diet consisted mainly of boiled rice and steamed fish and vegetables. That's standard stuff nowadays, but back then, when most players' idea of a nutritionally sound meal was plenty of red meat and fried potatoes, it was regarded as very weird indeed.

Budgie was a fine goalkeeper. I'd say that he was probably about four inches short of being a great one. To me there are three main things to look for in a goalkeeper: agility, decision making and size. Agility speaks for itself. Budgie was gymnastic in that respect. I recall he once brought the house down when we were staying at a hotel in Magaluf on an end-of-season tour. One of the other guests had been strutting around trying to impress the girls with his diving skills in the swimming pool, soaking those of us who were sunbathing while he was at it. Eventually Budge got so sick of this that he decided to put on a display of his own. He jumped up from his sun lounger and proceeded to walk around the pool and up the ladder of the diving board on his hands. When he got to the top he performed an immaculate dive with somersault and emerged from the pool to a spontaneous round of applause. By that time the show-off had got the message and disappeared.

Budgie's decision making was excellent. He watched every game he could and analysed every goalkeeper he saw, picking out strengths and weaknesses. He kept a keen eye on forwards, too, noting which foot they liked to strike with and the movements of the body that signalled a shot was on the way. The goalkeeper is in a unique position on the field. Even apparently routine decisions like whether to come out for a cross or not can decide the outcome of game. They are the only players who carry that kind of responsibility. Whatever he might have been like off the field, you never had any worries with Budge on it.

It was only his height that let Budgie down. As a striker you're always less confident when you face a really big goalkeeper like Peter Schmeichel, David Seaman or Chris Kirkland. Their presence is daunting. They literally do seem to fill the goal. Psychologically it has an impact on you. Budgie just didn't quite have that kind of massive build. And unfortunately no amount of sensible living or diving about after oranges could make up for that.

Budge was his usual ebullient self at Wolves. He pulled one memorable stunt at the Christmas party. The other players had decided to get their own back on him for all his practical jokes by trying to confuse him over what to wear. Half of us told him it was fancy dress and the other half that it was a black-tie affair. We should have known better. Burridge turned up wearing half of each. Literally. He'd divided himself down the middle. The right side of his outfit was a snappy James Bond-style tuxedo, the left side a ragged tramp's outfit. He was a one-off, no doubt about that.

But with the defence he had in front of him Budgie was on a hiding to nothing. We could have had Gordon Banks and Lev Yashin between the sticks simultaneously and it wouldn't have made a difference. Frankly, the club was a shambles.

We struggled right from the start, losing nine of our first twelve matches and drawing the other three. Even the usually loyal Molineux fans seemed to have thrown the towel in. When we played Villa at home in the local derby only 13,000 turned up.

We had some good old pros in that team and it's a measure of their character that instead of just throwing their hands up and giving in they were prepared to take responsibility and try and change things. One Monday after we'd been hammered 5–0 by Nottingham Forest – a really embarrassing afternoon – Kenny Hibbitt, Mel Eves, John Richards, me and a few others went to a pub near Molineux called the Goal Post to talk over what we could do to rescue things. We really cared about what was happening.

Kenny in particular had bitter experience of this sort of situation because he'd been at Bradford Park Avenue as a youngster when they dropped out of the League and he wasn't happy about having to go through it all again. We sat there for several hours discussing things we thought might help get our season back on track. Afterwards I went home to find a message waiting for me. It was Graham Hawkins. He wanted me to report to Molineux immediately. I phoned him and asked why. He said, 'The administrators have accepted a bid. You're going to Everton.'

It came as a massive surprise to me. I knew the Everton boss Howard Kendall and his assistant Mick Heaton had been to watch me in a League Cup match at Preston. My knee was swollen up like a balloon that night and I performed really badly. I couldn't believe that on the strength of that performance they'd come in for me. But they'd obviously seen something.

I went to see Graham in his office. He didn't want me to leave, but he had little choice. He told me to travel up to Goodison the next day. 'You better take your medical file with you,' he said, and handed me a folder that was as thick as my thigh. I took one look at it and thought to myself, 'Bloody hell, if I show them this there's no way they'll sign me.'

I had a big open fire in my house and that night I sat in front of it sifting through this folder and chucking documents into the flames. The next day when I travelled up to Merseyside I appeared to be a good deal healthier than I had been the day before.

When I arrived at Goodison Park the press boys asked me what I hoped to achieve. I said, 'To win trophies.' They didn't burst out laughing, but it was close.

I could understand their point of view. The man who had signed me, Howard Kendall, was unproven as a coach, and Everton were a struggling side. And that's putting it mildly. They were fifth from bottom of the table. In a League Cup tie against Chesterfield shortly before I signed they'd drawn just 8,066 to Goodison, the lowest crowd in the history of Merseyside's big two. Leaflets were circulating at home games calling for Howard to be sacked – '30,000 absent fans can't be wrong', one of them said. The manager had banned the press from the training ground. And to cap it all they'd just travelled to Anfield and been crushed 3–0 by Liverpool. Crisis was hardly a big enough word for it.

And me? Well, I was a forward with a dodgy right leg who'd watched his transfer value fall from £1.5 million to £280,000 in just over four years. Though I was still only twenty-seven years old there were a fair few people around who thought I was already past it. To the doubters signing me looked like the last reckless gamble of a manager desperately trying to save his job.

Once again my knee almost scuppered the deal. When I arrived with my heavily reduced medical file there was some amazement from the coaching staff that it was so thin. 'I thought you had an appalling injury record,' they said. 'Oh, no,' I replied casually, 'that's all been typically hyped up by the media.'

The medical people weren't that easily fooled. I was taken down to the hospital for a check-up that was easily the most thorough one of my career. A specialist and the club doctor both spent what seemed like hours poking and prodding at my leg. After that I was ordered to go and sit in the waiting room while they examined the X-rays. When they called me back in I suspected the worst, but they simply asked me what I would do if the move to Everton didn't come off. 'Go back and play for Wolves on Saturday,' I replied. The thought didn't exactly fill me with joy, but it was clearly the correct answer because they approved the transfer.

After the misery of Molineux the move to Merseyside gave me the lift I needed. When I first arrived in Liverpool Howard Kendall took me out for a meal in a local pub. I'd actually played against my new boss when I was at Villa and he was coming to the end of his career at Birmingham. He'd arrived at Goodison as player-coach. It was his first management position and, as I say, he was having a very tough time of it. Despite that, as we sat and chatted and he outlined his plans, it was plain that his enthusiasm for the game was still there. I found that really refreshing after the doom and gloom of Molineux. When you're around failure, as I was at Wolves, it starts to drag you down. Doubts creep into your mind. The less confidence you have the worse you play and the worse you play the poorer the team's results. It's a vicious spiral and you need a positive focus to pull out of it.

No matter what was going on at Everton, to me there seemed to be an energy about the place. I remember on my first day of training at Bellefield the left back John Bailey swung a cross. I met it with a good header and smacked it into the goal. At that moment my mood lifted. For the first time in years I was buzzing again. I felt good things were about to happen. Given the circumstances others might have seen things differently. And my arrival hardly provoked an immediate and dramatic improvement.

In my first game for my new club we beat Forest 1–0. Then, after losing to Arsenal and Norwich, we got a morale-boosting win at Old Trafford. I scored my first goal in a 1–1 draw with Aston Villa, but we then went on a terrible run that culminated in a 3–0 defeat to my old club Wolves at Molineux two days before Christmas. I guess we should have known we were in for trouble when David Johnson damaged a hamstring getting up from the dinner table on the night before the game. Wolves were the worst club in the division by a mile, they were already doomed, but they absolutely battered us. The pressure on Howard went up a notch. 'Kendall Out' chants and demonstrations against the manager were a feature of nearly every game we played home and away.

A lot is made of the way Manchester United chairman Martin Edwards refused to bow to the pressure to get rid of Alex Ferguson during the Scot's early struggles to bring silverware to Old Trafford. Rightly so. But in my view Philip Carter of Everton deserves full marks for sticking by Howard during that arguably even more difficult time. It would have been very easy for the chairman to opt for short-term popularity and pull the plug on Kendall, but he didn't. And like Edwards, he got his reward.

Evertonians point to different games as the turning point in the club's fortunes that season. Some will talk about the League Cup match against Oxford United. That game was played on the famous slope at the Manor Ground against a team that had already knocked out Manchester United, Leeds and Newcastle. I was cup-tied because of the game at Deepdale, but I watched from the stands. It was a tense affair. We were trailing for most of it and just as it looked as though we were going out, at nine minutes from time, Oxford's Kevin Brock under-hit a back pass and Adrian Heath nicked in, rounded the keeper and struck a shot that crawled just the right side of the post and into the net. Another couple of inches and that famous equalizer would have bounced out. When they talk about a fine line between success and failure, that is it right there.

The game against Oxford was important, definitely, particularly for Howard. If we'd gone down I think it's highly unlikely he would have survived. But as for the moment that transformed the team, I'd look at another fixture, one hardly anybody remembers – the League game against Birmingham City at St Andrews that followed the Wolves thumping.

Before the match against the Blues, Howard sat us all down in the team hotel and gave us a long and at times blistering team talk. He said, 'This is it. This is your last chance.' He accused some players in the side of not pulling their weight and said that if we didn't get a result that was the lot of us finished. He would bring in reserves and kids from the youth team instead. It did the trick. We went out and beat Birmingham 2–0. After that we only lost three more League games.

In the next match we were away to Stoke City in the FA Cup. There were 10,000 Evertonians at the Victoria Ground that day. Given how badly the side had been doing that was an incredible turnout. For his team talk before the game Howard didn't say a single word. He just opened the windows of the dressing room. We were right next to the away end and a thunderous noise rolled in through the open windows. It was all we needed. There was no way we could let them down. We won 2–0.

Howard's man-management on those two occasions was top class, but a few other little things had also made a big difference to the club. Firstly Howard's long-time friend and former Everton teammate Colin Harvey had been promoted from reserve to first team coach alongside Mick Heaton. That was a great decision. Mick was a nice guy, a bubbly personality and so soft-hearted that the lads nicknamed him 'Easy'. But he was more or less Howard's personal assistant. He made sure everything was taken care of for the manager. Harvey was much better on the tactical side.

Colin expressed himself simply and he spoke in the players' language. He could be rough when he wanted to be. His own Everton career had ended because of a hip injury and he still felt the pain from it. That didn't stop him racing around and flying into tackles in training. Colin had won a championship medal at Goodison and the sight of him putting himself through agony was a reminder to all of us just what it took to be a winner.

As a coach Colin never over-complicated things and he never gave you too much to think about at any one time. He wasn't one of those who make you sit down and watch a whole game and then say, 'OK, now let's analyse it.' He'd go home himself and pick out the passages of play he wanted to show you and put them on a tape. Then, on Monday after training, he'd call a few players upstairs to his office and for ten minutes or so he'd go through the video with them and together they'd work things out from that. Maybe Graeme Sharp and I would go up and he'd run through something he thought we ought to be doing, or maybe the weakness of some opposition defenders he'd noticed. He just homed in on those little details.

Colin was also very passionate and he didn't mess about. If he was annoyed about something everybody knew it. His arrival sharpened things up in training and in the dressing room. It was a massive appointment, one that had a major impact on everything that was about to happen at Everton.

I think there was a sense, too, that almost at the same time as Colin was moving up Howard finally discovered his best team. Whether that was good luck or good planning its hard to say. Howard wasn't an overly tactical manager. He liked his players to just go out and play. But he was a fiddler – if not quite a tinkerman – when it came to selection. He was trying different combinations all the time in an attempt to get the right one.

Peter Reid was the sort of competitor Colin Harvey liked and he was instrumental in getting him back into the team. Reidy had other supporters too. In those days Ian St John ran a famous football phone-in show on Merseyside local radio. After the defeat by Liverpool – a game Peter didn't feature in despite the fact that Howard sent out a five-man midfield – a guy phoned in and started complaining about the fact that Reidy wasn't in the side. 'There's no doubt about it that lad should be playing every week,' the bloke said. Ian St John asked the caller what his name was. 'Mike Reid.' 'Are you any relation?' Ian asked. The Saint was joking, but sure enough it turned out that Mike was Peter's brother.

Reidy had been struggling with niggling injuries all year. The turning point for him came in a home League Cup tie against Coventry that was played in front of a 9,000 crowd the week before I arrived. The Sky Blues were 1–0 up when Peter came off the bench and turned the game in Everton's favour. He was an ever present after that and did so well it's incredible to think that anybody ever doubted he should be in the side.

A few other things like that happened during my first few weeks at Everton, little bits of good fortune that might have turned out differently. Mark Higgins, a stalwart who'd been at Goodison for years, suffered a bad pelvic injury. Kevin Ratcliffe, who'd been bumping around playing in every position from left back to left wing trying to get in the side, came in as Mark's replacement basically because there was no one else available. He ended up becoming one of the best centre backs in the business, the youngest captain in the First Division and the most successful in the history of the club.

The story with Derek Mountfield was much the same. He came in from Tranmere and nobody took him seriously. Another spate of injuries and he was banged into the backline alongside Ratters. It was supposed to be a stopgap, but the pair of them gelled so perfectly that they were never separated through choice again. And if that wasn't enough Derek also discovered he had the knack of scoring important goals from set-pieces. If you've got a centre back whose guaranteeing you half a dozen goals a season you are fortunate, believe me.

Goalkeeper Neville Southall had been one of Howard's first signings when he took over from Gordon Lee. He was brought in from Bury and at first he'd been a bit overawed by things at Goodison. Everton was a huge club with a massive tradition and sometimes that can unsettle players. I even felt it myself a bit at times. There's pride in wearing the jersey of Dixie Dean, Tommy Lawton and Alex Young, but there's pressure, too.

Just about the only player who never seemed affected by that responsibility was Terry Curran. Terry had been brought in to Goodison on loan during Howard's first season and he'd helped the team stave off relegation. Everton hadn't been able to raise the money to buy him outright then, but they'd got him permanently a year later. Terry was a tricky winger and real cocky character. He'd been signed from Third Division Sheffield United, but from the way he carried on you'd have thought he'd been a star at the San Siro, not Bramall Lane. To hear Terry he should have been in the team every week and never have been dropped from it for any reason whatsoever. He was one of those players who was never quite as good as he thought he was. In fact if he'd been Pele he wouldn't have been quite as good as he thought he was.

Neville didn't have that sort of self-belief. It took him a year or more to settle and Howard even sent him out on loan to Port Vale at one point. By the time I got to Goodison, Nev was clearly feeling more confident. Kevin Ratcliffe told me that just after I signed, Neville went in to see Howard about a pay increase. The manager said, 'I'd love to give you a rise, but I don't have the cash. I've just spent it on Andy Gray.' 'Well, sell him then,' Nev replied

Although he wasn't in the John Burridge class, Nev was another big daft goalie. He had a sponsored car but he couldn't drive – his wife had to ferry him everywhere – and he once turned up at Wembley wearing his suit and a pair of flip-flops.

When I'd first come into the side Howard really couldn't decide between Neville and Jim Arnold as his first choice. They played practically alternate games until he finally settled on Nev. Jim was a good goalkeeper, and excellent shot stopper, but Howard could see there was something special in the

Welshman. He was right about that. Over the next few years Nev became the world's best goalkeeper. And that's not an exaggeration.

And then there was me. As I've said when I arrived Howard was almost on his way out. I was his last throw of the dice and the fact is that if he'd had a little more money to spend he wouldn't have bought me at all. He was after a Brazilian striker, Nunes, and he'd also inquired about Paul Mariner, but he didn't have the cash for him, so he got me instead. He'd come to watch me play at Deepdale that night and even though I'd been appalling he must have felt there was something still there that was worth a risk. I scored fourteen goals for him in forty-four starts.

So in the space of a few weeks Howard found a goalie, two centre backs and a central midfielder, and brought in a centre forward who'd been written off by practically everyone else in the game. And it all worked out. Good planning? Maybe, but I think luck had a big hand, too.

Next up for us in the FA Cup came Third Division Gillingham at Goodison. Despite all my positive feelings about Everton the tie almost put an early end to my career on Merseyside.

On Merseyside the Gills gave us the fright of our lives, forcing a 0–0 draw and coming close to winning when they hit the bar near the end. We travelled down to Kent for the replay the following Tuesday. We were having our usual pre-match meal when Howard asked me to step outside the restaurant for a minute because he wanted a word with me. 'I've decided not to play you tonight, Andy,' he said.

I was stunned. It was the first ever time in my career I'd been dropped. Admittedly I'd missed an easy chance in the first game, but apart from that I thought I was doing well.

I wasn't sure how to react. My initial feeling was to tell the manager to stuff it and walk out. I remembered that Andy King had done a similar thing a few weeks before when he was dropped. I hadn't agreed with him doing that because it affected the team. The spirit at Everton was great and the subs were a big part of that. We were one of the first clubs where the bench celebrated goals like the players on the pitch. So now even though I felt like walking I managed to check myself. I still had a job to do for the side. I took a deep breath and told Howard that I thought he was wrong and that his decision was unjustified.

The boss listened but said his mind was made up, turned and went back into the dining room. The choice was with me. I could either follow him and rejoin the team or turn my back and walk away. After some hard thinking I went back into the restaurant. It was one of the best decisions I have ever made.

After another draw – one that owed a hell of a lot to Neville's goalkeeping – we eventually overcame Gillingham 3–0. I had a hand in all three goals. On the coach afterwards Howard came up to me and congratulated me. He sat down and we had a chat and he told me he'd been wrong to drop me and that he'd never do it again. I told him he shouldn't say that because in football you never know what's going to happen next. As it turned out, though, he was true to his word, more or less.

We dispensed with Shrewsbury, and against Notts County in the next round I got a diving header to set up a semi-final against Southampton. It was one of the most amazing goals of my career. Sheeds took a free kick out on the left. He swung the ball into the box and it went just over Sharpy's head and landed about eight yards from goal. I knew instinctively that if I went for it with either foot I'd be stretching and I'd put it over the bar so, instead, I launched myself at it full length. It was about eight inches off the ground when I made contact, practically a half-volley, but it went into the net. In the League Cup the boys made it to the final but lost to Liverpool after a replay. There was no time to brood on that because a few days after that defeat we were running out at Highbury to take on Southampton.

That semi-final was extraordinary. I've never travelled to a game with a group of players who were so confident of winning in all my life. There was not a sign of nerves.

The windows of the dressing rooms at Arsenal open straight out onto the street. The whole area just seemed to be full of Evertonians. There was blue and white everywhere you looked. The fans were singing 'Tell your ma to put the champagne on ice, we're going to Wembley twice'. We opened the windows and waved to them and to our families who were milling around down below. It was almost a party atmosphere even though we still had the game to play.

I'm sure our attitude affected Southampton. In fact I know it did. Years later their manager Lawrie McMenemy told me that when the two teams were lined up in the tunnel he looked at his side – who were vastly experienced – and they looked like they were carrying the weight of the world on their shoulders; then he looked across at us – relaxed, full of belief – and he knew then that Saints had lost right there.

But it still took another brilliant save from Neville Southall to get us there. Nev had been sensational all season but in the first half he pulled off a series of saves that was exceptional even by his standards. The game went to extra time and we nicked it 1–0, with Adrian Heath getting the goal after Derek Mountfield had flicked on Reidy's free kick.

Heath – known as Inchy after the cartoon character Inch High Private Eye – had been Howard's first big buy. He'd got him from Stoke City for £700,000. Like Nev he had taken time to settle in. He'd been unsure whether to play in midfield or upfront and the price tag hadn't helped. For a while a few of the Everton players had felt the manager gave Inchy too much attention and support. They even took to calling him 'Howard's son'. When I arrived he was struggling. Before my first game against Forest I said to him, 'When we're out there and you see the ball coming to me get yourself around me and I'll make something happen. I'll head the ball on, or I'll knock a defender over and something will drop for you.' And sure enough it did. I got a knock-down, Inchy popped it in and from that moment on his whole bearing changed. He started to believe in his own ability. Eventually Adrian won everbody over. He was a brave lad with a knack of getting important goals. After a while he became so popular and well respected he was voted in as our PFA rep.

The journey back to Merseyside after the game was absolutely unbelievable. We boarded the coach and started up the M1 and M6. There were Evertonians, blue-and-white scarves flapping, everywhere. What we did as we drove along was to get the coach driver to overtake the supporters' buses very slowly. The fans inside would all be snoozing or boozing and as we pulled alongside we'd glance over at them. Eventually one would look our way and you'd see the realization dawning in his eyes. Then he'd start screaming and shouting and all the rest would come piling over to the windows on the right-hand side to wave at us. How the hell none of those coaches tipped over I'll never know.

By now the whole team was brimming with confidence. I don't think I've ever played in a side that had more belief in itself than we did. We were sure we would overcome Watford in the final because we simply felt unbeatable.

And it seemed to me that Watford were just pleased to be there. Everything that was coming out of the Watford camp in the build-up suggested that. They were delighted to have got that far and they were looking forward to a day out. For us it was about winning.

Watford had some good players – Maurice Johnston, George Riley, John Barnes – but they were a really inexperienced side. I think the back four were the youngest in Cup Final history – two of them were teenagers and the oldest, Steve Terry, was twenty-one. Trevor Steven took advantage and tore the full back, Paul Price, to pieces.

Howard had brought Trevor in from Burnley. The Turf Moor side had a reputation for unearthing top-class players – Ralph Coates, David Thomas and Leighton James amongst them – and the youngster was tagged as the next big thing after he'd played superbly for them in a televised League Cup match at Anfield.

Trevor was a quiet lad and like Nev and Inchy it took him time to settle. In fact it wasn't until that day at Wembley that he really began to put in the kind of performances that we all knew he was capable of from watching him in training. Trevor set up both goals. The first came when his drive hit Sharpy, who managed to control it and shot past Steve Sherwood.

My own goal caused a bit of debate. Trevor hit a high cross over from the right. Watford's keeper Steve Sherwood came to collect it. I was challenging for the ball along with my marker Steve Terry. The keeper was stretching with his arms away from his body to get it and I got my head in just quick enough to knock it out of his hands. As Sherwood followed through he collided with Terry and it was that more than anything I did that knocked him over. By this stage the ball had trickled into the net. Nine times out of ten the referee would have given a free kick to the defending team, but this time he got it right and pointed to the centre spot. People still tell me it shouldn't have been allowed to stand, but in my mind there's no doubt it was a perfectly legitimate goal. And it killed off the game.

As we did our lap of honour and took the applause of the fans I felt not only that we'd won the Cup, but also that I'd won a personal battle. In eight months I'd gone from sitting in the pub in Wolverhampton with Kenny Hibbitt debating how we were going to salvage the season, to doing a lap of honour at Wembley. Along the way I'd proved that I was still a top-class footballer and not the injury-prone has-been many had taken me for.

The move had allowed me to revert back to type. I'd become my confident, ebullient self again. It had been a fresh start and in just the right place. There's no way I would compare myself to Eric Cantona in terms of ability, but I think that just as Old Trafford was made for Eric, so Goodison was made for me. It brought the best out of me. Everything about it – the fans, the team, the history of centre forwards – was right. It was like it was meant to be.

Howard may have ridden his luck a bit in my first season at Goodison, but he was a shrewd judge of players. He proved that shortly after the Cup Final when he bought central midfielder Paul Bracewell from Sunderland.

The whole squad were taken aback by that news. Our midfield four of Steven, Sheedy, Reid and Kevin Richardson had been brilliant all season. Like most of the other players I couldn't work out the thinking behind the move. Richo was a really good player. Sitting in front of the back four, breaking up attacks and keeping it simple with his passing he was so effective it was impossible to see how anyone could be better.

Howard was spot on though. Brace complimented Peter Reid perfectly. Their understanding was terrific right from the start and you could almost guarantee that if somebody got past Reidy, Paul would be a few yards behind him waiting to get them. Brace wasn't the quickest player but he could run for ninety minutes and he put the opposition under such pressure that they ended up making errors. He was a terrific, neat and tidy, no-frills pro who only missed out on playing for England because of a mysterious ankle injury it took specialists over eighteen months to diagnose and cure.

Brace wasn't the only signing Howard made. He also brought in Pat van den Hauwe. I'd played against Pat when he was at Birmingham. I wasn't sure he was good enough for Everton. Once again, though, Howard had got it right. Pat turned out to be a great athlete, very quick. He played at left back even though he was right footed, and also slotted in at centre half when we had injuries and did a fantastic job there too.

Van den Hauwe was probably the only cockney-Welsh-Belgian I've ever played with or against and he was well-known as a hard man. He'd been part of the so-called Birmingham Five, a group of Blues players who terrorized virtually the entire Midlands in the early 1980s. He had a particular dislike for newspapermen. Generally the press would loiter around outside the dressing rooms after a game and we'd give them a few lines as we left to go home. The only thing they got from Pat was his meanest stare.

When Pat was called into the Wales team he finally agreed to do an interview with the *Sun*. 'I'll do it on one condition,' he told the reporter, 'You don't ask me any tricky questions.' The reporter agreed and then said, 'So, Pat, you must be very proud to have been selected for the Welsh side.'

The defender glared at him, 'I told you no tricky questions,' he snarled, got up and walked off.

Pat was an incredible guy. He was often spotted jogging near his home at Formby. Nothing unusual about that. Except that quite often it was four in the morning. He'd say to his missus 'I'm off to get the paper' at five o'clock on a Monday and not turn up home until Friday morning. Seriously. Nobody knew where he'd been in the meantime. Unsurprisingly, we nicknamed him Psycho-Pat. He wasn't everyone's cup of tea,

1. 'Aw The Boys', the Dundee United squad 1974–5.

2. *Right.* A fresh-faced youth at Tannadice, earning a princely £16 a week.

3. *Below.* My first senior goal, a thumping header against St Johnstone. You can just about see me at the far right.

4. Scotland's 'Team of the Year' for 1975 including a nineteen-year-old
Alan Hansen, and one of my heroes, Kenny Dalglish.

5. The Gray clan at home in Drumchapel. Willie, Mum, James and Duncan (standing).

6. The opening day of the first of my three spells at Villa Park.

7. *Left*. Saluting the Villa fans on my home League debut against West Ham.

8. *Below*. Hard to imagine a Premiership striker these days driving a Ford Escort, but I was happy with it.

9. *Opposite, top left*. Testing out the prototype of a new Scotland kit. Luckily it didn't catch on.

10. *Opposite, top right*. Looking smart and sober for a trip to the FA Disciplinary Committee during the 1976–7 season.

11. *Opposite, bottom*. My first trip to Wembley, for the 1977 League Cup Final against Everton. It took three matches to settle it in our favour.

12. Showing off the 1977 PFA Player and Young Player of the Year Awards.

13. *Above.* Recovering from one of my many knee operations.

14. *Right.* The offending cartilage.

15. Behind the bar at my ill-fated Birmingham night club, Holy City Zoo.

16. Taking it easy during the era of punk rock and the perm.

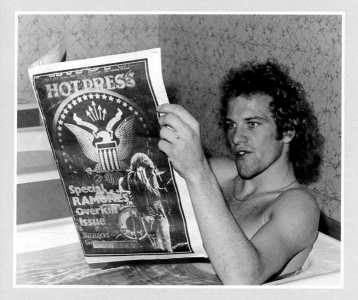

17. With Wolves' boss John Barnwell on the eve of becoming Britain's most expensive player.

18. The winning goal in the 1980 League Cup Final. My only thought, 'Whatever you do don't fall over.'

but we liked him. And whatever Pat got up to off the field, on it he kept his cool pretty well. He only saw red once all season, in a game against QPR when he got in a scuffle with Simon Stainrod.

When I first arrived at Goodison, Everton had been living in the shadow of neighbours Liverpool for over a decade. The team from across Stanley Park had been hoovering up domestic and European honours while Everton had won nothing since the days when Howard and Colin had played in the midfield alongside Alan Ball. The FA Cup win at last gave Evertonians something to cheer about, and although we'd lost that year's League Cup Final to Liverpool there was a feeling that the red tide was at last being turned.

As if to emphasize the point, on the first day of the 1984–5 season we beat Liverpool to win the Charity Shield. Unfortunately I was injured for that game and for the start of the League campaign. When I eventually came back it almost sparked a major dressing room row.

Like me Graeme Sharp came from the outskirts of Glasgow. He was a quiet lad who'd played as a part-timer for Dumbarton, scored a sackful of goals and been signed for Everton by Howard's predecessor Gordon Lee in 1980 for £125,000. I know that when Howard took over he didn't fancy Graeme as a player and he'd nearly sold him to Aberdeen. But Sharpy stuck it out in the reserves and eventually got his chance when the team suffered a bad run of injuries. By the time I arrived he'd established himself as a first-choice striker. That was another of Howard's little bits of good fortune.

Graeme and I struck up a fantastic partnership at Goodison, though I'd have to say he didn't exactly endear himself to me at our first meeting when he stuck out a hand and blurted,

'I used to watch you when I was at school!' There's nothing like being reminded of your age.

Graeme had a huge amount of ability. It was often suggested that he and I shouldn't play upfront together because we were too similar. That was a misreading of the situation. Because of his size a lot of people characterized Sharpy as a big target man, but he was actually a very skilful player, excellent on the deck and with a great first touch.

I think it's fair to say that when I'd first teamed up with him Graeme had been a scorer of great goals rather than a great goal scorer. He had the class but he lacked that extra bit of aggression you need inside the box. Graeme and I roomed together and we spent a lot of time talking about the game. I taught him a few tricks of the trade like jumping a little early so you get your body in between the ball and the defender. I gave him advice about leading the line and taking up positions. He made himself more positive in his runs and a little bit meaner, too. Within a couple of seasons it was a toss-up between him and Mark Hughes who was the best centre forward in English football.

For my comeback game at St James' Park I was handed the number nine jersey and Graeme found himself relegated to the bench. He was very upset about being dropped from the starting line-up. As we were getting changed he pulled me to one side and asked if he could have a word. In his hand he was holding a letter. I asked him what it was and he told me it was a transfer request. 'I'm giving it to the boss after the game,' he said.

Having nearly walked out myself after being dropped from the Gillingham game I could understand Graeme's feelings. On the other hand I'd swallowed my disappointment and as a result ended up with an FA Cup winners medal. I told Graeme to forget about it. It was the first time he'd been dropped from the team for months. He was bound to get another chance. He followed my advice and fortunately was straight back in the side for the following week.

I wasn't so lucky. I scored against Newcastle but also broke a bone in my foot. I was out of action for another six weeks. During that time Everton emerged as serious challengers for Liverpool's title. The team were playing brilliantly, so when I came back I had to content myself with a place on the subs bench. I wasn't content. I found it massively frustrating. I understood that Howard couldn't change a winning formula, but sitting watching and keeping myself match fit by playing in the reserves was never going to satisfy me however well my teammates were going.

It would have been easy for me to get depressed. Luckily Everton had a couple of guys around who could always lift the mood. One was the full back John Bailey, known as the Gnasher because his black hair stuck out all over the place and made him look like Dennis the Menace's dog. John is a bit of an unsung hero and in many ways typified that team. Bails was a Scouser, a true blue Evertonian, a big joker, a smashing lad who loved a drink or two, or three, or four. Bails had the habit of getting his words muddled up and he'd say things like 'I'm as happy as a log,' or 'He's as quick as a leper.' He had a terrific left foot and he was good on the ball and going forward, but he wasn't so strong defensively. Or as Bails himself once said, he was at his best 'just playing it off the collar'.

He'd actually won a cap with the England B team. He was very proud of that. 'I can see it as if it was yesterday, Andy,' he'd tell me, 'All of us in our white shirts lining up for the national anthem,' and he'd begin whistling the 'Stars and Stripes'. That was Bails. He came into training one day and told us all he and his wife had just had a Winchester delivered. He said the Winchester had cost him his entire win bonus but that it had been worth it because he had always wanted a Winchester and this one was top of the range. It took us days to work out that what he'd actually bought wasn't a gun but a Chesterfield sofa. Another time, Bails came into the dressing room after training and announced that he'd just signed a deal to go out and play in South Africa over the summer. 'Absolutely fantastic,' he said. 'Good signing-on fee, nice salary and I can take the missus out with me too.'

Jim Arnold, who read the broadsheet newspapers and was up on world affairs said, 'What about apartheid?'

'Two bedrooms overlooking the sea,' Gnasher replied.

Although Bails was a defender I'll always remember him for a bizarre goal he scored against Luton Town during my first season. He got the ball in our half and belted it up the field. The Hatters' goalkeeper Findlay came bombing out to meet it, misjudged the bounce totally and could only flap as it pinged up over his head and into the net. John didn't get many goals and he was ecstatic, jumping up and down and yelling, 'Even Pele couldn't score from his own half. Even Pele couldn't do that.' Just thinking about his celebration was enough to set the team laughing for months afterwards.

The other person who could always raise my spirits was the coach Terry Darracott. Terry was another True Blue. He was also as bald as a bowling ball. I'll never forget one time when we went up to Glasgow to celebrate Howard winning the Manager of the Year award. Terry was convinced that by the time the night was over we'd all have forgotten the name of our hotel, so he got the receptionist to scribble it on top of his head with a magic marker. When we got into a taxi in the small hours and the driver asked 'Where to?' Terry simply bent forward and pointed to the writing on his pate.

I also made my own contribution to brightening the lads' lives with an embarrassing moment during my first ever appearance on *A Question of Sport*. We had to identify famous football grounds from a photo. When mine came up I couldn't figure out where it was. 'Hillsborough?' I guessed, 'Loftus Road?' I had about six goes before the host David Coleman put me out of my misery – it was Ibrox. Now in fairness to myself I'd like to point out that firstly it was an aerial photo, an angle from which, never having flown over the ground, I had never seen it before, and secondly that it had been vastly modernized since I'd last played there. But no matter what I said in my own defence I knew it would do no good when I went in for training next day. And I was right. A few days later I got a big envelope in the post. Inside there was a photo of Rangers' ground with an arrow pointing to it and the words 'This is Ibrox' in big letters. It was from Derek Johnstone, or Big Ba as he was always known for some unfathomable reason.

I got endless stick about that mistake from the rest of the team. Luckily Reidy did his bit to put a stop to that. When he appeared on the show shortly afterwards he somehow managed to mistake Ossie Ardiles for Garth Crooks.

Despite my early blunder I've been on *A Question of Sport* quite a few times since. I really enjoy it. I like the banter. I know Sue Barker very well and Ally McCoist, of course, and John Parrott is a really good lad. It's nice to meet other sports people too. People like Frankie Dettori. But the funny thing is that no matter how often I'm on it the one appearance people never forget is that first one.

Sometimes in football one player's misfortune is another's opportunity. I'd been getting increasingly fed up with my subs role at Goodison when one of the first choice forwards Adrian Heath tore his knee ligaments in a game at Hillsborough. Inchy was a great lad. I wouldn't have wished any harm on him. At the same time his injury opened the way for me to make a return to the starting line-up. If I felt guilty it didn't last long.

By now the championship had reached the crunch. There was just a point between ourselves, Manchester United and Arsenal with Spurs and Southampton not too far behind. Everton hadn't won the title since 1970. Colin had played in that side along with Howard but neither of them liked to talk about it. I think both of them realized the sort of pressure that would put on the team. They made sure that at Goodison, unlike at Molineux, the past didn't dominate the present.

The key game for us that season came on 20 October when we went to Anfield. Everton hadn't won at Liverpool for fourteen years, but we completely shut them out. They didn't have a chance in the whole game. Sharpy got the winner for us with a fantastic strike from thirty yards at the start of the second half. It was as if we'd crashed through a barrier. Our confidence was sky high. The following week we thrashed – and I mean thrashed – Manchester United 5–0.

By November we were top of the League and we stayed there for the rest of the season except for a three-week spell over Christmas when our form wobbled. During that period we travelled up to Roker Park knowing that we had to win to maintain our momentum. We'd lost at home the previous week

3–4 to Chelsea and there were mutterings in some quarters that we were losing our grip.

I told everyone not to worry. I knew it would be all right because I'd never lost in a game at Sunderland. It was my way of giving everyone a boost. And it worked. We took it 2–1. What followed was an extraordinary run in which we won fifteen and drew two, conceding just nine goals. It was the sort of burst that killed off the opposition. Even Liverpool couldn't keep pace with it. We got to the stage where we felt we were never going to lose.

Unfortunately I'd also got to the point where I felt I was never going to score. Sharpy and Kevin Sheedy had been getting the goals, but no matter what I did I didn't seem able to find the net. I couldn't buy a goal. I was playing well enough, making a real contribution to the team, but as the weeks went by my confidence started to go. Goal scoring is a funny thing. I've found throughout my career that the more relaxed you are the more likely you are to get results. The minute you start trying to force it the trouble starts. But staying free of tension when you're on a barren run is easier said than done and my lean streak had lasted four months.

In February we played non-Leaguers Telford in the fifth round of the FA Cup. I shaved the bar with a header and squeezed a shot inches wide of the post. The nearer I got to scoring the more desperate I started to feel. I began to wonder if I'd lost my touch altogether.

Footballers by their nature are superstitious. I was no different from that. For example, I never started to get ready until exactly half an hour before kick-off. I'd just sit in my clothes and read the programme. Then at exactly half-past two, if it was a Saturday, I'd start to put on my kit. I also always came out of the tunnel fourth, which was a problem on the few occasions when I captained a side. Now, if you put me on the spot I'd say that sort of thing is all a load of nonsense, but there are times when you wonder.

The week after the Telford game we played Leicester City at Filbert Street. The match was being televised and before the game one of the TV commentators came into the dressing room to check some facts and figures. He said to me, 'Do you realize, Andy, that you've scored ninety-eight League goals since you came to England? If you could get the two you need today it would make a nice moment for us.' As a commentator myself these days I appreciate exactly what he meant. I joked that the way things were going I'd be lucky to reach my century by the end of the year, never mind the end of the match, but the idea fired something in me. Suddenly I got this feeling that today was going to be the day.

The team had been reshuffled because Sharpy was injured and so Trevor Steven partnered me upfront. As first-choice centre forward Graeme always wore the number nine jersey while I had to content myself with number eight. Since Sharpy wasn't around I took the chance to slip into my preferred shirt. We won 2–1. And the TV boys got their headline because I scored them both. You know the really strange thing? The TV commentator who told me about the ninety-eight goals was a guy named Martin Tyler. I kept a tight hold on the number nine shirt after that.

I suppose a lot of people's image of me as a player is of a guy diving to head the ball. That was my bread and butter. It's often said that a player should work on his weaknesses. But to me that's the wrong attitude. I think a player should work on his strengths and hone them. That's what I did with heading. I worked on it endlessly and I did well with it. I got a high percentage of goals with my head. Two of my best came later that season against Sunderland at Goodison. For the first, Peter Reid smashed one over from the right. I flew in full length at the near post, caught it well and smacked it into the top corner of the net. The second was more difficult because it came over from the left so it was on my weaker side. Paul Bracewell dinked it in, again to the near post, and I just got ahead of the defender, threw myself at it and it went into the opposite corner from the first one.

As I say, that was very much my style. It's something you don't see so much nowadays. Alan Shearer gets a lot of headed goals, but there are very few like him around. Thierry Henry, for example, who for me has completely reinvented the way a centre forward can play the game, has hardly had a header all year. When I was playing that would have been unthinkable.

We were on an amazing run, but the moment we really knew we could win the championship came when we travelled to White Hart Lane for a midweek game in March. Spurs had ten matches left to play, six of them at home, and they were regarded as favourites for the title. This was our big test. It was a titanic game. I put us in front. The goal was a pretty unusual one for me. Neville clubbed the ball down field and the Spurs centre back Paul Miller misheaded it on the edge of the D and it went square. I was running in and it fell in front of me about twenty-five yards from goal. It was sitting up beautifully. I just thought, 'hit it'. And I smacked it, only with my weaker right foot. Incredibly, it went like a rocket. I think the first time Tottenham's keeper Ray Clemence saw the ball after it left my boot was when it bounced back out of the goal. I ran up to him and I said, 'Don't worry about it, Clem. There's a perfectly good net behind you to stop that one.'

Trevor Steven got a second to put us 2–0 up. We were playing great. Then Graham Roberts smashed one in for them from about thirty yards to bring them back into it. With a few minutes left Nev once again proved his brilliance and his importance to the side. Mark Falco had a header from barely three yards out, bulleting towards the top corner and Nev flew across, full stretch, got a strong left hand to it and pushed it out. An absolutely unbelievable save. We hung on for 2–1 and when we left the ground that night we felt for the first time 'this is ours'. We clinched the title with five games to spare by beating QPR at home. Derek Mountfield and Sharpy got the goals in a 2–0 win.

That win was part of an incredible run of form. From Boxing Day through to May, we played seventeen games, winning fifteen of them and drawing the other two. We had the title wrapped up with five games of the season still to go. That's some record. We also made fantastic progress in the FA and Cup Winners' Cups and suddenly a treble looked a possibility.

The Cup Winners' Cup campaign had got off to an embarrassing start as we scraped past University College Dublin 1–0 on aggregate. We did much better against Inter Bratislava and we met the Dutch side Fortuna Sittard in the quarter-finals.

The first leg was at Goodison. We stuttered in the opening period and went in 0–0. We never looked like losing the game, but we didn't look much like winning it either. Things turned around in the second half. We won 3–0 and I scored a hat-trick that in a lot of ways summed up what my game was about. The first goal was a Peter Reid shot, the keeper spilled it and I reacted quickest and poked it in. The second was a cross from

Terry Curran that bounced between the goalkeeper, the centre back and myself. The ball was about two feet off the ground but I went for it with my head, full length. The keeper and the defender both came flying into me. We all ended up in a heap, but the ball found its way into the net. The third was a defensive error. I gambled on the centre back missing a through ball. He did and I smashed it in with my left foot from about twelve yards out.

People will talk about the second goal as being a brave one. It's a word that was used a lot about me in my career. It's flattering, but I'm not sure it's quite the right description. Brave is when you consider the consequences before you do something, realize how dangerous it is but do it anyway. I never did that. I wanted to get goals. When I saw the chance to score I was so focused on getting the ball in the net that I didn't notice the flying boots and never thought about what might happen to me. If I had I'd likely never have done it. It was purely instinctive. Once I was committed I couldn't pull out. Nothing could stop me, barring a brick wall. I was determined, certainly, and I was no shrinking violet, but brave? I don't really think so.

Playing in Europe was always a bit different tactically, though often the difference wasn't quite as great as some people made out. European teams tended to go in for man-to-man marking, which wasn't that common in England. As a striker I never minded a man marker, because generally I knew that if I could get beyond him even for a few seconds I was through on goal. It didn't matter if he stuck to me like glue the whole rest of the game, that one chance was all I needed to score. It was interesting to see just how strictly the marker took his job. Some of them would almost literally follow you into the dressing room at half-time. In that case it was up to you as a forward to drag them out of position and let the midfielders exploit any gaps that their absence left. It was just a simple thought process to work that out.

The other thing you had to watch out for in Europe, as I'd discovered playing for Scotland, was that the continentals had a lot of little tricks they used to goad opponents. Shirt pulling, for example, hardly went on at all in England then, but when you played in the European competitions you'd be getting tugged back all the time.

Shirt pulling is a pain in the neck and I feel that it is something that has definitely crept into English football post-Premiership. Corners and set plays have become farcical. Sometimes there are two dozen infringements going on simultaneously. The foreign players and foreign coaches have brought more good than bad into English football in the last decade, but this is one thing we could have done without.

Contrary to what some people will tell you, though, the idea that it's foreign imports that have introduced diving to Britain is nonsense. That's always been there. But in the past there were fewer cameras around to highlight it, so people didn't notice it quite so much. When I was playing in the First Division it was well known that people like Francis Lee and Trevor Francis would go down to win a penalty if the defender breathed on them. There's nothing wrong with that in my book. In a professional game your job is to help your team win. If an opponent leaves his leg out in the eighteen-yard area and you trip over it and get a spot kick, then you've contributed to victory.

We finished Fortuna Sittard off over in the Netherlands and that brought us up against Bayern Munich. The Bavarians had some brilliant players. Man for man in terms of technique and ability there's no doubt they were better than us. They had a fantastic left-winger named Ludwig Kogl, while Klaus Augenthaler, Soren Lerby and Lothar Matthaus were excellent if you gave them time on the ball, but if you didn't give them time they were vulnerable, as anybody is.

I missed the game in Munich. Howard played five in midfield. We stifled them and got a thoroughly professional 0–0 draw.

When we got them back to our place we took a different approach. We pressurized them high up the pitch and made sure the sweeper Augenthaler didn't get the chance to control the pace of the game. There were close to 50,000 at Goodison that night. The crowds were so thick outside the ground that we couldn't get the team coach through and we were late getting into the dressing room. When we ran out the roar that greeted us was thunderous. The atmosphere was absolutely incredible, the most intense I've experienced anywhere. The game mirrored it. If I had to take one match with me to my grave this would be it.

Bayern took the lead in the first half through Hoeness. With away goals counting double that meant a draw would be good enough to take them through. The strength of that Everton team was that no matter what the score was, no matter how badly we were being outplayed, we never ever thought we were beaten. That's a quality all great sides need. Manchester United's amazing comeback in the Champions' League Final is a prime example. They kept going when lesser teams would have given up because they were convinced something would happen.

In the second half we pressed Bayern all the way. We didn't

give them a second anywhere, and we played with a passion and a pace that absolutely paralysed them. Graeme Sharpe got the equalizer. Then with twenty minutes to go I scuffed in a second past Jean-Marie Pfaff. I knew we'd won it even before Trevor Steven added the third. Because when Lerby, the Munich captain, saw their substitute coming to the touchline he held up his hand. He'd had enough. He wanted to come off. When I saw that I knew we'd beaten them. Mentally they'd had it.

At the final whistle I went to shake hands with Hoeness. He didn't want to know. He just looked at me and screamed, 'That was not football. You are crazy men,' and stormed off.

In my view that was totally unjustified. The game had certainly been physical and I have to hold my hands up and admit that I'd played my part in that, breaking the centre back Eder's nose when we clashed heads going for the same ball. But in football sometimes you have to fight for your right to play. Bayern, for all their talent, couldn't or wouldn't do that. Not that it was all one-way traffic, mind you. I took a hell of a kicking from Pflugler early on, and while Kevin Ratcliffe's first half tackle on Kogl is the stuff of Merseyside legend, it's not so well known that Peter Reid took a whack on the shin from Lerby that needed six stitches. Reidy was receiving treatment for the gash when he noticed that the German bench was watching to see what would happen. Keen to send out a message to them about the sort of game they were in, Reidy grabbed a sponge, stuck it down his sock, jumped up and got on with it.

Everton were a good footballing side and sometimes we found ourselves on the receiving end. When we did, as Reidy showed, our reaction was a bit different from that of Hoeness and co. Another good example of that had come at Goodison in the game against Sheffield Wednesday earlier that season. The Owls were managed by Howard Wilkinson, then in full-on 'Sergeant Wilko' mode. They were a very hard, physical team who relied on the long ball. Twenty minutes into the game their winger Brian Marwood went in clumsily on Adrian Heath. It was the tackle that did Inchy's knee ligaments and allowed me back into the side. Brian wasn't a vicious guy and it was more of an accident than anything. But not long afterwards Peter Reid – who was a big mate of Heath – gave Marwood some of it back. Brian had to leave the field as a result.

At the time the press made a lot of it, claiming that Reidy had deliberately set out to injure Brian. That wasn't the case. Peter had certainly set out to rattle him, though. One of our boys had gone off, we were getting a battering and Reidy knew we had to do something. Sometimes you have to be strong and stand up for yourselves. If you don't you haven't got a chance of winning anything. Everton weren't a dirty side, but we played at a high tempo, we were physically strong and just about everybody except the two wingers could mix it if they had to. And sometimes in this game you have to.

We went into the FA Cup semi-final with Luton Town at Villa Park just three days after beating Bayern Munich in the Cup Winners' Cup. At that stage of the season if you're as successful as we were the fixtures pile up. It's tough, no doubt about it, but winning isn't supposed to be easy and there's no point whingeing about it. We didn't get any sympathy from Colin or Howard. Especially not when Luton scored through Ricky Hill. We were five minutes from going out of the Cup when Kevin Sheedy equalized with a free kick that was so far below his usual high standard it totally fooled the goalkeeper and bounced half a dozen times on its way into the net. It knocked the heart out of the Hatters and we got the winner in injury time through the goal machine, Derek Mountfield.

With the League title already ours we travelled to Rotterdam to meet Rapid Vienna in the final of the Cup Winners' Cup. The Austrians had a decent side that included the classy centre forward Hans Krankl and the Czech midfielder Antonin Panenka, who'd scored the winning penalty in the final of the 1976 European Championships. They'd beaten Celtic on the way to the final so they were no mugs. But again, the level of confidence in our side was frightening. When it came to matches nobody talked about ifs or buts or maybes. There was a certainty there that we were going to win. An absolute certainty.

It was the same against Rapid. We went out feeling that whatever they did we would better it. Whatever they scored, we'd score more. We dominated the game from the kick-off. They never posed a threat at all. They looked like they were in awe of us. It must have been one of the most lopsided finals in European history. How they got to half-time without conceding a goal I'll never know. They certainly shouldn't have done. I scored a perfectly good goal but had it wrongly disallowed for offside. Now sometimes in that situation, when you're really on top but you can't convert it into goals, there can be a tendency for a bit of panic to set in, especially when you've been unlucky with a big decision like that one. But there was never any danger of that happening with Everton. At the interval Howard was calm. He told us to just keep doing what we were doing and we'd score.

Sure enough we did. Graeme Sharp intercepted a back pass and chipped the ball across to me. It arrived at a decent height on the edge of the six-yard area and people will say it was a simple goal, but believe me when you've got to hit one on the volley to give your side the lead in a Cup Final it is never easy. Luckily I caught it nice and crisply and in it went.

The important thing for a striker is to get goals in big games. And that's the difficult thing, too. Plenty of people can score when their team's 3–0 up and there's nothing to play for, but doing it when the pressure is on is a different matter. When I look back I'm chuffed at my record of scoring in those situations, in Cup Finals and crucial League matches. It's easy to bang in goals against lesser lights, but what counts is getting them in crunch games. You should judge a striker by the quality of his goals – their importance to his side – rather than the quantity. That to me is the measure of a forward.

Shortly after I'd scored Trevor Steven added a second from a corner and we seemed to be cruising. But then amazingly Rapid, who'd done nothing but defend, went straight up the other end and pulled one back through Krankl. When that happens normally, you might say 'Oh, oh! Trouble here.' Their tails are up, nerves might have crept into our game. Not a bit of it. We simply went back on the attack and got a third through Kevin Sheedy. To me, that showed the resolve and quality of our side. We had no thought of losing. Ever. It finished 3–1.

Afterwards Krankl described Everton as 'possibly the best team in Europe'. That was a generous tribute, but you'd have found a few who'd argue with that 'possibly' at Goodison.

That was on the Wednesday night. On the Saturday afternoon we were at Wembley to take on Manchester United in the FA Cup Final. We'd played United three times already that season, beating them twice and drawing once, so we felt we had nothing to fear.

It turned out to be one of those games where an incident that should work in your favour somehow ends up working against you. We were having the better of things when Reidy intercepted a pass from Paul McGrath and began heading towards goal. He pushed the ball forward and with me running to his left and Graeme setting off to the right he only needed another touch and we were clear through. Peter got it, but a split second later United's covering defender, Kevin Moran, crashed into him and knocked him flat. It wasn't a malicious tackle. I don't even think it was deliberate. It was just mistimed. It looked bad, though, and Peter Willis became the first referee in history to send a player off in an FA Cup Final.

On a pitch the size of Wembley against ten men we should have been able to pass United to death, but it didn't happen. Instead the red card seemed to spark them to life and we ended up losing to a great goal from Norman Whiteside.

The FA Cup Final was a missed opportunity that rankled with me for years and I know Peter Reid, for one, felt the same. We were so close to the treble but it slipped away. It was a massive let-down and a game that may have had more than a little to do with the ending of my Everton career.

That season in winning the League and Cup Winners' Cup and getting to the FA Cup Final I think we maybe used sixteen to eighteen players. Incredible compared to the number a top side would use today. There was no thought then of what today we'd call squad rotation, or resting players. The only time Howard rested players was when the League was already won. Although I'd hated sitting on the subs bench I'm not sure he wasn't right about that. Continuity is important to the team and to the individual. As a player, especially as a striker, you want to play, particularly if you're in form. If you've just scored a hat-trick you want to carry that confidence over into the next game. But at the moment you're just as likely to find yourself left out of the following match. It's hard for the players. They're expected to be able to go in and out of the starting line-up yet maintain the same level of performance.

I don't want to sound like one of the those old pros who grumbles on about how things were better in my day, but I have to say I found it incredible last season when certain Premiership managers started grumbling about fatigue when we were only ten games into the season.

And I have to say that it also amused me when Arsene Wenger was complaining about Arsenal having to play three important games in a week. The way the Frenchman talked, saying it was 'disrespectful' to his team and so on, anyone would have thought it was something specially invented for Arsenal. But we went through it that year at Everton and so did Liverpool and Leeds United before us. And Manchester United didn't do the treble by putting their feet up for the last few weeks of the season.

To my mind the Frenchman made a mistake to go public with his views. I don't think it does the players any good to hear that kind of thing. Psychologically it has an effect. From my own experience I know that sometimes players are looking for excuses and if you offer them one the chances are they'll take it. If you tell them they're tired, then they'll feel tired and they'll use that as a reason for under-performing. Alex Ferguson's very aware of that. I noticed he came down hard on Gary Neville a little while ago when the defender blamed United's bad run on injuries and Rio Ferdinand's suspension. Fergie didn't want the players to have a get-out, or to start feeling sorry for themselves. Because if you start doing that you're likely to get punished, which was exactly what happened to Arsenal in the FA Cup and Champions' League.

Some people have suggested to me that that Everton side were a kick-and-rush team. That's unfair and untrue. You don't beat teams of the calibre of those we beat just by hoofing it up the field and running after it. You don't beat Manchester United 5–0, as we did, with primitive football. We were a very good side. At the back we had Neville, who at that time was arguably the best goalkeeper in the world; in the centre Ratters and Derek Mountfield, who were quick as you like. Gary Stevens at right back was a fantastic defender. Later, when he was at Rangers, Graeme Souness rated him as the best defensive full back in the world. Gary was also a wonderful athlete. He hardly ever missed a game through injury. So Gary was excellent and Pat at left back was, well, evil. The two wingers Kevin Sheedy and Trevor Steven were superb. You'd struggle to name a better pairing. They both had skill on the ball and great delivery. Long before Beckham came along Sheeds was a master of direct free kicks. Between them in the championship season they scored thirty goals. An unbelievable record. In the centre of midfield Reidy and Paul Bracewell were what every manager looks for in his midfield players. Both of them could tackle and pass.

That Everton side got on well together not just on the pitch, but off it as well. If somebody organized a night out at the Sefton or the Bulldog you'd get twelve or fifteen of us at it. We were all big mates and we had a great time. Certainly there were little groups within the squad. Myself, Reidy, Adrian

Heath, Paul Bracewell and Sharpy were a tight-knit little unit. We liked to go out and have a bit of fun. We were what we called the A Team, and then there was the B Team, which was made up of quieter, maybe more sensible lads like Kevin Ratcliffe, Gary Stevens and Kevin Sheedy. But it was more of a joke than anything else and it never affected the unity of the squad as a whole.

That kind of tight social bond doesn't always exist even in exceptional sides. You get great teams, who play terrifically together, where half the players can't stand one another. We've seen that with the German and Dutch national sides over the years. There were players there who practically had to be forced at gunpoint to eat in the same room as each other. The Manchester United team in the 1960s was full of divisions and Tommy Smith and Emlyn Hughes of Liverpool couldn't stand the sight of each other. But on the field they fitted together brilliantly. At Everton it was different and I think the fact that we were all close helped the team tremendously. Certainly the spirit there was the best I've ever known. I don't think there's any doubt that Reidy and I played a big part in the foundation of that. We were two footballers who hated losing. We brought a winning attitude and the other lads picked up the baton and ran with it.

Howard Kendall contributed, too. The manager always made sure that everyone in the squad felt involved, even the injured players. Everybody went on away trips no matter what condition they were in. It helped meld us as a unit.

The result was that everyone in the side was prepared to go that extra yard for their teammates. No one was selfish. No one took and didn't give. It's a quality you see in all the great sides. In Arsenal last season, in United's treble winning team, in the great Liverpool sides of the seventies and eighties. As Chelsea have maybe found, you can buy the players, buy the talent, but the one thing you can't buy is team spirit; that's something you have to build.

At Everton it was special. People talk about the quality of football in the Premiership now, but I really do believe that that side could have held their own with anybody that's around today.

We felt that we would have a great chance in the Champions' Cup the following year, but of course we never got the chance. Events in the Heysel Stadium in Brussels involving Liverpool and Juventus supporters resulted in English clubs being banned from Europe for the foreseeable future. Perhaps we deserved it for the behaviour of our hooligans over the previous decade, but from a player's point of view it was hugely frustrating.

Certainly it must have contributed eventually to Howard's decision to leave Everton and go to Athletic Bilbao, and to the break-up of the team he'd built. And if I'm honest I'd have to say it also played its part in my decision to quit Goodison. Because I think if I'd had a chance of playing in the European Cup I might have looked at things a little differently.

That summer my girlfriend Jan and I had found a nice house at Formby on the Lancashire coast and were looking forward to moving into it. Everton had just signed another striker, Paul Wilkinson from Grimsby, and with Adrian Heath back fit after the injury he'd suffered against Sheffield Wednesday I was a bit concerned about how I fitted into the manager's plans.

So a few days before we were due to move I went to see Howard at Bellefield, the club's training ground. I told him how much I loved it at Goodison but said that I was nearly thirty and didn't wanted to spend the last few years of my career playing reserve team football. I realized he couldn't guarantee me a first team place but, with four strikers now at the club, could he at least give me an assurance that I was still in contention for one? Howard replied, 'I think you underestimate yourself, Andy. There's always a place for good players at Everton.'

That set my mind at rest and we moved into our new house. We were unpacking some boxes a few days later when a Jaguar pulled up in front and out stepped the Everton manager. As I saw him coming down the path I turned to Jan, who was holding some plates she'd just unwrapped, and said, 'You might as well put those back. It doesn't look like we're stopping.'

As soon as I'd seen Howard I knew something was up, but he didn't get to the point right away. He had a look around, asked how we were and generally made a lot of nervy chit-chat before finally announcing that he'd had an offer for me from Aston Villa. 'What do you reckon? Do you think it's a good idea?' he asked, 'Do you want to stay?' I was standing surrounded by packing cases having just moved house from the Midlands to Merseyside. You might have thought that would have answered his question. I said, 'Why would I want to leave this club?'

He hummed and hah-ed a bit more before telling me that he was considering a move for Gary Lineker of Leicester City. He said he had to make a quick decision because Ron Atkinson at Manchester United was also preparing a bid.

I said that was his decision but that if he thought that at my age and after the season I'd just had I was going to be happy in the reserves he'd better think again. Howard said he didn't want to force me out. 'If I do, Andy, I'll get slaughtered for it,' he said.

He hovered about for a while longer making small talk, then he said, 'I think whether you decide to stay or not I'm going to go after Lineker.' I said, 'In that case, I'll make things easy for you. I'll go.'

Barely five minutes after Howard had left the phone rang. It was Villa boss Graham Turner. He told me he'd been given permission to open transfer negotiations with me. The decision had clearly been made long before the manager came to see me.

Looking at it from Howard's point of view I'd guess his mind had been made up during the FA Cup Final. With Moran sent off United were forced to play higher up the pitch and should have been vulnerable to balls hit over the top. There was a feeling that neither Graeme nor I had enough pace to make that work. In fairness to Sharpy and myself, I'd point out that at Wembley that afternoon both of us were knackered. We'd played in the Cup Winners' Cup Final in Rotterdam on the Wednesday, flown back to England and three days later were playing in the FA Cup Final. I'd defy any footballer to be physically at his best in those circumstances. But Gary Lineker was one of the quickest guys around and maybe that was in the manager's mind.

I think ideally Howard would have liked to keep me, but I knew it would mean sitting on the bench and I wasn't prepared to settle for that. I notice there are a lot of players around today who are happy to pick up their wages and a bit of silverware and play reserve team football. I was never one of them. I was playing at a time when players were punished with a spell in the reserves. Even at the League Champions I wouldn't have been happy starting as a sub.

Maybe if Everton had been in the Champions' Cup or the offer hadn't come from Aston Villa I might have thought differently. As it was within a week Lineker had joined Everton in an £800,000 deal and I was sorting out terms for my return to Villa Park. It's a decision I've never regretted even though if I'd stayed at Goodison in all likelihood I'd have picked up a second championship medal. I wanted to play first-team football.

Gary Lineker was a quality player and he scored forty times for Everton that season before moving on to Barcelona. You could say that vindicates the manager's decision to sign him. However, building a football team is about more than just assembling good players. It's about blending different men, getting the balance right. The best footballers don't always make the best teams.

That Everton side was a complex mix of characters. There were fresh-faced youngsters and battle-hardened old pros with a point to prove; skill certainly and talent, but also a lot of grit and determination. There were players who were quiet, some who could deal out a bollocking, and others who could lighten the mood with a joke. It's hard to say how, or why, it worked, but it did. The chemistry was right. We had a togetherness that was unbelievable. I felt I brought a will to win and a positive attitude to the team as well as my ability as a forward. And maybe that meant something. Because despite all of Lineker's goals, the following season Everton won nothing.

By the late summer of 1978 the joke going around Scotland was that Mickey Mouse had been spotted wearing an Ally McLeod wristwatch. It was cruel gag, but given what the Scotland manager had put me through a few months earlier I found it hard to have much sympathy with him.

McLeod had taken over running the national team from Willie Ormond the previous year. He landed the job after winning the League Cup with Aberdeen. His successor at Pittodrie was a certain Alex Ferguson.

With the World Cup coming up I was determined to impress Ally McLeod and earn the chance to go to the finals. I was struggling with a back injury at the time that meant I had to sleep on a board every night. Despite that handicap the season went well for me. I scored nine times in the first nine games, including a couple against the champions Liverpool at Anfield, and though I missed the middle of the season with knee-ligament trouble, I came back and did well in the last eleven matches.

At that stage I hadn't played for Scotland for eighteen months. That was partly as a result of the three-match ban for my little altercation with the Czech defender Anton Ondrus.

I'd made my international debut against Romania the year before after scoring a hat-trick for the U-23s, appeared again against Switzerland and got my first two goals for my country in the previous World Cup qualifier – a 6–0 thrashing of Finland at Hampden Park. I played really well that night. My first goal was a typical header from Eddie Gray's superb cross. My second was a bit special. In fact, it was voted Goal of the Season in Scotland. Kenny Dalglish crossed a diagonal ball from the right to the left-hand angle of the D. I managed to take it on my chest and as it dropped I smashed it across the goal-keeper and into the top corner. He didn't even move. It had taken him totally by surprise. And if I'm honest it took me a bit by surprise, too. Apart from scoring I also won a penalty and hit the post. I felt like I'd arrived. Then came the World Cup qualifier in Prague.

Scotland had a really good side. The midfield of Don Masson, Bruce Rioch and Archie Gemmill had just the right mix of skill and bite and up front I played alongside Leeds United's Joe Jordan – a real beast of a centre forward whose trademark was his missing front teeth – with Kenny Dalglish tucked just behind in the hole. The Czech's were the reigning European champions, but having beaten the Finns so easily we were confident we could match them and take another big step towards Argentina. Certainly by midway through the first half I felt we had the game under control.

I was being marked by Ondrus, a giant centre half, and I was taking a real kicking from him, too. With five minutes to go to half-time and the score still standing at 0–0, I was jogging along beside my marker when suddenly he cracked me across the cheek with his elbow and then shoved me over onto the turf. I bounced straight back up, caught up with him as he ran off, spun him round with my left hand and delivered a mighty right-hander Frank Bruno would have been proud of. Down Ondrus fell clutching his face. The referee's whistle went. And so did both of us.

I was disgusted with myself. It was the only time in my international career I'd got involved in anything like that and while there'd been provocation enough we'd been specifically warned to expect it by manager Willie Ormond. As the youngest player in the Scottish line-up I was the obvious target. Ondrus was an experienced pro. He'd carried out the initial assault when he'd seen the Italian referee wasn't looking, in the hope that if I retaliated I'd be the one that got caught. As it was the linesman had seen the whole thing from start to finish. That was small comfort to me, though, especially since in the second half Scotland lost all rhythm and composure and went down 2–0. For my part in the scuffle I received a three-match international ban.

I returned to Villa Park chastened by the experience. I was determined not to let anything like it happen again. And in fact I was only booked twice in the next eighteen months. As a professional you're always going to find yourself subject to provocation and you have to learn to ignore it. Look at the way David Beckham has mastered his temper since Diego Simeone did his dying swan act. If you're getting a hard time from an opponent as a forward, the best way to get your own back is by banging the ball in the net.

The ban had cost me three caps, injury had also played a part in my absence from the Scotland set-up and so, inevitably, had Ron Saunders. Right from the start the Villa manager had been reluctant to let me play for my country. He felt there was too big a risk of me aggravating injuries. Whenever I was selected for the squad Saunders put pressure on me to withdraw and time and again, reluctantly, I gave in.

Like the business with the PFA dinner, this is a case of me obeying the boss's wishes and living to regret it. No matter what anybody says playing for your country is the highest honour you can get in the game, but because of Saunders I never made the number of appearances I should have done. Between 1975 and 1980 Scotland played around forty games and I turned out in just about a quarter of them. That should have been my time, but it slipped away.

If it had happened these days it would have been different. FIFA rules now make it impossible for managers to force players to pull out of international games against their will. We've seen that recently with Nolberto Solano at Newcastle and Freddie Kanoute at Spurs. Back then it wasn't so easy to go against the wishes of your manager when it came to international fixtures. Clubs and the national FAs clashed often enough and the clubs invariably won.

If anything friction between the club and country has got even greater recently. Because of the foreign influence in the Premiership you have players jetting off to play in the African Cup of Nations and the South American World Cup Qualifiers, which are right in the middle of our season. But it's hard to see what FIFA can do about that. One way around it might be to have part of the year set aside for these sorts of tournaments.

Another obvious way of easing the problem would be to cut out meaningless friendlies at important times of the season. When you see England turning out in late March when the fixtures are piling up you can see why the managers of the big clubs get angry. And when you see the teams put out in friendly matches it's hard to justify them. I don't see why they shouldn't be cut back dramatically. If that isn't done then we are heading for real confrontation.

Despite my lengthy absence from the international scene I was selected for the World Cup pool from which the final twenty-two-man squad would be picked. Upfront Kenny Dalglish and Joe Jordan were automatic choices, so my main rivals were Rangers' Derek Johnstone and Joe Harper of Aberdeen. My scoring record was better than those of either of them.

McLeod came to watch me play against West Bromwich Albion at the Hawthorns. Villa won 3–0 and even though I didn't score I played a part in all the goals and felt I'd put on a good show. West Brom's manager Ron Atkinson agreed. Afterwards Big Ron congratulated me on my performance and assured me he was sure that I'd be going to Argentina along with Albion's winger Willie Johnston.

To be honest I didn't share Big Ron's confidence. McLeod hadn't picked me so far and I had a hunch he wasn't going to change that now. For whatever reason he just didn't seem to fancy me as a player.

The squad was announced in May. I went to a friend's wine bar in the centre of Birmingham and spent the day hanging around there. I guess part of me couldn't stand the thought of a local journalist phoning my home to tell me I'd been excluded. In mid-afternoon my mate went and rang the local paper to find out the news. I wasn't in it. Derek Johnstone of Rangers had been picked ahead of me. As it turned out he didn't play a single game in South America.

McLeod explained his decision by saying he was uncertain about my fitness. That might have made sense if it weren't for the fact that he'd picked Manchester United's centre half Gordon McQueen. Gordon still had his leg in plaster after missing most of the end of the season with ligament trouble. According to medical reports he wasn't going to be fit until – wait for it – the semi-final stage! How's that for confidence?

My non-selection might have caused an upset – most journalists had seen me as a certainty for the squad – but Scotland's confidence about the ability of the rest of the players was so high that my omission hardly raised a murmur of protest. With all the talent at his disposal the manager could afford the odd blunder. That seemed to be the Scots' view. McLeod did nothing to dampen expectations. He told anyone who'd listen that Scotland would never lose while he was in charge and when he was asked what he would do if the Scots won the World Cup he replied, 'Defend it!'

As it turned out the entire campaign in Argentina was a shambles, one I had to watch as part of the ITV World Cup panel alongside Paddy Crerand, Kevin Keegan and Elton John, who was then heavily involved with Watford. Within a couple of months of returning home from South America McLeod had resigned to take over as manager of Ayr United. He picked just one more team before that happened, for a game against Austria in Vienna and for the first time since he'd taken over I was in it. What can you do?

I'd made my debut in the Scottish senior side as a twenty year old when Willie Ormond was in charge of the team, in theory at least. Willie had been a great player, part of Hibernian's 'famous five' forward line. As a manager he'd led Scotland to the 1974 World Cup Finals and they'd been unluckily eliminated from a tough group on goal difference without losing a game. I'd come close to going to Germany after an excellent season with Dundee United, but in the end I was regarded as just too young.

Willie was quiet almost to the point of being shy. He was unassuming, a man of few words, rarely raised his voice and didn't elaborate tactically, just picked the team and let them go and play. All in all he was a very likeable guy, though I'm probably biased. It's hard to dislike someone who tells the press he thinks you're the Scottish Johan Cruyff.

Willie's main problem was that he struggled to control elements of his squad. And to be honest anybody would have. In those days I think it's fair to say the players ruled the roost in the Scotland side. Some members of the old guard such as Denis Law had gone, but men like Billy Bremner, Peter Lorimer and Jimmy Johnstone were still a big presence. Their reputations both on the field and off it were legendary, and justifiably so. Over a period of ten or twelve years with Leeds and Celtic, these men had battled hard all over the world and they were tough. These were guys who had done it all and knew what they wanted.

In fairness to them, I'd have to say that there wasn't a lot of emphasis on overall physical preparation in those days. It was something nobody thought much about. As a player you did your training and went to bed early on the eve of a match and that was about it. Diet in particular was never discussed. The knowledge just wasn't there. If we played on the Saturday and won a game we thought nothing of going into the players' lounge and having three or four pints of lager and then going out for a few more on the town. Now players know that if they drink alcohol in the twenty-four hours after a game it affects the way the body reacts and so a lot of them don't touch it.

I often wonder what would have happened if we'd had the

organization and planning that we have now with the players we had then. I think if you look at it, Scotland, with all the talent we had at our disposal in the 1970s, would have had a really frightening side on the field.

Off it, well, there were plenty of what you might call 'incidents' around that time. I missed the most famous one when a worse-for-wear Jinky Johnstone sailed down the Clyde in a rowing boat because I'd had to pull out of the squad with injury, but I was on the notorious trip to Copenhagen that resulted in Billy Bremner, amongst others, getting banned for life from the international set-up after a series of fights in nightclubs and bars. I wasn't involved in any of that. I was safely tucked up in bed in the hotel. I was still just a kid and to be honest I was too scared to go out on the town with those boys. They were huge, huge characters and they were intimidating. Not deliberately so. They weren't selfish and were happy to share information and to help the youngsters; it was just their presence, the knowledge of who they were. It made it hard for newcomers like me to settle into the squad. It was only really when younger guys like Frankie Gray, Kenny Dalglish and Alan Rough started to come through that I really felt at home.

In all after the sending off in Prague I didn't play for Scotland for two years. And after my unexpected game in Austria for Ally McLeod, Jock Stein took over and called me up for his first game in charge against Norway and then shortly after the League Cup Final win with Wolves, Jock brought me back into the side and I scored in a 4–1 win over Portugal.

As a manager I felt I never really saw the best of Jock. Born within a few years and a few miles of Bill Shankly and Sir Matt Busby in the Lanarkshire coalfields, it had been a hard road to the top for him. He'd begun working as a miner at sixteen, playing football part-time for Albion Rovers to top up the wages he earned at the coalface. It wasn't until he was twenty-seven that Celtic finally offered him terms as a full-time professional. Shortly after that his playing career was ended by a serious ankle injury. He went into coaching instead. Built a reputation at Dunfermline and Hibernian and then returned to Celtic Park. For thirteen years he lead the men in green-and-white hoops to one triumph after another – twenty-five trophies in all, including the 1967 European Cup.

Jock had left Celtic Park when the board tried to move him into a more general management position – nowadays it would be under the infamous title 'director of football'. He'd recently recovered from a near-fatal smash when a vehicle driving down the wrong side of a dual carriageway had crashed head on into his car. The Big Man was upset by the suggestion that he was no longer up to the job of coaching players and he quit. He was briefly in charge at Elland Road, but after just forty-four days in Leeds Ally McLeod's reign came to an abrupt halt and Jock was offered the job of national team boss.

To be honest I'm not sure Jock's health ever fully recovered from that horrendous accident. You could see what a giant of a man he was in football terms, but something was missing. I still had huge respect for him, as did the rest of the players. He was just one of those I'd loved to have worked with when he was really in his prime.

Maybe because of his background Jock couldn't abide anything he thought was extravagant. On one of my last trips with the Scotland squad I was sitting down to dinner with Graeme

Sharp in the team hotel. We studied the menu and when the waiter came to take our order I asked for a prawn cocktail. The next thing I knew Jock was standing behind me booming, 'You're from Drumchapel in Glasgow, laddie. What do you know about prawn cocktails? You'll have soup like the rest of us.'

He gave me a right dressing down. Jock was a man of the old school. To him ordering prawn cocktail was a sign of delusions of grandeur. It's funny to think how he would have reacted to some of today's players with their designer clothes and Lamborghinis.

Jock often came across to the public as a fatherly figure but he could be volatile, too. He didn't suffer fools gladly and was capable of losing his temper big time. He was a strict disciplinarian, but even he found it hard to control some of the Scotland players. I think he sometimes found that hard to accept. He'd ruled his great Celtic team with a rod of iron, but that was different. Most of the players he'd had under him then had grown up at Celtic Park; they'd come up through the ranks, so it was easier for him to control them, just as it is for Alex Ferguson with the boys who've come through the youth set-up at Old Trafford. But with hardened internationals – as with big money signings – it's much, much more difficult. If the senior Scottish players wanted to go out for a drink they would and if that meant breaking a curfew so be it.

The only time I really fell foul of Jock was after a game against Sweden in a World Cup qualifier at Hampden in 1981. We were playing poorly, really struggling, and I came on as sub in the second half and won us a soft penalty and we won 2–0.

After the game I was talking to reporters and they asked me about the spot kick and I said that in all honesty if it had been given up the other end I'd have been disappointed with the decision. The press boys made the most of that and the next thing I heard about it was when the squad was announced for the away tie against Portugal and I wasn't in it.

Jock phoned me up the same day and said, 'You are not in the side because of your remarks. As far as I am concerned that was definitely a penalty. Any talk that you somehow conned the referee is just pure bravado on your part and you should know better.' That was Jock to a T. I'd won him a penalty, helped the team to victory and he was dropping me for talking about it in a way he didn't approve of.

After my goal against the Portuguese I was expecting a decent run in the side. Unfortunately Scotland's next game against Northern Ireland clashed with a League game between Wolves and Arsenal.

Nowadays that would have presented no problem. FIFA regulations would have meant I'd have joined up with Scotland and my club would have had to get by without me. Not back then. Arsenal were pressing for a UEFA Cup place and if they could win their last two matches they might be able to squeeze into the remaining European spot ahead of Ipswich Town.

The Suffolk club therefore insisted that the FA force Wolves to field their strongest team. That naturally meant including me in the line-up, World Cup or no World Cup. Despite my presence Arsenal won 2–1, and I got injured and was ruled out of Scotland's next fixture with Wales. Arsenal meanwhile lost to Middlesbrough in their final game of the season and so Ipswich qualified for Europe anyway. My contribution to Bobby Robson's team's cause had been two Scotland caps.

I was called back into the squad for the next game, against

England at Hampden. I had never played against the Old Enemy at senior level and I was really looking forward to it and so were my family up in Glasgow. But on the Friday before the game Jock pulled me aside and told me that he was going to play Joe Jordan and keep me as a substitute. As I sat on the bench I at least had the thrill of hearing the Hampden crowd chanting my name. Unfortunately by the time I came on England were winning comfortably 2–0 and there was not much I could do to change the situation.

Two years later I finally did get a chance to play against England. This time it was at Wembley and for a long while it looked like it might have been the last ever game between the two teams at the self-styled 'home of football', but then Scotland and England met in the play-offs for Euro 2000. We also lost the game 2–0.

If missing out on the 1978 World Cup had been a big blow 1982 was even worse. Although I was at Wolves and we weren't a great side, I'd played in nearly all the qualifying matches and thought I'd done well.

There were a lot of good players in that side: Frank Gray, Archie Gemmill, Graeme Souness, Gordon Strachan, John Robertson. Partnering Kenny Dalglish was fantastic. I'd always been a great admirer of Kenny. I'd played against him when he was at Celtic, so I knew he was excellent. But you never really see just how good these guys are until you train and play alongside them. Kenny was sensational. He had huge talent and a great temperament, and his thought process was miles ahead of the rest of us. He could tackle, pass and score from thirty yards, or score from three yards. He could create goals and take goals. He could out battle people and out skill them. There wasn't anything he couldn't do. The guy was a genius.

In Jock's team I mainly played upfront with either Kenny or Steve Archibald, but sometimes I was paired with Joe Jordan. That didn't happen often because the feeling was that we were too alike. I'm not sure that was right, though we were both left-sided, combative, physical players. I doubt opposition defenders looked forward to facing us both. Joe was a rough, tough guy, but I never thought of him as a goal scorer. He got goals, but never enough. I always felt I'd score more than Joe and in club football I did. I think I'd have done the same at international level, too, but I just didn't get the chance.

Scotland topped a group that included Sweden and Portugal. Northern Ireland nicked the second qualifying spot, which I guess shows how times have changed. I was sure I'd be spending my summer in Spain, so when Jock called me at home and said he had decided to take Paul Sturrock of Dundee United instead, I was flabbergasted.

Looking back now I suppose I'd have to admit that maybe my domestic form had been patchy. Wolves were up and down and maintaining consistency was difficult. I was the sort of forward who was completely reliant on service, and in a poor team that was sometimes in short supply. So my international career stalled again and I spent another World Cup in the TV studios, this time at the BBC with Bob Wilson and Emlyn Hughes.

Things picked up again when I went to Everton. I started scoring regularly again and Jock Stein took note. After the Cup Winners' Cup-tie with Bayern Munich Jock came down to the dressing room to see me. He took me aside and said, 'I've seen an old boy turn the clock back tonight.' He wanted to include me and Graeme in the Scotland team to play England in the Rous Cup.

Unfortunately the FA intervened once again. The game was the day before Everton's match with Coventry. We'd already wrapped up the championship and the team were pretty much in a holiday mood. Coventry, though, were still involved in a relegation fight, so the powers that be at Lancaster Gate ordered Howard to field his strongest team and Graeme Sharp and I were pulled from the Scotland squad. Unsurprisingly, with the pressure off and the party on, Everton lost 4–1. And Scotland beat England. I never played in a senior victory over England and that was my last chance gone.

Scotland were playing Iceland a couple of days later and the squad had gone out to Reykjavik already. So straight after the game at Highfield Road, Coventry's chairman drove Sharpy and me to the airport in his Bentley and we flew out to join them.

I got to play in a 1–0 win, the first time I'd worn the national jersey since getting both goals and being named 'most valuable player' in a win over Canada in Toronto two years before. When it came to Scotland it sometimes seemed that the further away from home they were playing the better my chances were of getting a game. Unless, of course, it happened to be the World Cup Finals.

The events that occurred at Ninian Park, Cardiff, on the evening of 10 September 1985 are something no Scotland fan is likely to forget. Jock had guided Scotland to the 1982 World Cup Finals in Spain and now, three years later, we were on the verge of qualification again. Spain had run away with Group 7, despite a 3–1 hammering at Hampden Park, but all we needed was a point in Wales to ensure a play-off game against Australia – a contest that in those days we felt there was no way we could lose. The only problem was that a win for Wales would see Mike England's team through to the play-off in our place.

The Welsh were a good side. They had three of my Everton teammates, Nev, Ratters and Psycho-Pat at the back, and upfront Mark Hughes and Ian Rush were a strike force worthy of a place in Mexico. In Glasgow Rush had scored the goal that gave them a 0–1 victory.

Jock was so worried about the Welsh forwards he decided to play five at the back in Cardiff, with Willie Miller playing as sweeper behind Richard Gough and Alex McLeish. It had no effect. In the thirteenth minute at Ninian Park, Sparky gave his team the lead. The pressure was on Scotland. And we struggled to establish ourselves in the game.

At half-time an incident occurred that really stirred Jock up. Jim Leighton, our goalkeeper, lost a contact lens and didn't have a spare pair with him. Jock was furious. He hadn't even known Jim wore contacts. He was mad with Jim for not bringing a spare set, he was mad with Alex Ferguson who was Jim's club manager, for not making him aware of the situation and I guess most of all he was mad with himself because he hadn't known about it.

He had to call Alan Rough, who was out on the pitch with me and the other subs, and tell him to get stripped off. He'd wanted to have a full range of substitutes to choose from and now a change had been forced on him. I often think that had events unfolded differently that would have been Jim Leighton's last game for Scotland. It had upset Jock that much. When he came out of the tunnel he was really fizzing.

The second half did nothing to calm him down. We were struggling. Sitting on the bench I could feel the frustration beginning to mount.

As time ticked away Jock was bobbing up and down in the dugout. He'd a history of heart trouble, but in the atmosphere and tension of Cardiff the thought that he should relax was inconceivable.

I was sitting next to Graeme Souness, the Scotland captain who was out of the team because of injury, and we both sensed Jock getting more and more agitated. With about ten minutes to go one of the press photographers, Bob Thomas, appeared on the touchline. He must just have accidentally got in Jock's line of vision because the next thing we knew the manager had got up and almost bodily lifted him and moved him out of the way. For all he was volatile Jock was normally not a physical guy, so that was a sign of how worked up he was. How much the pressure was getting to him.

Rangers' winger Davie Cooper had come on and we'd started to do a bit better. But even so as the clock ran down we looked done for. Then, incredibly, in the eighty-first minute the ball bobbled into the Welsh penalty area and David Speedie hit a wild shot that struck Welsh defender David Phillips on the hand. I don't think there was much he could have done to get out of the way of it, but the Dutch referee, Jan Keizer, blew his whistle and pointed to the spot. I couldn't believe it. We'd put the Welsh out eight years before with a dodgy penalty and now it looked like we might be about to do so again. The Wales players surrounded the referee. The crowd was roaring. Davie Cooper placed the ball. When the protests of the Welsh finally stopped he strode up and struck his kick along the greasy surface, past the diving Neville Southall and into the net.

Pandemonium broke out on the field. From the corner of my eye I saw Jock try to get up, stagger slightly and then collapse to the ground. Stewards and staff hurriedly carried him into the players' tunnel and the attempts to revive him began.

Jock went off to hospital in the ambulance and after the

final whistle we trooped off the field and waited in the dressing room for news. The game had finished 1–1. We were well on the way to Mexico, but there was no thought of celebration. We didn't even get changed. We sat in silence for what seemed like hours. Eventually the door to the dressing room opened and Scotland's assistant manager Alex Ferguson, pale faced, stepped in. 'The Big Man didn't make it,' he said.

It turned out that was the last time I was selected for my country. Alex picked Frank McAvennie and Mo Johnston for the play-off with Australia. When the squad for the World Cup Finals was announced I was back at Villa and having a nightmare season. Alex phoned me at home in Sutton Coldfield and told me he wasn't taking me and I couldn't argue with that decision.

In all I played twenty games over a span of ten years and scored seven times. It could have been better, but then again it could have been worse. We had a lot of talent upfront then, first with Kenny and Joe and later with Charlie Nicholas, Archibald, McAvennie and Johnston. The fact that my Everton teammate Sharpy, who scored 150 goals in the English First Division, only got a dozen caps shows the competition there was in those days.

I think it's fair to say that Scotland under-achieved for much of that time. We had the talent, there's no doubt about that. Alan Hansen, Souness and Dalglish were fantastic footballers who would have got into any side in the world. People often point the finger at the goalkeeping situation – something that wasn't helped by the way Jimmy Greaves always used to high-light errors by Scottish keepers on the ITV show he did with Ian St John – but I think that's totally unjustified. Guys like Roughie and Jim did a decent job for us.

At one point we were certainly hampered by the clamour for a so-called 'Tartan XI' amongst sections of the fans and media. That is to say a Scotland team made up of players drawn entirely from the Scottish League. Those of us who played in the English Football League were branded 'Anglo-Scots' as if somehow we'd become half-breeds because we were living in England. The suggestion seemed to be that somehow we had deserted our country. What rubbish. In my opinion a Scot has to be a bigger patriot when he or she lives south of the border than if they live in Scotland because you are constantly having to defend your corner. You don't have people in the dressing room at Hibs or Celtic giving you endless stick about being a Jock. Or at least you didn't in those days. Besides, most of the best Scottish players were playing in the First Division at that time, so leaving them out was helping nobody but our opponents. Sometimes it seems the only time us Scots are guaranteed to get a shot on target is when we're aiming at our own feet.

To my mind, though, the real problem was that we never really had a strong enough manager, a guy who could really pull us together as a unit. As I say, I don't think Jock was at his best when he took the job because of that horrendous accident.

Most of the time we had no real organization. We played off the cuff as individuals not as a team, and relied purely on skill. If we won games it was because we had superior players to the opposition. But a good team is better than the individuals that form it. It's more than the sum of its parts. I never felt that was true of Scotland. And by the time it was, under Andy Roxburgh and Craig Brown, we didn't have the quality of player any more.

There are signs that may be changing. We have the best

crop of youngsters coming through that we've had for a while, boys like Everton's James McFadden, David Marshall, Stephen Pearson of Celtic and Manchester United's Darren Fletcher, and hopefully we can turn that into something.

Whether Berti Vogts is the man to do that, I'm not sure. No disrespect to the guy. He did well with Germany in Euro 96. But my view is that a Scot should be in charge of the Scotland team. I find it incredible that the SFA turned to a foreigner when somebody with the experience and record of Walter Smith was sitting around twiddling his thumbs.

I feel exactly the same way about England. Sven Goran Eriksson has done a half-decent job, but I don't believe he's done any better with the players he's got at his disposal – world-class talent like Owen, Gerrard, Scholes and Beckham – than half a dozen English candidates, guys like Harry Redknapp or Sam Allardyce, would have done. I'm not being xenophobic. The Italians or the Germans wouldn't have a foreign manager and I don't think we should either.

I never got to the World Cup Finals as a player but I've been lucky enough to attend the last two as a broadcaster. So far Sky has never obtained the rights to cover a major international championship but I've worked on radio off and on down the years and they've been kind enough to take me along. In some ways radio is less pressurized than television because you don't have to worry too much about your appearance – which is just as well in the case of some radio commentators, believe me. On the other hand, you don't have the pictures to tell the story for you and you have to fill practically every second of air time. It's swings and roundabouts.

In France 1998 I was working for Talksport commentating alongside Alan Parry. I'd done some Champions' League games with Alan for the station earlier that year and it had gone off pretty well. I enjoyed working for Talksport. In a lot of ways it reminded me of the early days of BSB. There was a flying-by-the-seats-of-our-pants feel about things, a sense that you were one step from plunging off the deep end. You never knew what would happen next. One minute you'd be sitting doing a live feed from the stands in Montpellier or Lyon and suddenly you'd look up to find one of the black leather-clad French police marksmen pointing his rifle at you and telling you to move along because you weren't authorized to be in that section of the ground at that time.

Often there weren't even enough media passes to go around and I'd find myself sneaking into the press zone past lines of gun-toting French coppers waving a plastic accreditation badge with a picture of Clive Allen on the front of it. No disrespect to Clive but he doesn't have my looks. One of the other guys who worked for the station, reporter Dave Roberts, went one better getting into several matches posing as Chris Kamara. Chris is about six feet three and black, while Dave is five feet eight and white. But they both come from Middlesbrough, so maybe that was what fooled security.

The atmosphere in France was fantastic except for those horrendous few days in Marseille when England played Tunisia. Later some people said that what went on was exaggerated by the media. Don't believe it. I was there and I'd have to say that it was one of the most frightening experiences of my life. We were having lunch in the Old Port when the rioting kicked off. Being in the centre of a mob of English football hooligans is no joke, especially if you're a high-profile Scot. We made it back safely to our hotel, which fortunately was nearby. There was a guy lying stabbed and bleeding on the pavement outside and tear gas coming in through the windows. It wasn't an experience I'd ever care to repeat. I went to Korea/Japan for Radio Five Live and covered the Republic of Ireland's matches, which were preceded by a major controversy.

Managers don't always pick players because they like them as people. They pick them because they think they will do a job for them. I'm sure Ron Saunders didn't like me and I certainly didn't like him. But that didn't stop him playing me and it didn't stop me giving everything I had whenever I went out on the pitch in a Villa shirt. That's why I couldn't believe the public row that went on between Republic of Ireland manager Mick McCarthy and Roy Keane before the competition.

Keane deserved to be punished for the things he said publicly, but the situation that led to him saying them should never have been created. Instead of sorting the matter out in what amounted to a public meeting McCarthy should have dealt with the matter head to head in private. He shouldn't have dragged the rest of the team into it. The Ireland boss should have told Keane 'You can't stand me and I don't much like you, but we're here for the same purpose, so let's just focus on that.'

There are often players in teams who are disruptive or difficult, but if they're talented then it's up to the manager and the coaching staff to find ways of accommodating that. Eric Cantona had been kicked out of practically every club he'd played at. Sir Alex gave him a bit more leeway, put up with some of his wilder antics and reaped the dividend. That's something a good manager needs to do. He has to be able to judge which players are worth it, obviously. But frankly, anybody who thinks the Republic were a better side without Roy Keane is crackers.

I was out in the Far East for six weeks and it was a fabulous experience. The feeling in Seoul when Korea played was tremendous. The Koreans were great, really hospitable and friendly, but I think it's fair to say that they are not the world's biggest drinkers. Two cans of lager and they are steaming. This may not be great news for the Korean brewing industry, but it means a party only takes half an hour to really get going. After they defeated Spain the whole of the downtown area of Seoul was just a rolling sea of red shirts and even redder faces. Absolutely brilliant.

I travelled up to the final in Japan to see Brazil beat Germany. In my view it's a game England were more than capable of reaching. Although I didn't attend the quarter-final in Shizuoka I watched on TV and felt that they played poorly.

A lot has been made of Sven Goran Eriksson's failure to give guidance from the bench. I'd go along with that. But in some ways the problem was deeper. England just seemed overawed by the Brazilians. I couldn't understand why. Felipe Scolari's side were decent, certainly, with one or two good individuals, but it was hardly Pele and the side of 1970, was it?

It's been said that when they were chasing the game England ran out of ideas. I'd go along with that. With ten minutes to go, trailing against ten men, I'd have at least expected them to start bombarding the Brazilians with high balls into the penalty area. It's a crude tactic, but you've only to think back to Manchester United's incredible victory over Bayern Munich in the final of the Champions' League to see how effective it can be against opposition who aren't used to it. As it was England hardly got the ball in the box at all. It was a limp display all round and given the quality of many of England's young players and the fact that they'd beaten the other finalists, Germany, 5–1 in the qualifiers, a really massive opportunity missed.

My second spell at Villa ended in the summer of 1987 with the arrival of Graham Taylor. You could say it resulted from a clash of personalities – I had one and he didn't.

On the day the future England manager took charge he sat the whole squad down in the canteen at Bodymoor, the Villa training ground, introduced himself to us and began to talk. What seemed like three hours later he stopped. When he'd finished I turned to the lad sitting next to me and said, 'Can you tell me what he just said?' And the guy just shook his head and said, 'I'm sorry, Andy, I've no idea.'

A little while after that Graham called me into his office and sat me down. He said, 'How do you see this season going, Andy?'

I'd had a poor time of it the previous year. I'd had injury problems. I'd started just nineteen games and scored only once. But I was still feeling positive. I told him I was looking forward to the kick-off and that I was sure that if we all worked hard we'd bounce straight back up to the top division.

He said, 'I'm afraid you won't be here. I'm letting you go.'

I asked him why he was doing that. Despite a bad run I felt I was still good enough to do a job for the side, especially in the Second Division. He told me the decision had nothing to do with my ability. He said, 'I feel the other players in the squad like and respect you too much.' That was why he was getting rid of me. He saw me as a threat to his position at Villa.

The fear that some of the older players – the ones who'd been part of the set-up for as long as I had at Villa Park – might cause trouble wouldn't be uncommon in a manager coming in to a club. The difference is that usually the new man would get a feel for the situation and get to know the individuals involved before they decided what action to take. Taylor judged me without knowing me. I didn't like that.

I told him I thought he was wrong. That he was making a bad decision. As my parting shot I added, 'And one day I'll be sitting there in that chair.' I did too, even if it was only as Ron Atkinson's assistant.

I'm not usually one to hold a grudge and I might have forgiven Graham Taylor, but then he had the nerve to try and sell me to Birmingham City.

Taylor had built Watford up from virtually nothing. He'd taken them from the Fourth to the First Division, to the FA Cup Final and into the UEFA Cup. You have to admire him for that. But in all his time at Vicarage Road he'd never actually won anything except the Fourth Division title. And he'd never dealt with big-name players.

I got the impression that Taylor didn't like having stars or strong characters in the dressing room. In his second spell at Villa Park he cleared out people like Paul Merson and filled the side with players who were uninspiring but did as they were told. He was like Ron Saunders in some respects.

I always felt because of that attitude he was out of his depth at the highest level. It showed when he got the England job. At

Watford his preferred tactic was to try and bring the front men in early with long balls banged over the top into space behind the defence. He took the same approach in international football. By then I was working for Sky doing analysis on international games. I picked up on something Taylor's England were doing. One night I said, 'Now I'm going to show you the kick-offs from all of England's matches since Graham Taylor took charge.' In each clip the same thing happened. England knocked the ball back to the edge of the centre circle and then somebody lumped it out of play as far into the opposition half as they could hoof it. His team were kicking for territory like it was a rugby match. In international football, where possession is everything, that was Taylor's tactic. What more can you say?

In truth, though I certainly had no intention of going to St Andrews, I can't say I much wanted to stay at Aston Villa. My return to Villa Park had not been a huge success. They say you should never go back and this proved why. My Sky colleague Martin Tyler will tell you that when it comes to matches I played in, if I scored I can always remember it, if we won I'll probably remember it, if we drew I might remember it and if we lost there is absolutely no chance whatsoever of me remembering it. He's about right, too. Which means my recollections of the next few years are a little bit sketchy.

Because of the way I had left Everton I reported back for training at Villa Park determined to prove Howard Kendall wrong. I was confident I would. Villa had some talented individuals. A few members of the European Cup winning side – Nigel Spink and Allan Evans – were still around and Gary Shaw was there. I'd played with Gary once in the reserves during my first spell at Villa when he was a young kid and I was coming back from injury. You could see then what a talent he was. He had incredible ability. Unluckily he'd suffered a terrible knee injury playing against Nottingham Forest, had a lot of surgery and when I came back to Villa Park he was hardly ever fit.

I'd had knee problems myself and I knew how it felt. I sat down and talked to him about it. I said to him that maybe he'd have to adjust his game a little bit. That because of the injury he wouldn't be able to do all the things he'd done before. He'd have to tailor the way he played. I'd begun doing that myself during the last year of my spell at Wolves. I'd started doing more work outside the box. I'd scored less goals as a result, but felt I'd made a bigger all-round contribution.

I explained all that to Gary, but he was still only in his mid-twenties and maybe because he had so much ability he found it hard to come to terms with the idea of cutting his cloth to suit. He was a big loss not only to Villa, but also to English football.

There were other decent players at Villa Park, too: Simon Stainrod, Garry Thompson, Neale Cooper – but despite my early season optimism things didn't work out. The side never gelled, the atmosphere at the club was poor and my own form was patchy to say the least.

The manager who signed me from Everton was Graham Turner. Graham had done well in the lower divisions with Shrewsbury. He was a smashing lad, but the Villa job was way too big for him. I think he knew that himself. He'd prove that he was a good manager down the League again with Wolves and Hereford. He was happiest in himself at that level.

It goes without saying that coaching talented players is different from coaching less talented ones. But that's something that cuts both ways. Quite a lot of top-class players have found it a struggle to drop down and manage in the lower divisions.

Generally speaking I'd say it's true that the best footballers don't make the best coaches. Look at Arsene Wenger and Sir Alex Ferguson – neither of them had great playing careers. There are exceptions like Kenny Dalglish, but by and large I'd say that the naturally gifted players find coaching hard because they've never really had to think about the game. And that makes it very hard to teach the skills they have. The classic example of that is Bobby and Jack Charlton. Bobby had a God-given talent, while Jack had to really work at it.

I do think, though, that no matter what sort of a player you were, if you've played only at the highest level then that is where it is easiest for you to manage. It would be very difficult for me to coach in the Third Division because I never played there and I don't understand the nature of the game and the players at that level. I'm not saying it can't be done. My teammate Neale Cooper has done great at Hartlepool, for example, and Brian Little has done well in the lower divisions, too, but it's difficult. Look at the way Tony Adams has struggled to make an impact at Wycombe Wanderers.

I know from my own experience that players think differently at different levels in the game and it's not always easy to adjust to that. When I was at Cheltenham very late on in my career, for example, I'd make runs into positions where I'd expect the ball to be delivered – where it would have been delivered at Everton or Rangers – only to find it had been hit somewhere else entirely. Thought processes are not the same as you go up and down the League ladder. Graham Turner understood the game at Gay Meadow or the County Ground but I'm not sure he ever really got a handle on it at Villa Park.

The other really big difference is that the quality of opposition in the lower divisions is plainly not as good. I think that the teams we were playing in the First Division, the ability of their players, really frightened Turner. If Graham Taylor couldn't handle his own side, I always felt Graham Turner couldn't cope with his opponent's.

The season began badly and got steadily worse. When a team are struggling the manager needs to give the players a lift. That's the strength of someone like Bolton's Sam Allardyce. Even when the Trotters have looked down and out Big Sam has always managed to rally them for one more effort.

Graham Turner, though, was a man who wore his heart on his sleeve. If we played badly on Saturday, on the Monday when we came in for training we'd be greeted with a long face. At one point I actually took him aside and told him that it was having a detrimental effect on the team. I said, 'If you come in flat as a pancake the team are going to feel the same way. They're looking to you for leadership.'

It did no good and soon he seemed to have his chin permanently down on his chest. His despondent attitude spread through the whole club. That's not to say he was totally responsible. Far from it. And I admit my own goal-scoring form didn't help. Despite playing in forty games that season I failed to reach double figures – one of the worst returns of my career.

We escaped the drop by winning crucial home games against Ipswich and Chelsea at the end of the season. That should have given us confidence, boosted the whole club. Management is a balancing act. Sometimes it can work to talk down your team's chances. George Graham was master of that during his years at Highbury and David O'Leary used the same methods successfully during his early days at Leeds. By and large, though, the players and the fans don't want to hear talk about avoiding relegation or battling for survival. They want a manager whose ambitions match their own. That's especially true at a big club like Villa.

But instead of capitalizing on our escape, building on it and talking up our chances for the coming campaign, Graham just let the team slip back into the same gloomy rut we'd been in before. Barely a month into the season we were battered 6–0 by Nottingham Forest. It was humiliating. The feeling at Villa Park began to remind me of the final days at Molineux. There was a sense of doom about the place.

It must have affected me more than I thought because early on in that season I got so desperate that I attempted to commit suicide, or at least its football equivalent – I tried to do Jimmy Case.

Back in those days every team had a hard man. I've already mentioned Birmingham's Joe Gallagher, who ended up playing alongside me at Wolves. Micky Droy at Chelsea was another monster of a guy with muscles in his spit, and his teammates David Webb and Ron 'Chopper' Harris would both have kicked their own grannies for tuppence. 'Six feet two, eyes of blue, Big Jim Holton's after you' was still rumbling around Old Trafford, Arsenal had the infamous Willie Young, who got more bookings than Frank Sinatra, and Billy 'Bonzo' Bonds was knocking lumps out of people at Upton Park.

All of these guys were rugged, but undoubtedly the hardest man I ever came across was the Liverpool midfielder Case. He was a real beast, tough as old boots. I'd had a few encounters with Jimmy in the Merseyside derby, but by the time I had my moment of madness he'd left Anfield and was playing for Southampton.

For whatever reason I got it into my head that I was going to take Jimmy out. Now I couldn't tackle a fish-and-chip supper, so what gave me the idea that I could take on a pro like Jimmy, God alone knows. It was master versus pupil, and have no doubt about it, I was the schoolboy. The first chance I got I steamed into Case. I went at him from about twenty yards away with everything I'd got. Gave him a real thrash. But Jimmy had seen me coming and had taken the appropriate measures. I found myself lying on the turf with my knee throbbing like a blind cobbler's thumb and Jimmy standing over me giving me this sort of knowing look.

In boxing a fighter tries never to show when he's really hurt, and back then a similar attitude prevailed in football. If someone rattled you the first thing you did was bounce back up again as if to say, 'Is that the best you've got?'

I managed to do that, but it was obvious I wasn't going to last. I limped around for as long as I could, until eventually the pain got too much and I was substituted. If I thought I'd denied Jimmy the satisfaction of knowing he'd put me out of the game I was sadly mistaken. As I headed for the touchline I heard a cry of 'Andy! Andy!' When I looked around there was Case smiling sweetly at me and waving goodbye.

If Jimmy was the hardest man I encountered the most frightening was definitely Norman Hunter. By the time I joined Villa from Dundee United Norman had left Leeds, a piece of news that must have cheered up every striker in the First Division. Norman is one of the nicest guys you can meet *off the field*. On it, though, he was a different proposition.

My only encounter with the legendary 'Bites Yer Legs' came when I was still at Dundee United and played for a Scotland Representative XI against Leeds United. It was supposed to be a friendly but when it came to football I don't think Norman recognized that word. Early on I came short to collect a pass with Hunter tight on me. The ball arrived and just before I could control it, it took a bobble, bounced up onto the top of my foot and spun over my head and over Norman's, too. Quick as a flash I spun round and past him and away after the ball. Moments later up comes Norman, face like thunder, 'You little bastard,' he said, 'If you ever do that to me again I'll snap you in half.'

Even at that age I was pretty combative; ready to mix it with anybody, but believe me Norman was scary. I didn't exactly go down on my knees and beg for mercy, but I came pretty close. I looked up at him and squeaked, 'I didn't do it on purpose, honest. It was an accident. I'm really not that good.' Luckily he let me off.

Despite those two encounters I'd have to say that the hard men centre backs never really gave me that much trouble. I found that the best defence was usually to front up to them. Then you found the bark was often worse than the bite. Kenny Burns of Birmingham City and Nottingham Forest had a pretty rough reputation. He'd played as centre forward at St Andrews but then switched to the back four. There were a few around like that in those days. Dave Watson at Man City, one of the best defenders in the Football League, had also begun as a big target man at Sunderland. I'd guess it was a case of setting a thief to catch a thief.

I remember the first time I played against Kenny at St Andrews. He made no attempt to disguise the fact that he intended to sort me out. His first few tackles were real rattlers. When I got the chance, I gave him a whack back. I said, 'Every time you boot me I'll boot you. We can carry on like this all day if you want, or we can play football. What's it to be?' Kenny chose to play, which from my point of view was a poor decision because Kenny was a bloody good footballer. In fact, I'd say he and Larry Lloyd at Forest, along with Roy McFarland and Colin Todd at Derby County and Alan Hansen and Mark Lawrenson at Liverpool, were the most difficult defensive duos I came up against in my career. McFarland and Todd were particularly good. They were an excellent pairing who complemented one another perfectly. They knew each other's strengths and weaknesses, which is the biggest thing. Both of them could play football, too, which was unusual in those days. Roy would attack the ball and win it and Colin read the game brilliantly. Toddy hardly ever tackled. He anticipated and intercepted and he could make you look a real fool with it.

Midway through my second season back at Villa Park, with the team not so much flirting with relegation as bringing her home to meet the parents, Graham was sacked and the chief coach Ron Wylie took over as caretaker boss. Ron was bright and cheery and he picked things up for a brief while before the new man, Billy McNeill, arrived.

When I heard the news that McNeill was coming I was really pleased. I thought it was a brilliant appointment. I'd grown up in a house in Glasgow where nobody would eat the Penguin biscuit in the green wrapper. In other words we were Rangers through and through. As a result I had spent most of my childhood and teenage years hating Billy McNeill. I knew him as the captain of Celtic's Champions' Cup winning team, a tall, imposing guy who strode around the field never giving my hero Colin Stein a kick and picking up trophy after trophy. Later I'd played against him in Scotland. The man was a giant in all senses. My hatred had gradually turned to respect. At Villa I was sure he would turn things around. He was a winner.

He was a leader. As manager of Celtic he'd won half a dozen trophies. I expected great things from him.

I could not have been more wrong. To me McNeill the manager was a huge let-down, one of the biggest I have known in my career. From day one at Villa Park he gave no direction. He brought no enthusiasm. He didn't motivate. If you tried to spark off him you got nothing back. The drift begun under Turner simply continued.

A few months after the new manager arrived we got hammered 4–1 at Highbury. After the game we were sitting in the dressing room feeling devastated. Billy breezed in and said, 'OK lads, see you all on Monday,' and breezed out again. Monday morning it was five-a-sides and nothing said. We lost again the following Saturday at Hillsborough and it was the same thing: 'OK lads, see you all on Monday.' That was it. Where was the leadership? As far as I was concerned Billy McNeill turned up and that was about all.

Years later I wrote a newspaper article about my time with Billy at Villa. To me it was a well-thought-out and considered account of my experiences. Unfortunately the sub-editors chose to headline it 'Billy McDuff'. Billy was not happy about it and we've rarely exchanged a word since. Still, I stand by what I said then – he was a massive disappointment.

I'm sure McNeill must have cared. He must have done. But he didn't appear to care and from the point of view of the players that's disastrous. The relegation that had seemed inevitable practically from the start of the 1986–7 season was soon confirmed. We finished eight points short of safety. Before Billy arrived at Villa he'd taken Manchester City to the bottom of the League. He was in charge of two teams that were relegated that season. Off he went. In came Graham Taylor. Out went Andy Gray.

Taylor's fear that I would lead some sort of dressing-room coup against him was total rubbish, but at least allowed me to team up at last with Ron Atkinson, who'd just taken charge of West Brom for the second time.

I'd known Big Ron socially for about a decade. The Midlands football scene was a small world and the players and staff from the various clubs all socialized together. When I'd been at Villa the first time around we'd had some really bruising encounters with City, but afterwards we'd meet up with Keith Bertschin and some of the other Blues players and all have a drink together.

When Ron had been manager at the Hawthorns, building that great Baggies side around the talents of Bryan Robson, Brendan Batson, Laurie Cunningham and Cyrille Regis, we'd bumped into each other quite a bit. Although Ron is well known for his one-liners, gold jewellery and champagne Charlie lifestyle, at heart he is a real out-and-out, serious football man and we'd always got along well.

Ron, of course, had tried to sign me once before when he was at United. This time he got me for a fee of £25,000. I was part of a massive process of wheeling and dealing the Big Man had begun the minute he'd taken the reins at West Brom from my old pal Ron Saunders.

The Baggies were in a real mess not just on the field, but also off it. There'd been a series of boardroom upheavals and the financial side of things was a shambles. It must have been quite a culture shock to the Big Man when you consider that when he'd left Albion to go to Old Trafford they'd been one of the top six clubs in England with a playing staff valued at tens of millions of pounds. Now the Baggies were nailed to the bottom of the old Second Division and sometimes seemed to be struggling to raise the coach fare to matches.

Ron felt that what was needed were a few old pros who'd bring in a positive, winning attitude to the place. Along with myself he also pulled in my old Villa teammate Kenny Swain, ex-Man United man Arthur Albiston and the former Ipswich and Arsenal midfielder Brian Talbot. The Villa winger Tony Morley and Watford's big George Riley, who I'd played against for Everton in the FA Cup Final, were already there. I think the average age of the squad was something like thirty-four, so you can see Ron was banking on experience not speed. But with the addition of youngsters David Burrows, Carlton Palmer and Don Goodman, who'd come through the youth team and the capture of defender Chris Whyte, later a mainstay of Leeds United's Championship winning side, from the US there were signs that Albion were getting a decent side together.

Well, decent is maybe not quite the appropriate word. Because there were also a couple of what you might call 'characters' at the Hawthorns. One of them was a left winger named Robert Hopkins, who was notorious in the Midlands. When he was at St Andrews Hoppy had been part of the Birmingham Five along with Pat van den Hauwe – the others were Tony Coton, Mick Harford and Noel Blake – and a right wild bunch they were.

Hoppy had decent ability, but he would lose it in a big way, not only on the field, but with his teammates socially as well. He was forever getting into fights and scrapes. And I tell you when he went he was genuinely frightening. You wouldn't want to cross him. Many tried and came off second best.

Hoppy was a mad keen Blues fan. He used to give me a

shedload of stick about being a Villa player because he said City were for the real Brummies while Villa were for what Roy Keane would call the 'the prawn sandwich brigade'. Funnily enough, Hoppy had actually started his career at Villa Park when I was there first time around. He'd never really got out of the reserves but he claimed that was deliberate. 'Reserve games finished at 3.45, Andy,' he used to say, 'So if I legged it I could get to St Andrews for the second half.'

As if Hoppy wasn't enough of a handful on his own we had Tony Kelly, too. Tony was a Liverpudlian. He was an excellent midfield player, bundles of skill, wonderful passer, but ate too much, drank too much, carried a lot of extra weight and couldn't get around the pitch as he should have. So he didn't have a great attitude and he was also another out-and-out nutter.

Before the start of my second season at the Hawthorns, Ron decided to send the first team off to the Algarve for training. Something cropped up at the last minute and he was unable to come himself, so he called me into his office and said, 'You're the senior pro, Andy. When you get out to Portugal you're in charge.'

Thanks, boss.

It was not an easy job for one man. In fact, a riot squad would have struggled to cope. The minute we hit the airport tarmac all hell broke loose. On the bus to the hotel Hoppy smacked Tony Kelly, who responded by hitting him across the head with a bottle. I ended up knocking Tony unconscious after catching him in a nightclub peeing onto a potted plant, and various hire cars got wrecked. It was an absolute nightmare.

When I got back I went to see Ron in his office. I said, 'How do you control that lot when they've been on the drink?' Ron said, 'You don't. And judging by the list of complaints we've had you didn't.'

We staved off relegation and there was a chance that the side was developing into something. I know the manager felt so, too. The trouble was that the club was in a deep financial hole. Money was so tight that Ron would sometimes volunteer to do an after-dinner speech at the team hotel as a way of paying for our overnight accommodation. That was typical of Ron: a) because he loved the sound of his own voice, and b) because he always wanted the best for his lads.

As a result of the financial pressures no sooner had the various new signings begun to gel than Ron was forced to sell one of them. And that was how I came to realize one of my greatest football ambitions.

One day at the start of the 1988–9 season Ron called me at home and said, 'Someone's just been on the phone inquiring about buying you.'

'Who?' I asked.

'Have a guess,' Ron said. 'Which team have you dreamed about playing for since you were a kid?'

'Oh my God,' I replied, 'You mean . . . Real Madrid want me.'

'Have another guess.'

'Milan?'

Ron told me to stop being stupid, 'It was Graeme Souness. He wants you at Ibrox. He's offered twenty-five grand. I've said I'll let you go up and talk to him.'

I said, 'I'll walk there if necessary.'

Of course, the minute Ron had asked the question I'd known what he meant. Or at least I'd hoped I did. But I was superstitious and hadn't dared say the name in case it turned out not to be true. Playing for Rangers. I couldn't believe it.

It had almost happened once before. When I was at Dundee United the Rangers boss Jock Wallace had tried to sign me. Years later Jock told me how he'd phoned Jim McLean and said, 'I want the boy Gray.' Jim knew that he'd probably get more for me from Rangers than from an English club. I was a proven goal scorer in Scotland. He also knew what the consequences of such a deal would be. So Jim replied, 'You must be joking. If I sell him to another Scottish club I'll be slaughtered. If he goes anywhere it'll be to another league.' And that was that. By this late stage of my career I thought any other chance of realizing my boyhood ambition had long since passed me by.

As it happened Graeme Souness had only brought me in because of injuries to his first choice front pairing of Ally McCoist and Kevin Drinkell. Souey was fond of saying, 'A footballer's body is his only asset.' But he knew they could have other attributes, too, ones that were just as valuable. As Graeme said to me, he'd bought me as much for the banter in the dressing room as for what I could offer on the field. But I wasn't too worried about that. I was pushing thirty-two years of age and it was clear that even with the injuries to key strikers I was only going to be a bit-part player. For once, though, I wasn't belly-aching about being on the bench. Because Ron was right – pulling on the blue jersey was something I'd dreamed of when I was a kid.

I'd been brought up in Drumchapel on the outskirts of Glasgow. Drumchapel was a big new post-War housing development that has got a pretty tough reputation these days. But back when I was growing up it was considered a bit of a working-class paradise because unlike in the inner city there were big expanses of grass for kids to play on. If your family was rehoused in Drumchapel in the 1950s you thought you'd won the lottery.

My family had a fourth floor flat. There were five of us living there, my mum, me and my three elder brothers Willie, James and Duncan. My father William had left home when I was two and my brothers made it pretty plain they didn't want him coming back. Willie had been sixteen then and he'd taken on the mantle of man about the house, going out to work as a gas-fitter to bring home a wage. Mum worked as an office cleaner and then as a cook at a local school.

My mother was from the Isle of Lewis in the Outer Hebrides. Like most of the Islanders she was strict Free Church of Scotland. As everyone knows, football loyalties in Glasgow are divided along religious lines and so given our background it was inevitable we'd follow the Gers.

Loyalties were taken seriously, often to silly lengths. As I say there was always a row in the flat over which of us would be forced to eat the Penguin biscuit that came in the cursed 'Celtic' wrapper. A friend of mine, Eddie Hayes, once helped his mum to decorate the home with balloons for Christmas only to have his dad return from work and systematically burst all the green and white ones.

My brothers were all good footballers. When I was still at primary school James turned professional with the new local club Clydebank. He was a right-winger and had a couple of seasons in the Scottish League. He used to take me to home games with him and I'd get to hang around in the dressing rooms and even make the half-time tea. James had the potential to be a good player but his temper let him down and he was forever getting sent off. So no family resemblance there, clearly.

I was football mad from practically the moment I could walk. I used to go out and play with my brothers. Because I was so little that meant they always stuck me in goal. It drove me mad, especially since every time I let one in they'd taunt me by calling me Frank Haffey – Celtic's keeper at the time. I'd beg them and beg them to give me the chance to play outfield, and in the end when they wouldn't I'd run up the stairs and complain to Mum until she came down with me and ordered them to let me have a turn out of goal. They'd agree, of course. But the minute she'd gone back in doors I was back between the goalposts again.

Because I was the youngest I also had to go to bed earlier than the others. I dreaded the moment when the window of our flat opened and from way up there on the fourth floor I'd hear my mother shouting, 'Andrew! Andrew!' Mum never called me by anything other than what was known then as your 'Sunday name'.

We didn't just play out of doors, either. When Mum went

off to her cleaning job in the evenings leaving Willie and James in charge, my brothers would wait until she'd disappeared down the stairs and then move all the furniture into a corner and make a goal out of the dining-room table. Because I was just about still small enough to stand underneath it without cracking my head I was tagged as keeper again as my brothers played three goals the winner with a tennis ball. God knows what the neighbours must have thought.

One Christmas Mum gave the four of us a Subbuteo table-football set, something we'd been pestering her for. We played on the kitchen table. My competitive streak was just as strong then as it is now. Playing against boys so much older than me inevitably led to frustration. Whenever I conceded a goal I'd be so angry I'd grab all the players and start packing them away in the box. Most matches seemed to end with Mum bundling me off to bed in tears.

Luckily things were better at school. I got my first winner's medal under the management of Mrs McArthur of Lochgoin Primary. From there I moved on to Kingsridge Secondary. At one time that was considered the best football school in Scotland. Danny McGrain and Alex Miller were other former pupils. At one time they could have fielded an Old Boys XI made up entirely of professionals. By the time I was fifteen I was a regular in the school side playing as centre forward. I made the Glasgow Boys team and went on to play for Scotland Schoolboys.

My biggest break, though, came when a friend, Brian Paton, asked if I'd like to join him playing for the local juvenile side Clydebank Strollers. I went along with Brian expecting to be a substitute, but one of the other players didn't turn up and I was put straight into the team. I scored a hat trick on my debut, became a regular and we went on a fantastic run that took us through to the local cup final, where we beat our biggest local rivals Kilbowie Union 3–2. While I was playing for Strollers I was selected for the Scottish Amateur Youth side and for Scottish Juveniles and, best of all, I caught the attention of Maurice Friel, the Dundee United scout.

With my duties for Strollers, school and representative teams there were times when I played three matches a day. That's something the academy system at professional clubs has been designed to cut out. When you're a growing lad, putting that kind of strain on muscles and joints and bones that are still pliable can have serious consequences. In the past a lot of talented kids played too much football in their teens and ended up permanently injured and lost to the game forever. The effect of what coaches now call overplay was something that was rarely considered in those days. Boys like myself played as many games as they could and never thought of the consequences.

As I say Mum came from Lewis in the Outer Hebrides. My brother James was born there, too. Every summer we'd make the long journey up there, taking the train to Mallaig and the ferry to Stornoway. We'd stay for five to six weeks in the little village of Back with my maternal grandparents, the Murrays.

It was a massive change from Glasgow, but I loved it. In a lot of ways it was a very strict and old-fashioned world. My grandparents were very strict church-goers. On Sundays everything was religion. My grandfather, who doubled as blacksmith and school caretaker, wouldn't tolerate any entertainment on the Sabbath and my grandmother was even stricter. On Lewis the swings in the children's playgrounds were padlocked up on Sundays. We weren't allowed to play, or read any books except the Bible. You could get out of bed and go for a walk and that was about it. You certainly couldn't listen to pop music and that was a particular passion of mine at the time.

As you might expect there was a lot of church going. However, the services were all conducted in Gaelic, a language I didn't understand, so I was excused attendance at Kirk. But I was expected to sit quietly in a chair at home until the rest of the family returned. I always waited until they were safely out of sight and then tuned the little transistor radio that sat on a shelf to Radio One. When I heard them coming back I turned it off again. I had to be careful, though. When my grandfather got back from the service the first thing he'd do was put his hand on top of the radio to check it wasn't warm. If it was he'd shake his head and go 'Tut, tut, tut.' Luckily the radio was too high for my grandmother to reach, because if she'd thought I'd been listening to the charts on the Sabbath she would have gone ballistic.

Because of the dark nights and a total lack of floodlights, football on Lewis was a summer game. The village had a team that played in the local league and cup competitions. In 1972 when we'd arrived for our usual two-month break, the captain of the side that had been in the doldrums, asked my mother if I could play the game. He was hopeful because Mum's four brothers had all been decent footballers and had quite a reputation on the island. I was the youngest child and Mum was always singing my praises, so of course she told him I was very good indeed and I found myself picked for the team as striker.

The facilities at Back didn't amount to much more than a pitch cut out of the sand dunes and a couple of sets of goalposts. The players changed in their cars. Despite that the locals took it seriously enough.

Back had never done very well in the League but that season we won the title in a play-off against Lochs despite being 3–0 down at half-time. We'd also made our way through to the final of the island's major knock-out competition, the Isle of Heather Cup. Our opponents for that clash were Back's local arch-rivals, Point.

The problem was that the summer was coming to an end and I had to go back to school in Drumchapel to start studying for my O-levels. Undeterred, the club decided to fly me out to Stornoway for the game. I felt like a proper footballer for the first time, being flown up for the big games. Mates at school would ask, 'What are you doing at the weekend, Andy?' and I'd say, 'Oh, my team are flying me out to play a cup final.' It made me feel very important. It was also the first time I had ever been on an aircraft.

It has to be said that the decision was not entirely popular with some of the villagers, who regarded me as an outsider and felt the club shouldn't be wasting its money on my air fare. To make matters worse the final ended in a draw and it was me who got our equalizer. That meant a replay the following Saturday. Once again the club forked out for my flight.

For the replay over 2,000 supporters lined the touchline, practically the entire population of both villages. We were 0–1 down at half-time, but I got an equalizer in the second period and we went on to win it in extra time. My two goals in the final cost the villagers £50 a piece, but judging by the celebrations that followed they seemed to think they were worth it. My mother still has the medals from my double-winning year. They're the only ones in my collection that are inscribed in Gaelic.

When I was playing at Villa and Wolves I went up to Lewis

regularly. It was great to be able to get right away from things and relax, but I haven't been back for some while. Both my grandparents are dead and I have no real reason to go there. But I'd like to take a trip up there sometime and take my daughter Sophie with me. I think it would be quite sobering for her, though I'd guess that these days the kids in Back have their PlayStations and pop music. Maybe even on the Sabbath.

When I wasn't playing football I was invariably watching it. And that meant Rangers. On Saturdays my brothers and I would get the number nineteen bus to Govan and walk the forty-five minutes to Ibrox, where Willie would usually lift me quickly over the turnstile and I'd disappear into the crowd before the gateman could intervene. We always stood in the same place – in the Rangers end, Cairnlea Drive, stairway thirteen, halfway down. In those days Rangers still adhered to old-fashioned standards similar in some ways to those on Lewis. Even in the 1970s the players had to keep their shirts tucked in and their socks pulled up. Moustaches and beards were banned. Rangers were smart. They were good, too. They had 'Slim Jim' Baxter in midfield, Willie Henderson on the wing and John Greig in defence – all excellent players. But the guy who really caught my eye was Colin Stein, who arrived in 1968 from Hibernian for £100,000, the first six-figure fee ever paid by a Scottish club.

Colin was a targetman, physically strong, fearless and rugged. At one time almost every club had one. Alan Gilzean, Joe Jordan, Derek Dougan, Wyn Davies, John Toshack, Malcolm Macdonald – the list was pretty much endless. Supermac was one of the first English strikers I remember noticing. I played against him for Villa when he was at Arsenal, but this was back in the days when he really made his name at Newcastle. I was playing for Dundee United down at St James' Park in the Anglo-

Scottish Cup. We were doing really well, playing the Magpies off the park. The crowd had been really quiet, then all of a sudden for no apparent reason they started roaring and bawling. I looked around and I saw this great steam engine of a man with thighs like tree trunks rumbling up and down the touchline doing his warm-ups. It was Supermac. He came on a few minutes later and absolutely battered us. He was very fast and so powerful that he knocked big guys like Jackie Copland over as if they were made of tissue paper. We lost the game, but by the end we were just glad to get off the field in one piece.

Nowadays you don't see too many of that type of forward about. In fact I'd say that in the Premiership the guy who now wears Supermac's old shirt at St James', Alan Shearer, is just about the last of the breed. I've got a lot of time for Al. I work with him regularly and he's great. The public perception of him is of a rather dour, boring bloke. But that's just a front. It's something he learned from Kenny Dalglish at Blackburn. Kenny was always of the opinion that you should present a blank face to the media. Just like Kenny, away from the spotlight Al's terrific company. Now he's on Sky he's started building a TV persona for himself and I'll think you'll see attitudes to him changing.

Colin Stein scored eight goals in his first three games for Rangers, including two hat-tricks. He became my idol. I thought he was fantastic. If anyone is responsible for me being a striker it's him.

It was at Ibrox that I got to know my father a little. He'd left home when I was a toddler and, as I say, he wasn't exactly welcome back in the family home. He never made a single visit to the flat in all the time I lived there. When I was nine, though, he started taking me to games. I caught the bus up to

Anniesland, which was where he was living in Glasgow at the time. We got on well enough, but meeting someone once a month is not the way to form a close relationship. When I was thirteen or so he drifted out of my life again. I never had what you'd call a father and son relationship with him. We never even played football together.

When I became a player at Dundee United I started to see Dad again and he enjoyed coming to watch me. He died when I was at Villa. He had cancer and was in hospital in Glasgow undergoing chemotherapy when I last saw him. I sat on the side of his bed and asked him if there was anything I could get him. He said, 'Well, you know, Andrew, I've always wanted to shave with one of those electric razors.' I went straight out and bought him one. It was the only thing he ever asked me for.

My brothers and I went regularly to home games at Ibrox. As I got a bit older I started to go separately from Willie, James and Duncs with my school pals. That was who I was with on 2 January 1971. I'd gone in as usual and taken up my regular spot on the Cairnlea Drive stairway. It was an Old Firm game. With eighty minutes gone Rangers were losing and for some reason I decided to leave early. Ten minutes after I'd gone a series of barriers collapsed on stairway thirteen and sixty-six fans died. Fifty-seven of them died of traumatic asphyxia, some lost their lives on their stomachs with their heads pointing down the slope towards the pitch. Others were killed standing up, squeezed out of their shoes by the crush.

As I sauntered home I knew nothing about what had happened. But my mum had been at home listening on the radio. She knew all four of us were at the game. She knew where we stood in the ground. She was petrified. There were no mobile phones in those days, of course, so she had no way of checking if we were all right. She just had to sit in the flat and wait for us to walk in through the door. Thankfully we all did. But I can't imagine what she must have gone through while she was waiting.

It wasn't the first time such a thing had happened at Ibrox. In 1961 two fans had been killed and another seventy injured on stairway thirteen. In 1967 another eleven people were taken to hospital. Two years later twenty-nine more people were injured. Add to that Heysel, Bradford, Hillsborough. You look at the stadiums we have now – comfortable, safe – and it's horrendous to think how many people had to be maimed and killed before we got to this stage.

As a player Graeme Souness was incredibly talented and incredibly tough. He had a reputation for fancying himself a fair bit, too. Our Scotland teammate Archie Gemmill famously said that if Souey was chocolate he'd eat himself. Graeme was big enough to acknowledge the truth in that and laugh about it. Which shows he's not as arrogant as some of his enemies have made out.

He was certainly single-minded and determined, though, and he was prepared to back his own judgement even if everybody was yelling that he was wrong. That showed when Souey signed Mo Johnston. Maurice was the first Catholic to play for Rangers for 113 years. He was also a former Celtic player. It was an amazing piece of business. And it caused a massive furore in Glasgow and across Scotland. But Graeme – whose wife was Catholic, incidentally – didn't flinch. Neither did Mo and he took immense amount of stick from both sides.

I'd left Ibrox by the time the deal went through, but I had an idea something was going on. At the end of the season we played Celtic in the Scottish Cup Final at Hampden. I was gutted because despite the fact that Ian Durrant, Neale Cooper, Ray Wilkins and Derek Ferguson were all injured I hadn't even made it onto the bench. I'd been sure I would be selected and maybe get a run-out in the game because I was the only goal scorer we had in reserve. But at the last minute Graeme – who'd hardly kicked a ball all season – decided to pick himself as one of the subs.

The truth was Souey had a bit of thing about the Cup. He hadn't won the FA Cup with Liverpool, and since he'd been at Ibrox, Rangers had made a habit of getting knocked out early by underdogs like Hamilton Academicals and Dunfermline. And we nearly did again that season when we only just scraped past Raith Rovers after a replay.

As a result of all this Graeme had begun to think he was jinxed in the Cup. It was all a lot of nonsense, really. Football throws up these kinds of things all the time. Bob Paisley, one of the most successful managers in the history of the game, didn't win the FA Cup either, and neither did Brian Clough. My own career had been blighted in a different way. When I was sixteen playing for Glasgow Boys away to Manchester Boys I'd scored. Little did I realize it at the time but that goal – a header at the Stretford End – was the first and last I would ever get at Old Trafford. Maybe it's just as well Big Ron didn't sign me for the Red Devils from Wolves after all.

However silly it was – and that wasn't something I'd like to have put to Graeme, by the way – Souey believed in it. He thought there was a hoodoo. And obviously he saw this as his last chance to lay it to rest once and for all. So he picked himself as sub. And we lost 1–0 to a Joe Miller goal. To cap it all we had a decent goal of our own disallowed, Ally McCoist missed a total sitter and the guy who made the mistake that lead to the goal was Gary Stevens, who'd been our best defender all season.

Afterwards we sat miserably in our dressing room listening to the noise of the Celtic celebrations coming through the walls. Then Graeme strode in, face like thunder, and hurled his loser's medal into the corner. He said, 'Let them have their party and enjoy themselves now, because this summer something's going to happen that will change the face of this club and change the face of their club forever.'

Like the rest of the squad I didn't know what he meant at the time. But a few months later it became clear that what he was referring to was the signing of Mo Johnston. The irons were already in the fire that day at Hampden. Mo was preparing to knock back a return to Parkhead and come to Ibrox instead.

Having grown up in Glasgow as a rabid Rangers fan I'd have to be totally and utterly honest and say that if I hadn't lived in England for most of my adult life I might – might, mind you – have been one of those Gers supporters who set fire to their season tickets and burned their scarves in protest at the signing of Mo Johnston. When you're immersed in that sort of culture it's very hard not to get caught up with it. But I've spent over a quarter of a century south of the border and while I do still believe that the tradition of Rangers – and of Celtic, too – is a massive part of the identity and fabric of those clubs, I also think that you have to move on.

And there's no doubt that Souey was right when he said the signing changed the situation not only at Ibrox but also at Parkhead. Graeme knew that the bar on signing Roman Catholics worked against Rangers and made things easier for the club's main rivals. Celtic had never operated any kind of sectarian policy. If they had the history of Scottish football would have been very different. The Celts' greatest manager, Jock Stein, was a Protestant and so was one of their best-ever players, Kenny Dalglish. Because Celtic judged players and staff purely on merit they had traditionally drawn from a bigger pool of talent than Rangers.

When I was a kid playing for junior teams if a scout came up to you after a match and asked what school you went to you knew straightaway that he was from Ibrox. And you can bet if you'd answered 'St Patrick's' he wouldn't have bothered making a note of your name. Jock Stein always said Rangers' policy made his life a whole lot less stressful. Because if a good youngster emerged in Glasgow who was a Catholic the Celtic manager knew he didn't have to lose sleep over whether there'd be any serious rivals for his signature. And if a Catholic player came up for transfer from another club he knew he wouldn't get in a bidding war that would hike up the price; he'd get them cheap.

It was a completely ridiculous situation. Despite the initial fall-out when the Johnston signing was announced it seems that many Gers fans must have felt that way, because the protests that were threatened never really materialized. Mo came into the side and in his first season did a great job for the team. And that was that.

Nowadays with all the Italians, Portuguese and Brazilians who've played for Rangers since that time it's hard to imagine such a situation ever existed at all. Graeme broke the mould. It had to happen. But it took a strong man to do it.

Even before the Johnston signing there's little doubt that Graeme's arrival at Ibrox in 1986 had had a massive effect on the Scottish Premier League. His experience of playing in Italy had given him a different perspective on training and the whole culture of club football. When he was at Sampdoria he'd been impressed with the way the club looked after the players and the way the players took care of themselves off the field, the whole *rituro* system. In Italy, Souey noted, the players remembered their job at all times, and they watched what they ate and drank and went to bed early. Graeme believed in all that, that level of high professionalism. He brought the same kind of attitude and attention to detail to the job at Rangers. He even took the players for pre-season training to Sampdoria's camp at Il Ciocco.

His transfer policy had also turned the world upside down. Until Souey came in, Scottish clubs sold players to England. Nobody went the other way unless his career was finished. That was more or less set in stone. Yet suddenly here was Graeme buying top English stars like Terry Butcher, Chris Woods, Ray Wilkins and Mark Walters.

He had overturned a century or more of tradition with the help of millionaire chairman David Murray, who'd taken control of the club a few months before I arrived, his own reputation built at Anfield and the Heysel ban. The fact that playing for Rangers almost guaranteed European football was a huge selling point for the club.

Terry Butcher and Chris Woods were two of Graeme's first signings when he took over at Ibrox in 1986. Woodsy had been brought in from Forest for £600,000 and he was soon England's number one. Butcher was the captain of the national side and widely regarded as one of the best defenders on the planet, justifiably so. He cost £725,000 from Ipswich. That was a massive signing for Graeme, not just because of Terry's ability, but also because of what it signalled about Rangers. Manchester United had wanted Butcher, and so had Everton, but he'd chosen Ibrox instead and that sent out a message to the rest of football.

Terry was a ferocious competitor – the sort of guy who tended to react to defeat by booting his foot through the dressing-room door. It was lucky Rangers were successful or the joiner's bills might have bankrupted the club. Put him at the back with Richard Gough and my old Everton teammate Gary Stevens, who'd been brought in for £1,000,000 a month or so before I arrived, and it's plain you've got the makings of a very solid back line.

Ray Wilkins was another great buy. Ray had been brought in from Paris St Germain for £250,000. He'd played for Manchester United and Milan and won eighty-four caps for England. So that tells you he was no mug. During his career Ray was often criticized for being negative. When he was at Old Trafford Ron Atkinson nicknamed him 'The Crab' because he sometimes opted to pass sideways just a little too often. But Big Ron had also rated Butch very highly. I back that judgement. Not that we don't still wind Ray up about his reputation. Whenever he comes to do work at Sky we always arrange the chairs in a straight line and tell him, 'We thought this would suit you better, Ray, because you don't have to look forwards.'

Some people think that the silky way Butch played the game and his relaxed demeanour indicate that he isn't as great a competitor as somebody like Terry Butcher, who really wears his heart on his sleeve. That's a mistake. Ray was as passionate about winning as anybody I've played with.

Some might say that ultimately bringing in all the foreign players had a detrimental effect on the Scottish game. I'm not so sure. I think that until Graeme arrived at Rangers there was a danger of the Scottish League becoming like the League of Ireland. Interest in the SPL was at an all-time low. You were looking at a situation where Rangers were sometimes only getting 10,000 for home games – an unheard of situation. Somebody had to stand the thing on its head and Souey did that. The great thing was that everybody else – especially Celtic – had to catch up. And while there was a lot of talk of Rangers 'buying' the title, the fact is that he never spent more than £1.7 million on a player.

Graeme's policy of buying from England and later from Europe has been criticized for starting the flood of foreigners into the SPL. From his point of view it's hard to see what else he could do. He wanted Rangers to be a force in European football, not just in Scottish football. To achieve that he needed a squad of high-class players and, because of the size of Scotland, to do it with only Scots in the side he'd basically have had to field the international team. There was not much chance of that. And besides, Souey was looking at the bigger picture. He'd spent his whole career in England and never lost sight of the fact that he'd won the European Cup in a Liverpool side that had just three Englishmen in it. If Bob Paisley had operated the kind of policy some people felt Graeme should adopt – home players only – you can bet they wouldn't have needed quite as much silver polish at Anfield.

In the end I'd have to agree that the influx of foreign players into Scottish football since that time has not benefited the game. Quite the opposite. I'm not talking about the quality players who've come in. Having stars like Henrik Larsson, Alan Thompson or Ronald de Boer playing in the SPL can only improve the standard. My concern is with the mediocre overseas players who've been brought in for only one reason – because they are cheap. Nobody wants to see average foreign players holding back home-grown talent, but too often in recent seasons that seems to have been the case, not just in Scotland but in the English Premiership, too.

When Rangers can send out a team without a single Scot in it, as they did under Dick Advocaat a few years ago, then I'm sure I'm not the only one throwing my hands up in despair. But I don't think you can blame Graeme Souness for creating the situation. When he shopped abroad he only bought good players like Terry, Chris, Butch and Trevor Steven. Souey didn't just buy foreigners either. He'd also snatched Ian Ferguson out from under the nose of Liverpool, and while I was there he invested in a young lad from Clyde named Tom Cowan who Forest and Coventry were after.

I'd say that far from being detrimental, Souey's input revitalized Rangers and the SPL. By the time I returned to Glasgow Ibrox was full again, which often meant we were playing in front of the day's biggest crowd not just in Scotland but in Britain. Planning had already begun for a new tier on the main stand to increase capacity to 52,000 and the stadium was widely acknowledged as the best in Britain. From the situation in the early-1980s that was quite a turnaround.

Souey threw down the gauntlet and Celtic have responded magnificently to the challenge. Parkhead, like Ibrox, is now a fantastic stadium, and Martin O'Neill has built a great side to play in it. Inevitably, this has led some to suggest that the Old Firm should join the English Premiership. I'd love to see it. And I'd guess that the clubs are keen to see it as well because I don't believe they built those two grounds just to play Dunfermline. But the logistics of it mean it will never happen. I can't see UEFA and FIFA accepting it, for one thing. If they did I suspect we'd be going down the Great Britain international route and I can't see the Scots or the English voting for that.

A few years ago I thought the way out for the Old Firm would come through the formation of a European League. I thought that was something that was inevitable. With the G14 group of powerful clubs clamouring for one it seemed a certainty. Not any more. It's become clear that it just wouldn't be economically viable. You only have to look at the attendances for the Champions' League group stages to see that. Teams like Milan and Juventus are playing in half-empty stadiums. The domestic leagues in the bigger countries attract far higher attendances. Fans are excited by the idea of beating their local rivals far more than the thought of a win against the champions of Belgium.

It's a pity, because at the moment the SPL just isn't competitive. The other clubs simply can't compete with Rangers and Celtic. I'm not being disrespectful. It's simply a matter of economics. The revenues of both the Old Firm clubs are massive compared to those of their main rivals from outside Glasgow. The wages the big two can offer compared to the rest means they will always suck up the best talent from across the country. Financially it isn't a gap, it's a chasm. And it looks like it will stay that way.

My overall impression of Graeme was that he was a man who got what he wanted. As a player he never shirked anything, never pulled out of a tackle, and when he asked somebody to do things he expected them to do them. He could be fierce, no doubt about that. And he certainly wouldn't tolerate any dissent. Shortly before my arrival he'd sold Graham Roberts because the former Spurs midfielder had made the mistake of arguing with him in front of the rest of the team. Graham Roberts was a whole-hearted battler and he was a massive favourite with the fans at Ibrox. But if he thought that made him fireproof Souey proved to him that it didn't. Not only did he sell Roberts. He also waited until he got the right price for him, which meant the Englishman spent the last part of his Rangers career playing in the reserves.

Although Andy Cole and Dwight Yorke might not agree, I believe that since those days Graeme has mellowed a little. He's no longer the sort of guy who can start a fight in an empty room. He had major heart surgery and his experiences as manager at Anfield – where his head-on approach made him too many powerful enemies – have changed him. He's done well since leaving Liverpool and it wouldn't surprise me at all if he were destined for bigger things.

Graeme's assistant at Ibrox was Walter Smith. I'd played with Walter for two years at Tannadice. He's a Glaswegian, a life-long Rangers supporter and a lovely lad. I say that even though chasing his over-hit passes at United reduced my playing career by at least eighteen months. At Dundee United I'd always thought Walter would go on to become a coach. He was that type. Always looking to learn more.

Graeme had brought Smith in from Dundee United, where he'd been working under Jim McLean. It was a shrewd appointment, because when he'd come in at Ibrox Souey hadn't really known the Scottish scene. He'd captained his country, but he'd not played any club football there. So he'd realized he needed a guy who knew what was what and was also a good coach. And that was Walter.

In general I didn't get to see too much of Souey as a manager at Ibrox because I was more or less part-time. I trained with West Brom during the week and flew up to Scotland the day before games. I'd get there on Friday mornings in time to train with the team. Go to the game on Saturday, usually as a sub, and fly back to the Midlands on Sunday. It was an arrangement that suited everybody. Everybody, that is, except for my club colleague Ally McCoist.

Coisty thought I should be a permanent presence in the dressing room. So one day when I wasn't there he turned up with a life-sized cardboard cut-out of me and propped it in one corner. He said the two-dimensional dummy had better movement than I did. Every morning when I was in England, Ally would spend a few minutes in the dressing room holding a one-sided conversation with the cardboard cut-out saying, 'How are you, Andy? Where did you go last night? Oh, really, that sounds exciting, but we better not let the boss know.' I guess it kept the little fella amused.

Ally and Graeme didn't always see eye to eye and there was the occasional clash. I'm not sure exactly why. Ally was a megastar at Rangers. He was handsome and charismatic, and I think in Souey's eyes he sometimes traded on that and coasted a little. I wouldn't go along with that. Certainly on the field I never saw Ally give less than his best. Off the field I'd agree he enjoyed himself. Graeme had that Italian thing about a footballer being a footballer twenty-four hours a day and perhaps he thought Ally was sometimes more interested in being Ally McCoist twenty-four hours a day.

Ally was really funny, very sharp and a great presence in the dressing room. He could turn any situation into a joke, even one that had gone against him. One Friday morning Graeme delivered his team talk for Saturday, announced who was playing and Ally wasn't in the starting line-up. Souey left the room and we were all sitting there wondering how Coisty would take being dropped when suddenly he jumped to his feet, clapped his hands together and said, 'Right, where is he? Where is he? Where are the hidden cameras? Where's Jeremy Beadle? Come on, I know you're there Jeremy. You can't fool me. Drop Ally McCoist? I don't think so. This is obviously one of your silly TV show's practical jokes.'

Ally was another of those whose contribution to the team was more than just what he did on the pitch. And he did plenty on the pitch. He was a great goal scorer. People have said that part of that was luck. There's a bit of truth in that. Sometimes it seemed Lady Luck wasn't just smiling on Ally, she was right there sitting on his shoulder grinning. If the ball came into the six-yard box and hit Ally on the backside you could almost guarantee it would bounce into the net. But there's nothing wrong with that. Luck's an underrated commodity. To be successful in anything, particularly sport, you need it, because the margins between success and failure are so small. In cricket how often do you see a batsman who's been in for a couple of overs edge the ball, the slip fielder spill the catch and the batter go on to get 200? It's the way it happens. As Napoleon said, 'Don't give me good generals, give me lucky ones.'

Ally had a whole lot of self-confidence, too, and that was great because it rubbed off on his teammates. I remember going up to play Dundee United in a Scottish Cup quarter-final replay. In the draw at Ibrox Ally had missed at least five gilt-edged chances and Souey had really laid into him about it, telling him he was a complete dud. In the dressing room at Tannadice the other lads started giving Ally stick saying it was all his fault they had had to travel up to Dundee on a freezing Monday night when they could have been at home watching telly. In typical style Ally immediately apologized and said not to worry, he intended to sort it all out by getting the winner this time around. And in the forty-ninth minute he did just that.

Make no mistake: Ally also has incredible talent. He was exceptional. He could win games on his own just with the quality of his finishing. When Ally was still at St Johnstone, Jim McLean had been to watch him. I spoke to Jim shortly afterwards and he was really excited. He said to me, 'I've seen this kid Andy and he is a natural. The best young forward I've come across in Scotland in the ten years since you left.' Jim was interested in taking Coisty to Tannadice, but Ally went to Sunderland instead. He didn't have a great time in England and the fact he didn't has led some people to question his ability. But I think when you look at his record with Rangers, domestically and in Europe, and internationally with Scotland, it speaks for itself. Sunderland maybe came too early and perhaps it wasn't the right club. From my own experience of playing and training with Ally I have no doubt he could have been brilliant in the English top flight. Maybe he could have given it another shot, but at Rangers he had everything he wanted. He never felt he needed to move.

I got on great with Ally. In many ways we're quite similar personalities. I've always enjoyed locking horns with him across the studio on *A Question of Sport*. I don't see him too often socially these days. He works for ITV, which means that professionally our paths don't cross too often – maybe they will at the Champions' League Final this year. We're never in the same place at the same time.

I did get to work with Ally on the film *Shot at Glory*, which also starred Michael Keaton and Robert Duvall in supporting roles to the great man. I got a call from the film people asking if I'd do the commentary with a guy named Rob MacLaine up in Scotland. The people who were making the movie were American and they didn't have much idea about what they called 'soccer'. They'd show me clips they'd filmed and I'd point out anything that wasn't authentic, like Robert Duvall talking about the players sitting in 'the locker room' and they'd redub it. The most bizarre thing about the whole experience was watching Ally in the football scenes playing in a green-and-white hooped shirt and having to sit in a mock-up of the Sky Studios describing him as 'the Celtic legend'.

Ally's first-choice strike partner that season at Ibrox was Kevin Drinkell. Graeme had bought him from Norwich for £500,000 shortly before I arrived. Kevin was an old-fashioned centre forward, big, strong and fearless – the sort of all-out trier Rangers fans have always loved. He also smoked like a trooper. Loved a fag, one of the few players I've known who did. Maybe Kevin wasn't an international class forward, but he scored forty-nine goals in fifty-four games for Rangers, which is some record.

The crowd at Ibrox adored Kevin, but they didn't actually call him by his name. Rangers supporters had a thing about certain names. In Glasgow Drinkell and another Englishman, midfielder Nigel Spackman, were rechristened by the fans. They didn't like the name Kevin and they particularly didn't like Nigel. They thought it sounded wrong for a Scottish footballer. So instead they named the pair Rab Spackman and Billy Drinkell.

Coisty and Billy were both out of action when I arrived at Rangers that autumn, so one of my first duties was to sit on the bench at Hampden for the Skol Cup semi-final. Graeme was short of strikers but it didn't matter, because Mark Walters took apart opponents Hearts single-handed. He scored twice and set up the other for Scott Nisbet in a 3–0 win that booked us a place in the final against Aberdeen.

I'd known Mark since he was a kid at Villa. He's a smashing lad, very talented, good balance, two wonderful feet and his attitude was first class. He was incredibly level-headed. And he needed to be. Souey had bought him from Villa for half a million and Mark was the first black player Rangers had had for fifty years, and one of the few in the SPL at the time. That unfortunately meant he attracted racist abuse and banana skins from morons across Scotland. I thought he handled it all calmly and with incredible dignity.

When Mark was younger there had been a feeling in the game that he was what was called a non-fancier. That meant that if you rattled him early he lost interest. I know when I was in teams playing against Villa at that time I'd always tell the defenders to clatter him the first chance they got in the hope it would put him off. A lot of players tested Mark's bottle, rightly so, and when he was starting out he didn't like it. But by the time he got to Rangers he'd really toughened himself up. He didn't let opponents intimidate him any more. And believe me in the SPL plenty tried.

Often skilful players rely purely on their ability. They don't have the ugly side to their game that can take them on a bit further. Mark was possibly a little in that category. If you look at the really great ball players, Jimmy Johnstone, Denis Law, George Best, they were spiky customers who didn't take kindly to being kicked and were likely to exact their own justice before the ref could intervene. Davie Cooper, who was also in the Rangers squad at that time, fitted into that category. Defenders knew they couldn't kick Davie and not expect to get one back.

Maybe Mark could have done with a little more of that kind of fire. He proved he could take the rough stuff but maybe he needed to dish it out a little too.

The final against Aberdeen was played in front of 72,000. It was game that had a bit of added edge to it. We'd travelled up to Pittodrie a few weeks before and lost for the first time that season. The defeat was overshadowed by the fact that the Dons defender Neil Simpson had caught Ian Durrant with a tackle after the whistle had gone and totally smashed the young midfielder's knee. The surgeon described it as the worst sporting injury he'd ever seen. He said the only time he'd seen a leg so badly damaged before was in a car crash. And that was it. Ian's career effectively ended that day.

We didn't realize it at the time, of course. The team all thought he'd recover. Rangers, aware of how special he was, spent a huge amount of time and money on treatment for him. But though he did come back he was never half the player he'd been. It was a tragedy because players of that ability don't come along too often. Durrantie was really special. When I first arrived at Ibrox I used to watch this wiry kid in training and think, wow! He really could play. He was mobile. He had great vision and incredible stamina. He was one of those players who seem to gain energy as the game goes on.

Ian had only been in the Rangers team for a season and a bit and already he was a regular in the Scotland midfield. Souey rated him as a greater talent than Paul Gascoigne and I'd say there's no doubt about that. To me he seemed destined to become the best footballer Scotland had produced since Kenny Dalglish. I know Graeme saw Durrant as the man Rangers would build a team around for the next decade. But it wasn't to be.

As a result of that tackle there was a danger that the Skol Cup Final might turn into some sort of grudge match. Certainly that was the talk in the media. But Souey sensibly played that down. He told the players that the best revenge for Ian Durrant would be to see us lift the trophy and we did just that thanks to a couple of goals from Coisty and another from Ian Ferguson.

I got my own first goal in the blue jersey at Love Street. It was arguably the most important I scored that season. We were trailing 1–0 to St Mirren, which would have been our first defeat of the season and a blow to the team's confidence, especially since Aberdeen were breathing down our necks. I came off the bench with twenty minutes to go and struck the equalizer in the eighty-seventh minute. I got a few more after that, including a couple at Dens Park in the penultimate match of the season. It was nice to get my final goals in professional football in the city where it had all started for me.

Playing in that team was superb; there was great camaraderie and really high-class talent there. I got a championship medal, and a few goals including two at Ibrox. It's fantastic to realize a childhood dream. Especially when the reality doesn't disappoint you. And it didn't.

The Rangers fans really took to me, which was great. They knew I was one of them. They knew when I pulled on the blue jersey it was a Rangers supporter pulling on that jersey. I wasn't just fulfilling my fantasy but theirs as well. People talk about there being a particular type of player that the fans at Ibrox love – aggressive, whole-hearted, in your face – I don't hold with that particularly because they also worshipped Ally Mc-Coist and Jim Baxter, but that is the sort of player I am. I think fans at all clubs, not just Rangers, respect that. What supporters want to see is guys who give everything they have. If you do that then they appreciate it and they're prepared to forgive a bad performance. You can't guarantee form, but you should guarantee effort and I believe I always did.

The reception I got at Ibrox from the supporters is something I'll never forget. But the truly fantastic thing about that season was how much my family enjoyed it. It was as much a buzz for them as it was for me. They are all diehard fans and because I was a Rangers player they could turn up on match day and find tickets waiting for them. I could take them into parts of the ground they'd only ever heard of and introduce them to everyone, the players, the staff, the manager. They loved every minute of it. For me that was wonderful. It was the cherry on top of the icing on top of the cake.

10

At the end of the 1988–9 season my contract with Rangers finished. I knew one season was all that Graeme would offer me and that was fine by me. It has to be said, however, that beyond a summer holiday I didn't have clue what I was going to do next.

My plan – if you can call it that – was to go to my home in Worcestershire and wait for the phone to ring. Now I was a free agent I was sure I'd get an offer from somewhere, a short-term playing contract maybe, or a coaching job. I sat down and waited. And waited. And nothing happened.

As a player I'd always tried to keep my feet on the ground. When I was at Villa and was injured, in bad form or generally feeling down, I'd get up at 6 a.m. and drive down to the main bus station in Birmingham. I'd park the car for ten minutes or so and sit and watch the people standing with their sandwiches under their arms going off to work. It was a way of reminding myself how lucky I was. Usually while they were on the way to the factory floor footballers like me were still lying in bed.

In many ways professional football cushions you from ordinary life. Everything is taken care of for you by the club. They make your travel arrangements and your doctor's appointments. If you're unhappy at your place of work they sort out a move to another one. If they want rid of you they don't just hand you a P45 and push you out of the door, but arrange another job for you somewhere else. There are down sides, of course, as there are with any profession, but generally it's a comfortable, sheltered life.

So when you finish in football and suddenly all that back-up, all the support, is removed, it comes as a massive shock to your system. You're used to the buzz of training, to being around a load of noisy lads, getting told what to do and where to go. Now with what seems like no warning at all you're all on your own. It's bewildering. Depressing.

That summer was a really sobering experience for me. I was out of work, thirty-two years of age and hadn't any idea what I was going to do with the rest of my life. And so I sat there. Finally one day in July the phone did ring. It was a guy named Andy Melvin.

I'd met Andy when he worked for Scottish Television. I was at West Bromwich Albion and Andy had come down with a couple of other people from STV because the legendary Scots commentator Arthur Montford was retiring and they wanted to run the idea past me of going back to Scotland and taking over from him. We talked about that off and on for a few months at which point I signed for Rangers. Wearing the blue jersey put an end to any chance of the STV job because it effectively alienated half the TV audience in Scotland. But I'd done a few other things with Andy Melvin after that, little interviews and bits and pieces of commentary, and he'd enjoyed my way of talking about the game and my enthusiasm for it.

I'd had a fair amount of television experience as a player, mainly thanks to Scotland's habit of not selecting me for World

Cups, and being on TV had never bothered me. I've never been nervous about it. I've never looked at a camera and felt phased or worried. Because of that I've always been able to be myself on air, and luckily people have liked that. There are a lot of ex-players coming into TV these days and when they ask me for advice that's what I always tell them, 'Be yourself.' Because the worst thing you can do is to try and be something you're not. Anyone who's fake or insincere, the camera will pick that up right away and beam it into the viewers' living rooms. I was always natural on camera, the same off air as I was on it, and I think that was one of the things Andy Melvin liked about me.

So Andy said, 'What are you doing at the moment?' I said, 'Do you want me to be brutally honest? Absolutely nothing.' He asked if I was intending to play on and I said that I'd been hoping to, but that at the moment it seemed increasingly unlikely. Andy said that in that case he had a proposal.

While I'd been at Ibrox Andy Melvin had been poached by the new TV company British Satellite Broadcasting to head up their sports operation along with a guy from the BBC named Brian Cowgill, who had a great reputation as a real TV vision-ary. BSB were looking for commentators and Brian had asked Andy if he thought they should try and get Ian St John, who was pretty much the top name at that time, from ITV. Andy had said, no, he thought they should get me. And that was why he was phoning.

I met Andy and Brian in London at one of the airport hotels. They told me all about BSB, the company with the squarial satellite dishes. They'd come very close to getting the rights to cover the League, only to have them snatched from under their noses by Greg Dyke, then at LWT, for what now seems like the bargain price of all time, £11 million. But they had succeeded is securing coverage of the FA Cup, Scottish football, England internationals and Serie A in Italy.

They told me their ideas of how the coverage was going to be shaped. I remember Brian's big dream was for the 'God slot'. He wanted to put live football on BSB on Sunday, kicking off at about 6 o'clock when there's nothing on terrestrial TV except religious programmes. It hasn't happened yet, but you can see it would be massive if it ever did.

Andy and Brian were both certain about one thing – the football on BSB wasn't going to be like anything there'd ever been before. The first big change the pair intended to make was in the commentary style. The normal British system was to have a commentator alongside an expert summarizer who was cued in every ten minutes or so. Andy and Brian felt that didn't get the best out of either of them. So they were going to have two commentators working together in tandem. It was a style borrowed from America, where it was used very successfully for the NFL. They told me that they wanted me to be the John Madden figure, the ex-pro who supplies the analysis. In the US in those days Madden used a chalkboard to explain moves live on air during games and I actually did that for a while on BSB. I'd have to say it was a lot more difficult for me because our brand of football moves a fair bit quicker than gridiron.

Andy and Brian felt I could take the Madden role and also do some presenting, generally learn the trade and over time become their football man.

I went away to think about it. I hadn't ever considered a career in broadcasting. I'd still been thinking in terms of playing or management. But now I thought, 'Why not?' To be in at the inception of something, pick up a new skill, seemed like a

19. Playing for your country is the greatest honour in the game
and scoring makes it even more special.

20. The controversial strike against Watford in the 1984 FA Cup Final. In my view the referee was spot on.

21. Enjoying the FA Cup win with my favourite supporters.

22.Goodison glory. Celebrating my goal in the classic Cup Winners' Cup semi-final clash with Bayern Munich. The greatest match I ever played in.

The 1985 Cup Winners' Cup Final against Rapid Vienna

23. *Opposite, top*. Defensive duties. Something's going on behind the wall but only Trevor Steven and I seem to have noticed.

24. *Opposite, bottom*. I net one. I'm not sure where the defence has got to.

25. *Right*. Celebrating our victory in the traditional manner.

26. *Below*. Sharing the glory with an Everton fan. They deserved it. In the home leg against Bayern they practically sucked the ball into the net.

27. Return to Villa Park. Manager Graham Turner, chairman Doug Ellis and a lion look on.

28. *Left.* The cherry on the icing on top of the cake. Lifting the Scottish title with boyhood idols Rangers.

29. *Below.* Getting my opinions across without the aid of a microphone as assistant manager at Villa.

30. *Right*. Working for Sky is a lot like being in a football team and I'm proud to wear the jersey.

31. *Below, left*. Alongside striking partner, co-commentator Martin 'The Voice' Tyler.

32. *Below, right*. And with the skipper Richard Keys.

33. Playing golf with Darren Gough.

34. With my partner, TV presenter Suzanne Dando.

great opportunity. And to be completely truthful it was the only job offer I'd had. So I called Andy Melvin and said, yes.

Andy had taken a big gamble on me and he became my mentor. Over the past fourteen years he has taught me everything I know about broadcasting. Just as Jim McLean was instrumental in me succeeding in football, so Andy has been fundamental to building my career in television. Without either of them it's doubtful if I'd have achieved anything.

A few years ago Andy decided to move into senior management at Sky. It was sad day for us. I think it's fair to say that we've found it impossible to replace him. That's not to downgrade the contribution of those who came after him, it's just that they were big boots to fill. Andy had great drive and he knew what he wanted. He is the man who made the decisions that forged the identity of the channel. For five or six years he set high standards of professionalism and discipline for the rest of us. Martin, Richard, myself and everyone else at Sky Sports owe the guy an enormous debt.

BSB's offices were at Champion studios in West London. Andy and Brian worked there assembling the staff ready for the channel's launch in February. They put their team together like a football manager would, with the same care and attention. Around the same time they hired me they brought in Richard Keys. Keysie was a football nut, a Coventry City fan, who'd worked on local radio up in Merseyside for years covering the game before taking up his position on the TV-am sofa. He'd been sitting on that thing five days a week for five years getting gradually bigger and bigger and I think the chance to get involved with sport again came at just the right time for him.

I didn't know Richard, but we hit it off from day one and have had a great professional relationship ever since, partly I suspect because Richard knows I don't want his job and I know he doesn't want mine.

Over the years Keysie has grown to become, in my opinion, the best sports presenter in the business. People may throw up the name of Des Lynam. To me Des does an altogether different job. Most terrestrial channels have a build-up to games that lasts from fifteen to twenty minutes. For the Champions' League Richard is sometimes on air for two hours. On Sundays he does an hour pre-game and an hour at the back end of the show. Now that is some effort. The biggest compliment I can pay him is that I can't imagine anyone else sitting in his chair doing that job.

Richard doesn't use an autocue, just handwritten notes he commits to memory, and yet he never ever misses. He makes the odd mistake, of course. His classic was a few years ago at Villa Park. Villa had played Sheffield Wednesday and Richard was wrapping up and getting his countdown for the end of the show. He's saying, 'Well, not exactly a classic match.' And the countdown is going 18, 17. 'But from Villa Park we leave you,' 10, 9 'with the scoreline,' 6, 5 'Aston Villa one . . .' and then there's this terrible little pause because he's forgotten which team Villa have just played, 4, 3. But he knows he's got to hit his cue, so quick as a flash he says, 'The visitors one,' and up comes the music. And that's Richard, a consummate professional.

Probably the hardest thing to master in TV is carrying on talking while the producer is giving you instructions through your earpiece. It's something that takes a bit of getting used to.

Richard and I work well together on that sort of thing. I know, for instance, that if he's getting the countdown in his ear and there's forty-five seconds of the show to go then that is an awkward length of time for him to fill, so I'll chip in with something and take it down to ten seconds, which gives him time to formulate what he's going to say to close the programme. Little bits of teamwork like that remind me of playing the game. And at BSB and now at Sky there is a real team feel. Andy Melvin was the manager and Keysie is the captain. I'm the centre forward. Funnily enough, though, my and Keysie's best moment of cooperation came not at Sky but on ITV.

Celebrity is a funny word. It's not one I particularly like, especially when it's applied to me. I don't think of myself as a celebrity and I never have. I'd like to think that if I am famous it's for what I do, whether that's being a footballer or a broadcaster, and what I've achieved on the field and in television. I don't live a celebrity lifestyle and I have very few famous people as friends. My friends are ordinary, everyday folk. I've never courted publicity and I've never wanted to be the subject of newspaper headlines unless they were related to my work. Inevitably, fame has come because of the jobs I've done. I enjoy what fame brings and what it's given me, make no mistake about that, but it's not something I've ever actively gone looking for and my life doesn't and never has depended on it. Others may want to live their lives in the spotlight but I don't. I've been asked to do 'I'm a celebrity this' and 'I'm a celebrity that' and I have turned them all down. It's not me.

The only celebrity show I did do was *Who Wants to Be a Millionaire*. The wife of one of the producers on Sky Sports works on the show and she asked if Richard and I would go on it. We agreed. It was a chance to win a massive amount of money for charity, it's a good programme and I know Chris Tarrant quite well from his days working in the Midlands.

Waiting to go on was absolutely nerve-racking. I hadn't been so frightened about anything for years. I think we were both terrified of making fools of ourselves and walking out with a thousand pounds. The people ahead of us hadn't done very well, which made it worse. Now Richard is pretty intelligent and it seemed to me that he would know things that I didn't and I would know things that he didn't. So we hoped we'd be all right. Just to make sure, though, when we got to the nominating of the friend for the phone-a-friend section we nominated Judith Keppel, the woman who won the million. We got her phone number from a contact, gave her a ring and asked if she'd be our friend for the evening and she agreed. Early on we got a film question about Marilyn Monroe and we weren't sure of the answer. So Chris asked us what we wanted to do and we said we'd like to phone a friend. He asked who our friend was and we said 'Judith Keppel.' Chris though it was a wind-up. He said, 'Come off it, you don't know Judith Keppel.' We said, 'Yes, we do. She's one of our mates.' He said, 'How long have you known her?' We said, 'Oh, at least an hour.' So he phoned the number we'd given him and sure enough Judith answered, got the question right in a split second and off we went again. The next question, for £32,000, was a poetry question, so I had no chance. But Richard thought he knew it. And then he wasn't sure. And then he was. And then he wasn't again. It took us twenty-six minutes to answer that one.

Eventually I said to Richard 'Come on, let's just go for it. What have we got to lose?' He said, 'Well, £15,500 each for our charities.' I said, 'Look, if we get it wrong, then I'll pay the £15,500 to my charity, Sparks, out of my own pocket.' I expected Keysie to say the same but he just started coughing and spluttering.

He got it right in the end and we ended up with £64,000, which was not a bad effort, especially for someone who failed his highers.

That was to come. Back in the summer of 1989 my striking partner, the second commentator, still had to be signed. Andy asked who I thought they should get in to sit alongside me. He already had somebody in mind, but he wanted to get my opinion too. I gave it some thought. Brian Moore, John Motson and Barry Davies would obviously have topped a lot of people's lists, but I remembered covering a game – it was the Sherpa Van Trophy Final, would you believe – with a guy from ITV named Martin Tyler. I'd enjoyed working with Martin. He loved his football, and had a nice way with words and a great voice. I'd also felt we had the makings of a good understanding. We'd got on great. So I put that to Andy. And it turned out that Martin was his first choice as well.

They went off to see Martin. Martin had worked for Meridian and LWT and had risen high enough in the pecking order at ITV to do the commentary on the World Cup Final in 1982. Initially Martin wasn't convinced about joining us. He was worried that BSB might collapse and leave him out in the cold. But I guess he also knew that because of Brian Moore – who was pretty much unassailable at ITV – he was never going to get the chance to be number one and do all the big domestic and European games. So as with Richard and myself the offer came at just the right time for him, and after some persuasion from his agent he came on board.

Like me Martin was a striker, or at least that's what he tells anybody who'll listen. He played in the old Isthmian League for Wycombe Wanderers and Wimbledon. He even turned out for the famous Corinthian Casuals. The guy is a football fanatic and a workaholic and I'm sure if he had his way he'd cover every game on the planet. His secret ambition is to do all fourteen Champions' League games simultaneously.

To me the Voice, as we call him, is far and away the best in the business. He's got a fantastic style about him and he makes it all sound effortless. Believe me, though, it isn't. The work Martin puts in when he's preparing for games is incredible. Ask him how long it takes to do the research for a match and he'll reply, 'How long have I got?'

Nowadays, admittedly, there's not as much time for preparation as there used to be. We're covering so many games a season with Sky that sometimes just remembering which ground to turn up at is a big achievement. But Martin still keeps at it. He feels he needs to know everything he can about the players – how many children they've got, what their wives are called, what cars they drive, where they buy their newspapers, their whole history. Because if the game's a poor one he needs some way to fill the air time and that's when these facts and bits of trivia come in handy. Martin will tell you that despite all the research he does he actually likes it best if he gets to the end of the ninety minutes and finds he hasn't used any of it. Because that means it's been a really good game.

While Martin concentrates on those sorts of details I focus more on the topical. I know the information from this season: how many games each player's started, how many goals he's scored and that type of thing. But in the main my job is to react to the game. And because of the nature of football you never know what you're going to see next.

The more relaxed, free-flowing commentary style Andy and Brian introduced worked well from the outset. It's flexible and conversational and it allows me to instantly reflect on events or pick up on things the Voice might have missed. To work like that you have to have a really good understanding. Martin and I are very much like a forward partnership in that respect. We know each other's style, our interplay is good and over the years we've grown to be able to anticipate each other's moves.

Martin joined us all at Champion studios in September. And so with five months to go before launch day the three stooges were now in place. Little did we realize that fourteen years later we'd still be there.

11

I don't know if it was some sort of test but one of the first tasks Big Ron Atkinson gave me as his assistant at Aston Villa was to take charge of the pre-season trip to Germany. We had training facilities and series of friendly matches arranged over there, but Ron couldn't come himself because he had one or two transfer deals to complete in England.

Paul McGrath is a lovely, gentle, shy man and as a footballer arguably one of the best we've seen. Certainly Ron reckoned the £35,000 fee he'd paid to take him to Old Trafford was the best-value deal he'd ever done.

At Old Trafford Macca had suffered a series of knee injuries so bad that in 1989 United had actually wanted to declare him a write-off and claim on the insurance. Yet somehow the big Irishman managed to keep going for another decade, which tells you something about the guy. He was a competitor.

Because of his fragile body Macca's training schedule amounted to nothing more than a bit of light jogging or walking around the pitch. Off the field he required special treatment, too. His history of problems with what my old chum Graham Taylor might call 'refuelling' are well documented. Fergie had cleared him out of Old Trafford along with Norman

Whiteside for just that reason, which is how he came to be at Villa in the first place.

When BBC TV signed Paul up for the 2002 World Cup they ended up sending him home the day after he arrived in Korea after a boozing session on the flight over. Which, come to think of it, probably makes him the only guy with a press card ever to be dismissed for drinking too much.

My first encounter with Macca was on this trip to Germany. Of course, I knew about his reputation. I also had Jim Walker, the Villa physio, with me. Jim was the guy the Republic of Ireland team used to take with them on trips basically to baby-sit Macca. He knew Macca's ways and the defender liked and trusted him.

We had been in Germany for less than forty-eight hours when Jimmy Walker came knocking on the door of my room. It was about 11 o'clock at night. Jim told me that Macca had climbed out of his bedroom window and done a bunk.

I didn't feel I could phone Ron up and tell him I'd already succeeded in losing his best player, so I asked Jim, 'Where will he have gone?' Jim replied that in all likelihood he would have headed into the city centre and holed up in the first bar he found.

There are cities in the world where you can count the bars on your fingers even if your name's Captain Hook, but believe me when I tell you that the port of Hamburg is not one of them.

It was a long shot, but I was desperate, so I said to Jim to come with me and we'd go into Hamburg and try to find Paul.

We got in a taxi and asked the driver to take us to a street where there were a lot of bars. The driver dropped us off somewhere along the Reeperbahn and incredibly as I was paying him who should I see reeling down the other side of the road but Macca.

I pointed him out to Jim and asked what we should do. 'Don't make a move towards him,' he said, 'If he sees you coming he'll think he's done wrong and that he's in trouble and he'll run for it. What we'll do is follow him at a distance until he goes into a bar. We'll let him get settled and then we'll walk in all nonchalant as if we're just out for a quiet drink ourselves and act surprised that we've bumped into him.'

And that's exactly what we did. Macca went into a bar. We gave him time to have a couple, and then in we went ourselves, ordered our drinks, looked around and went, 'Good heavens, it's Macca! Fancy meeting you here big fella!'

We bought him a few drinks, had a chat and then I looked at my watch and said, 'Come on guys, it's getting late. We'd better be away to our hotel.' And Paul came back with us good as gold.

That was Macca. He could give you problems but there was no doubt he was worth it.

Ron had called me up to ask me to be his assistant when he took charge at Villa Park in the summer of 1991. I'd been with him as a player at West Brom and I know he felt that I had the background, character and ability to do well as a manager.

By now BSB was up and running. I was presenting a lot of Scottish and Italian football and the magazine shows that went around them. It was a learning process for me. I was starting from scratch but the good thing was that because basically we had no viewers at all you could make plenty of mistakes and get away with it.

I wasn't sure if I'd be allowed to do both jobs but I asked my bosses at BSB what they thought and they were great. They said they didn't see that it would interfere with my work for them – which was mainly Sundays and weekday evenings – and I should go ahead and do it.

So off I went to Villa Park again to join Ron and his other assistant, Jim Barron. I'd known Jimmy since our days at Wolves together. I'd even played under him for a while when he was manager at Cheltenham Town. It was just after I'd signed up for BSB, and because the launch date was several months away I was able to bring my career to a gradual halt training with the lads at Whaddon Road and turning out in the Conference. I enjoyed my time with the Robins, though I have to say you get kicked a fair amount at that level. I got my last goal in competitive football with them and I was really pleased when they made it up into the Football League a few years ago.

On our first day at Villa Ron and I had an informal get-together of the staff, so we could meet everyone. We invited all the youth team and the kids in for a relaxed training session in the morning, and some of the first-team players came in as well to show willing. Before it kicked off Ron and I discussed things. He said to me that we would take our time. We'd have a good look at things for two or three months and then make decisions on where the team needed strengthening.

After about half an hour of five-a-side Ron called me over. He said, 'Remember what I said this morning? Well, forget about it. We're starting today.' It was that bad. I think within a fortnight we'd brought in half a dozen players and shipped out eight. Amongst the new guys were Shaun Teale, Ugo Ehiogu, Paul Mortimer and Kevin Richardson. Not a bad selection, and it had the desired effect. It freshened up the club and gave everybody a lift.

We were also looking for a goalkeeper and a little while

afterwards we got one. The signing of the Australian Mark Bosnich was a typically cute piece of work from Ron and I played my part in it. Bozzy had spent his teenage years with Manchester United, but he was eventually sent back to Oz when he turned seventeen and his student visa expired.

Ron had heard through the grapevine that Mark wanted to give English football another crack. To check whether he had the talent I put in a call to Jim Leighton, my old Scotland teammate who was now a senior pro at Old Trafford. Jim's verdict was simple, 'He's the best young goalkeeper I've ever seen.'

There was one slight problem: Bozzy didn't have enough international caps to satisfy the criteria for getting a work permit. From what we'd heard it seemed that United expected Mark to stay in Australia until he'd played enough times for his country and then come back and rejoin them. Ron snuck in before them, though. He found that Bozzy had a Mancunian girlfriend and persuaded him that it would be a good idea for him to marry her. Visa problems sorted out Mark flew into Heathrow and joined us. United weren't happy and complained to the FA, who fined Villa £35,000. Not a bad price for a goalkeeper of that quality.

Eventually Mark did go to Old Trafford, of course, but things didn't work out. It was plain from the start that the chemistry between him and Alex Ferguson wasn't good. The talk at the time was that Bosnich maybe wasn't Fergie's choice, that it was the club that were buying him, not the manager. I don't know how much truth there is in that, but it certainly seemed strange for Alex to go after someone who, in his eyes, had previously let the club down.

I spoke to Mark a few times on the phone during that

period. He was unhappy about being dropped from the first team by Fergie. I told him not to worry about it and to stay positive. At Villa Bozzy had always worked really hard in training and I told him to keep doing that and to concentrate on the weaker aspects of his game. One of the things that didn't help Mark with Alex was that he had terrible feet when it came to dealing with the ball.

Because of the back-pass rule we're now in an era where a goalkeeper has to be able to control and kick a football like a defender. In his first few games for United Bozzy was embarrassed a couple of times by his inability to do that. And I told him so. I said his kicking was rubbish when he arrived at Villa Park and that in the decade since it hadn't improved at all. I told him he should go back in the afternoon after training and get someone to keep rolling balls to him over and over again until he was absolutely sick of it. Because in the end that is how you get better. Unfortunately, by then I don't think Mark's heart was in the game any more. He'd always had a liking for the bright lights and he'd been plastered all over the newspapers as a result during his time at Villa.

A move to Chelsea was never going to help on that score. London had too many temptations. Once again he ended up on the front page instead of the back page of the papers. It came during a particularly nasty time for football, with various other allegations being made against Premiership players. Football attracts a lot of bad publicity, but it's worth remembering that there are prats in all walks of life. Just take a look around any town centre on a Friday or Saturday night if you don't believe me. The point here is that stardom brings with it responsibility. When I was a player the rules were drummed into you: remember who you are, what you are and who you represent. Most players understood that then and most players understand it now. Unfortunately it appears Mark wasn't one of them.

It's sad to see what's happened to him since. At some point he's going to look around and realize his career has gone. He should have been one of the best goalkeepers in the world. At Villa he was absolutely immense. He was a fantastic athlete and a nice lad who just never sorted out his priorities and that's a real shame.

One of the main parts of the assistant's job is to act as a buffer between the players and the manager. You lend a sympathetic ear to the team's grumbles and try and soften the blow a bit if something the boss does goes against them.

At Villa I found I was also acting as a buffer between the manager and the chairman, Doug Ellis. Right from day one Ron let it be known he didn't much care for Ellis. He felt Doug was a meddler and an interfering busybody who was forever sticking his nose into things he knew nothing about. That was Ron's opinion and he did nothing to hide it. He refused to let Ellis on the team bus and discouraged him from coming to the training ground or into the dressing rooms.

Now Doug Ellis has a bad reputation in football. The attitude to him is probably summed up by former Villa manager Tommy Docherty's old gag, 'They told me Doug Ellis was behind me. I said I'd prefer him in front of me where I can see him.'

Doug is universally known as 'Deadly'. A lot of people think that title refers to his habit of sacking managers. In fact, Jimmy Greaves gave it to him when he was presenting a fishing show on Central TV. Greavesie spotted the way the Villa chairman – a mad keen angler – quickly despatched any fish he landed and said, 'Blimey, it's Deadly Doug.' The nickname stuck and Ron for one felt that Ellis was a wee bit too proud of it.

I always got on all right with Doug Ellis, though. It's true that he sometimes told you unlikely tales and his fishing stories could go on a bit, but all in all I thought he was OK. I'd known him for a long time, too. Right from when I'd first walked through the doors of Villa Park as a nineteen-year-old.

Admittedly the chairman had his little ways. Was he obsessed with money? I'd say so. I remember one time when I was a Villa player introducing him to a girlfriend of mine. He said, in that fruity voice of his, 'And where do you come from, my dear?' She replied, 'Malvern, Mr Ellis,' and Doug responded, 'Ah yes, Malvern. £20,000 an acre I believe.'

Could he be pompous? Definitely. He had a yacht in Majorca and when Villa were out for pre-season training on the island he used to love to invite all the players onto his boat and show it off. One time we were there and Doug's son Simon was with him. At one point the chairman said, 'Simon, be a good boy and throw the anchor overboard.' Simon said, 'But, Dad . . .'

'Don't argue, just do as you're told and throw the anchor overboard.'

'Really Dad, I don't think . . .'

'Simon, I don't want to hear any more, will you please throw the anchor overboard.'

So Simon did. Of course it wasn't attached to anything, so it just sank like a stone.

Doug watched this and after a pause said, 'Simon, go and fetch the anchor.'

The classic Doug story is the one about an incident that occurred during the war. It's a story that's been told and retold so often around the Midlands and embellished so much in the telling that it's become part of folklore. Even if it isn't true, everybody now believes it is, possibly even the Villa chairman himself. From what I can recall of it Doug was playing for a British Army team against some Italian POWs.

'So there I am. Lined up alongside some of the greats – Tommy Lawton, Frank Swift and so forth – on a pitch in the North African desert in front of a crowd of 2,000. Within minutes the crowd of 15,000 were applauding rapturously as I carried the game to the opposition. Soon the 25,000 men in the crowd were chanting my name. And that was when it happened. As the crowd of 30,000 looked on the ball came to me on the edge of the penalty area. As the 40,000 watchers could immediately ascertain it was too low for me to head it and too high for me to attempt a volley. A hush descended over the 50,000 spectators as they asked themselves what the young maestro would do. Instinctively I flung myself into the air and somersaulting gymnastically kicked the ball with thunderous power into the top corner of the net. As the 75,000 fans exploded into spontaneous applause I picked myself up, dusted myself down and said to myself, "My word, Douglas, you have just invented the bicycle kick."'

As I say, despite all that Doug and I got along fine. I liked the man. And one thing is for sure – he loves Aston Villa. A lot of people, including many Villa fans, will find that hard to believe, but it's true. Doug wants what's best for the Villains and he has done everything he can to achieve that short of hawking the club. He has never built up debt. And when you see what's happened at Leeds you'd have to say that that is a good thing.

On small matters Doug certainly can be penny-pinching.

No doubt about it. He'd come into the players' lounge and notice a plate of uneaten sandwiches and say, 'Is nobody having these? Maybe we shouldn't provide them any more if they are just going to go to waste.' But if you examine the record you'll see that under his chairmanship Villa are the seventh biggest spenders on players in the history of the Premiership. They've laid out in the region of £115 million. You can't accuse a guy who pays £7.5 million for Bosco Balaban of being a skinflint.

Brian Little, John Gregory and Graham Taylor have had money, but they haven't always invested it wisely. I've mentioned Balaban and you can add Stan Collymore, Savo Milosevic and Mark Draper and a load of others to that list. So maybe the responsibility lies not with Doug but with the managers.

Now of course, Doug appoints them and maybe he hasn't always done so wisely, Graham Taylor's second spell at the club being proof of that. I think the chairman thought the club needed stability and he wanted to appease the fans after John Gregory had gone. He brought in Graham again and I thought that was a huge error of judgement. You can't ignore Juan Pablo Angel, who even when he was struggling at the start plainly had all the attributes of a quality player, and instead go out and spend £5 million on Peter Crouch and £2 million on Marcus Allback. The fact that David O'Leary came in and without adding much to the squad had them challenging for a Champions' League spot tells its own story.

So Doug has spent the money. But it seems to me that there are people in Birmingham who will not be happy until Ellis has left Aston Villa. Buck Chinn is a name I first heard when I joined the club as a player from Dundee United, and he has been involved in trying to get rid of Doug Ellis practically ever since. Now his son is involved, too. It wouldn't matter if Villa won the title, the FA Cup and the Champions' League. Every time something goes wrong, or there's a problem at Villa Park, up they pop and blame Doug for it. That fragmentation has worked against the club. I can't help wondering where Villa would be now if the energy that's gone into all this in-fighting had actually been channelled into something positive over the last twenty years.

Now there's talk that Ray Ranson, a guy I played against when he was at Birmingham and Man City, is looking to take over at Villa. It's maybe the first real challenge to his ownership that Doug has faced since he became the majority shareholder. But he can easily turn down any offer. He doesn't need the money and Villa is his life. When he leaves Villa Park it will be on his own terms.

Whatever I thought, the fact was that Ron just couldn't stand Ellis. Along with a lot of other people, I tried to persuade the manager to be a bit more diplomatic when dealing with the chairman. Ron's response was that he refused to bow and scrape to anyone. Fair enough. But there's a line between refusing to kow-tow and treating a person with contempt, and at times I felt that Ron jumped across it with both feet.

I think Ron like a lot of others had gone into Villa Park with the view that he wasn't going to let Ellis push him around. To me that's the wrong attitude. If you look for conflict with him then you're going to get nowhere. You've got to win him over. When David O'Leary took over at Villa I spoke to him about this. I said, 'Get him on your side, because if you do that you'll find he's a very different guy.'

That was what I tried to do as Ron's assistant. I tried to

tickle Doug a bit. On match days I'd always go up to his office and give him the team sheet before it went out to the press so that he would be the first to know. It sounds stupid, I know, but the chairman always likes to know the team before anyone else. It makes him feel important.

I felt doing that kind of diplomatic stuff was the wise course of action. Ron had told me early on that if I was serious about football management I'd have to get used to being sacked, but I didn't think that meant going out of my way to make sure it happened. Because the fact of the matter was that if it came down to a battle of egos there was only ever going to be one outcome. I told Ron that many times. I said, 'In this fight we can score a lot of points, but we can't win.' Ron and I worked for Doug, and I always felt that when it came down to it the chairman would simply bide his time and when the right moment came Ron would go. Which is how it worked out. Villa did well under Ron for a couple of seasons but the minute they got into bother – bang! – out came the P45.

Ron's arrival at Villa Park had in itself been controversial. He'd been managing Sheffield Wednesday and doing very well there. They'd just won promotion back to the top flight and beaten Manchester United in the League Cup Final when the Aston Villa job came up. Villa were Ron's club; he'd supported them as a kid, he lived locally in Worcestershire and it was where his heart was. He'd found it a difficult decision to make, but he'd made it. Sheffield Wednesday's fans were understandably unhappy about it and they'd denounced him as a Judas.

So naturally what does the League fixture computer throw up as Villa's first game of the 1991–2 season, my debut in management, but a trip to Hillsborough. I thought, 'Great, my first match on the staff and I'm sitting on the coach next to a guy with a price on his head.' Actually, I didn't sit next to Ron on the coach. I told him if the sniper's bullet missed there was no way it was hitting me and I sat in the back with the rest of the boys. As it turned out, though, the atmosphere was nowhere near as bad as we'd been lead to expect and in many ways the game proved to be a nice introduction for me.

The Sheffield Wednesday keeper was Chris Woods. I'd played with Woodsie at Ibrox and I'd noticed that from free kicks and corners if you dropped the ball on top of him and put him under a bit of pressure he sometimes made mistakes. I told this to the lads in the dressing room. I said I wanted the first few corners to be in-swingers and for one of our forwards to make sure he was right next to Chris when the ball came in. They did that and sure enough Woodsie flapped at one of them and Cyrille Regis knocked the ball into the back of the net. A silly little thing in a way, but it gave me a good feeling and we went on to win the game 3–2.

Ex-players will tell you that it's hugely frustrating watching a game from the dugout and that's true. On the other hand it's a terrific feeling seeing a team you've trained playing well and watching things you've worked on and talked about coming off. I really enjoyed coaching the players at Villa.

There was only one I couldn't get along with and that was Dalian Atkinson. Ron loved Dalian. In his eyes the forward he'd bought from Real Sociedad that summer could do no wrong. Even when he messed up Ron would make a joke of it. The manager laughed about his lack of work rate. Generally Ron was prepared to forgive players just about anything if they had talent. I remember him asking me one day if he should try and sign Matthew Le Tissier from Southampton. I told him no. Ron got down a Rothman's and pointed out Le Tissier's excellent goal-scoring record for the Saints. I said I didn't care how many he'd scored, in my opinion he was still a lazy sod.

The same applied to Dalian. His attitude stank. He had a huge amount of talent, no doubt about that. He had skill, power, speed and scored some fantastic goals. But to me he was never really making the effort. He didn't want to learn. He wouldn't listen. I remember one time he'd been out for a few games with a minor injury. I was trying to gee him up in training. I said, 'Come on, Big Man, the team's playing well at the moment. If you want to get back into it you're going to have to show something, or the gaffer won't pick you.' And he just turned to me and said, 'I don't care if he doesn't pick me. If he doesn't pick me I'll get a transfer and go somewhere else.' And that just summed up Dalian Atkinson to me.

We had a good season, finishing seventh in the League. It might have been better. We could have, maybe should have, won the FA Cup that year. We made it through to the quarter-finals and travelled up to Anfield.

That day Ron and I had had one of our few disagreements about selection. We had debated all week whether to play Tony Daley or a youngster named Steve Froggatt on the wing. Froggattt was left-sided, very quick and very direct. He'd been terrorizing defences coming on as a sub, and I wanted to go with him because I felt that Tony Daley let us down too often in the big games. When we needed him he went missing and I felt he was likely to do that again at Anfield.

Ron wasn't so sure. I could understand his dilemma. Froggatt was an unknown whereas Daley was an England international and he was also a big favourite with the crowd and that is a big influence on the manager. So it was a huge decision. Because if you leave Daley out and you lose people are going to seriously question your judgement. You're going to get hammered. In his career Ron made a lot of bold choices, but on this occasion he played safe and went for Tony Daley.

The way the competition had played out it was obvious that Villa and Liverpool were the two strongest teams left. I spoke to the lads in the dressing room before the match. I told them, 'Whoever wins this game wins the FA Cup. So that's where you are today. Because mark my words that is what is going to happen. If you let this chance pass you by you may regret it for the rest of your lives. If you lose to Liverpool today it will be them collecting the winners' medals at Wembley instead of you.'

We lost 1–0. Tony Daley was poor. We took him off after an hour and brought on Steve Froggatt. He did brilliantly. He tore the defence to shreds, but the chances went begging. And later that season Liverpool beat Sunderland 2–0 in the final.

As I say that was one of the few times Ron and I disagreed. I liked his attitude to the game and the way he set about things. He worked incredibly hard and he took his job seriously.

Ron was a great man manager. I could understand why the players and staff loved him and wanted to do well for him. A lot of managers these days arrive at a club and tell people to 'judge me after three years'. Gerard Houllier, Claudio Ranieri and and Jose Mourinho have all taken that line. That wasn't Ron's approach. He built sides quickly. I admired that about him. It meant he often grabbed cups and was great at getting teams out of the mire. Unfortunately his sides never seemed to mount sustained challenges in the League. I know Villa came second under him the season after I left, and when he was at Manchester United they had that ten straight wins at the start of the season, but coming close is a lot easier than finishing top. We've seen smashing teams like Kevin Keegan's Newcastle and Leeds United under David O'Leary play wonderfully, get lots of totally justifiable praise, yet win nothing.

One of the talents that all the truly great managers – Shankly, Busby, Bob Paisley, Fergie – share is an ability to pick their teams back up again when things have gone badly. If you can't do that you won't win the title, because even a really good team is going to suffer a dip in form during a long season. When things get shaky the boss has to rally the players, restore confidence and get them back on a winning run. It sounds simple, but it's not. Ron had that knack, though for some reason it never translated into titles. But as I say he was a brilliant guy to work with as an assistant and to work for as a player and I certainly learned an immense amount from him.

Not that we haven't had our run-ins since. The Big Man has sometimes been critical of my analysis and we also had one very public falling out live on air. That was in March 1996 when Ron was manager of Coventry City. They were struggling near the bottom of the Premiership and there was a lot of discontented muttering from Sky Blues supporters about the job the manager was doing. One of the supporters doing the muttering was my colleague Richard Keys. Richard, as I say, is a huge Coventry fan.

Richard and I were presenting *Monday Night Football* and Coventry were playing Southampton. Keysie had spoken to Ron before kick-off and asked him what he thought City would get from the game and Ron had replied, 'We'll get what we deserve.' So Richard had stored that up. There wasn't much in the game. Southampton won 1–0 with a scrappy goal from defender Jason Dodds. In my view the only real difference between the two sides was that maybe one or two of the

Saints players wanted it more, so I said that at the end of the game.

All through the match Richard was wearing his Coventry hat. He wasn't the detached presenter. He was a fan on the terraces and he got more and more frustrated with what he was seeing. After the game we got the interview with Ron, and Richard was still fuming. His first question was, 'So, what next for Coventry?' Ron replied sarcastically, 'Tottenham on Saturday.'

That riled Keysie even more. He said, 'Well, you said before the game you'd get what you deserved and you got nothing. Is that what you deserved?' Ron began to answer, but Richard interrupted him, which is something he would hardly ever do, 'Hang on a minute,' he said, 'I'm sitting here with Andy Gray and he says you got what you deserved.'

I thought to myself, 'Thanks a lot for dragging me into it, pal.'

Well, when he heard that Ron went ballistic. He said, 'I don't care what he thinks. He can sit up there playing with his silly machines and talk all he likes. I am manager of this side. If my players need whipping I'll decide when to do it, not him or anybody else'. And then suddenly he remembered something. He said, 'Hang on a minute, fellas. Who was your man of the match?'

When I told him it was the Saints goalie Dave Beasant, Ron said, 'That says it all, then, doesn't it? Thank you and good night.' And he took off the headphones the interviewees wear and hurled them away and they went – wallop! – right off the head of one of our reporters. Being Ron, of course, instead of storming off he rushed over and offered profuse apologies.

I had the feeling that at Villa I was being groomed as Ron's successor. Having been the assistant manager I know that that wouldn't have been an easy step to make. In many ways being assistant manager is the best of both worlds. You work with the players day-to-day and it's easy to build a good relationship with them because you don't make any of the decisions that really hurt them. It's the manager who drops people, or tells them they're no longer part of his plans.

As the boss it's impossible to get too close to the players. You have to maintain a distance from them. The manager doesn't have a social bond with the team. Coming to terms with that is one of the biggest problems many new managers face. They have been players themselves and they've been used to that camaraderie and suddenly they find they can't get involved. They need to distance themselves from it. That can be difficult. I know Howard Kendall at Everton had trouble adjusting to the situation at first, but he learned how to do it.

Assistants are much closer to the players than managers. That's why so many can't make the transition. Colin Harvey at Everton was a brilliant coach and a great guy but when he took charge at Goodison after Howard left he couldn't cope. Brian Kidd was the same when he left Old Trafford for Blackburn. Could I have done it? We'll never know because events off the field were about to reshape my life.

As far as I was concerned I was able to work for BSB and for Villa. It was tough, admittedly. I was doing six days at Villa and then rushing off to London to present Scottish football. There was added pressure as well, because BSB had been taken over by Sky to become BSkyB. It was called a merger, but to be honest that wasn't how it felt. We all knew BSB was in trouble naturally. The squarials hadn't caught on and the fact the company was losing something like £10 million a week was all over the newspapers.

It was an uncertain time for us all. The only fortunate thing from where we stood was that Sky at that time didn't actually make programmes. They bought in programmes like *The Simpsons* from other stations and broadcast them. So they basically had no capability for doing what we were doing. And as it turned out a dozen years down the line from the merger, practically all the people who were involved with BSB's football coverage are still working at Sky.

Despite all those factors I still I felt I was handling it all pretty well. Unfortunately Doug Ellis wasn't so sure. What happened was that all through the season I would get memos from Doug expressing his concern that I was spending so much time doing television work. He'd say, 'I saw you on TV again last night, Andy. That is the fourth time this week.'

What the chairman didn't seem to realize was that BSkyB – who still didn't have the rights to cover Football League games, remember – had hours to fill and not enough programmes to do it, so they would repeat stuff endlessly. I'd do a show on a Sunday and they'd put it out again on Monday, Wednesday and Friday. And that was what Doug was watching, repeats.

Towards the end of the season I got another memo from him saying, 'Clearly my previous memos have fallen on deaf ears. We must get together when the season comes to an end and discuss where your loyalties truly lie – with Aston Villa or with Mr Murdoch.'

Well, as chance would have it, that summer something happened that made the decision for me. All season there had been talk at BSkyB about the rights to cover the new First

Division, or Premiership as it was about to become known. We knew the company would bid for it but we didn't honestly think they stood a chance of getting it. We were sure the terrestrial channels would carve it up between them as they'd done in the past.

But to our surprise and delight we got it. The price had risen a little. Sky paid £304 million, £214 million of that for the Premiership, which is quite a hike from that £11 million of four years before.

What happened was a reverse of the situation that BSB had found themselves in previously and it was the result of a lot of behind-the-scenes dealing that included the careful wooing of chairmen like Chelsea's Ken Bates, who'd been keen to accept the original BSB offer, and Ron Noades of Crystal Palace, whose teams were not at what you might call the top table. There was a need to convince them that we could do the job, because contrary to what a lot of people might think the decision wasn't just about money; it was also about the company the chairmen thought they could trust to deliver. After all, anybody could offer vast sums of cash. The big question was whether they could sustain it and honour the commitments they had made. As the Nationwide League found out to its cost a couple of years back with OnDigital, you can't always turn promises into cash.

Many might have thought that after what had been going on in football in the late 1980s – the disasters, the hooliganism, the dwindling crowds – Sky had taken a huge gamble in investing so much money in the game. But the management had clearly recognized the incredible potential there was for live football in this country. And they also judged, quite rightly, that in the UK if you are a sports channel that doesn't have football, you're effectively shovelling water with a sieve. Football is a massive, massive slice of the sports market in this country. People like cricket and rugby union certainly, but nothing attracts the same interest as football. You only have to look at the amount of space the newspapers devote to it to see that. By and large the game gets twice as much coverage as all the other sports put together. So if you don't have football there's not that much else that will guarantee an audience. Sky knew that and they also knew that the terrestrial cartels had never paid a realistic market price for their coverage. If it was a gamble it wasn't a very big one.

I got a call from Andy Melvin to say that Sky had won the bidding. Naturally he was over the moon. He said we needed to get together and discuss what that was going to mean for me. I met up with Andy and David Hill from Sky and they told me that there was now going to be a huge amount more work. In fact they were talking about a full-time job. They said they felt that I was fundamental to Sky's coverage and that there was no way they could continue compromising with Villa over my services. So Andy, like Doug Ellis, was asking me to make a commitment one way or the other.

I talked to Ron about it. He asked me what I thought. I told him I enjoyed the job, loved being around the club and working with the lads, but that to be honest I felt I had to give television a go. The Premiership was just starting up and it was a fantastic opportunity. Ron agreed with me. He said if he was in my position he'd do exactly the same.

I think if I'd been a manager it would have been different, but I was an assistant. While the Big Man talked about eventually stepping down or moving sideways, so I could take charge, I knew how much he loved his football. I knew that day might still be a fair way off. Given the nature of his relationship with Doug the odds of Ron still being at the club five or six years down the line didn't make it a very attractive gamble. And so that summer I left Villa Park for the third time.

12

When you're an ex-player it's hard to find the same adrenalin rush you got from the game. For twenty years you've had the buzz of running out in front of a crowd, of scoring goals, and suddenly it's taken away from you overnight. Mentally that can be difficult to cope with. I'm lucky because live TV really does give you that buzz. Nothing can match playing in a big game in front of a packed ground, but the job I do now comes close.

The excitement of that first live Premiership game on Sky was unforgettable. It was a beautiful, sunny afternoon by the Trent and Brian Clough's Nottingham Forest were taking on Liverpool. We went on air at around 2 p.m. with a two-hour build-up to the match. Keysie was at the helm in one of his beautifully coloured jackets – which when I come to think of it was probably made out of the same fabric as the GMTV sofa. I did the first section in the studio with him and then walked up to the gantry to join Martin. It was genuinely bloody nerve-tingling. A Cup Final. We'd been doing live football for a couple of years, but not like this. This was where it really mattered. This was what our future was going to be all about. How well we did it, how well we packaged it and presented it would determine whether we survived.

The game was a good one. Forest were neat and slick, good passing and movement, and Liverpool were still one of the best sides around. Teddy Sheringham – or Edward as Cloughie insisted on calling him – got the first ever Premiership goal on the new channel and it finished 1–0. We went off air at 7.30 after five and a half hours and everybody was elated. It had happened, nothing had gone wrong and we felt fantastic.

When Sky gained exclusive rights to live coverage of the Premiership there was widespread pessimism about what that would mean. We were perceived as cowboys funded by Aussie cash. Certain people thought we were all glitz and glitter and no substance and we wouldn't do the game justice.

The truth was altogether different. I can tell you from experience that there isn't anyone involved with Sky Sports who isn't absolutely serious about football. I don't mean that we're po-faced about it, just that we all really care about the game. I believe that from that first match onwards we've taken football coverage in this country to new levels. Before we came along TV football programmes had hardly changed in Britain since ITV introduced the first pundit panel – and that was for the 1970 World Cup.

Along with Andy Melvin, one of the main men responsible for the innovations was David Hill. David was in charge of the whole sports operation at Sky. He was a big, brash, noisy Aussie. His office door was permanently open and through it came wave after wave of effing and blinding, usually delivered at maximum volume. David never bothered with the phone. If he wanted to see you he just yelled. And even if you were halfway home you heard him. David's energy levels were amazing and for the first few years he really tore into things

The guy was an Australian, as I say, and he knew absolutely

nothing about football. If Richard, Andy and I were sitting discussing something and David came sneaking up and sat down besides us we'd say, 'Dave, we're talking about football. You know nothing about it. Eff off.' And he'd say, 'Fair point, fellas,' and off he'd go.

But in a weird way the fact that David didn't know anything about the game was a really big help, because he didn't have any preconceived notions about how to present it. He'd come up with ten new ideas for covering the game every day and usually nine of them were total crap. But the remaining one was interesting, so we'd give it a go.

One of his biggest innovations was the Monday night football. The idea was another one that was picked up from the US. Monday night is the big night for the NFL in America. It's become so important over the decades that now it's almost part of the national identity. Basically the thinking behind it is that people are back at work, it's not a time for going out, or socializing, so you give the public something to sit down to after supper and watch. David wanted to do the same thing in the UK and establish a sort of long weekend of football, which is what we did.

David suggested all sorts to get the thing going. One of them was the Sky Strikers cheerleaders. The girls put on a fantastic display and added a touch of glitter and glamour to the whole occasion. They were greatly appreciated, not least by some of the staff. On the days when the girls were working Richard and I got to the ground at about 10 a.m., which, coincidentally, was just when they started to rehearse. Mind you, the Strikers didn't always get the kind of reaction you might expect. One night at Highbury when they ran out the Arsenal fans started chanting, 'Are you Tottenham in disguise?'

At half-time to keep everyone entertained we had the giant inflatable sumo wrestlers or bands playing. Again it didn't always work out as planned. Sonia, the British Eurovision runner-up, was jeered so badly at Highfield Road that the poor girl came off in tears, and when the Shamen appeared at Highbury around the time they'd had a big hit with Ebeneezer Goode they were booed off before they could finish the first song. Whoever had booked them hadn't realized they were well-known Spurs fans.

For the grand finale we put on a massive firework display just after the whistle. Or at least we did for a while. Then one day at the Dell, Southampton's old ground, a few of the rockets went astray, flew over the grandstand and nearly blew up a local garage. After that they sensibly cut out the pyrotechnics.

Some of the best ideas in those early days were really simple things, though, like the clock in the corner of the screen – which was something David Hill came up with. We introduced that. No one had thought of it before. It's hard to imagine watching a match on any channel nowadays without the clock telling you how many minutes have been played, but incredibly that's the way things had been for the previous fifty or so years. Viewers had to rely on the commentator to tell them how long was left.

David Hill left after three years to go and run the American football coverage at Fox and Vic Wakeling came in. I'd known Vic for a long time. He's a north-easterner and I've always got on really well with him, though unfortunately these days the only time we seem to see one another is when we're negotiating contracts. Vic had started at BSB doing a sports news programme. Because we didn't have the rights to show any footage, this ended up being more or less like televised radio.

So he'd been around more or less since the beginning of things. David's shoes were big one's to fill, but Vic did that. He's a very different character from David, much quieter, but in his own way just as effective, and we kept on with a policy of introducing new ideas.

As I say not everything we tried worked out but a lot of things did. It was a question of attitude. We were a new station, one that was prepared to rip up the rule book on how football was covered. I feel the terrestrial channels had got into a deep rut. Their attitude was very much 'this is the way football has always been covered, so that's the way we'll carry on doing it'. We brought fresh ideas and innovations. We were prepared to try things and if they failed, well, so what?

We also worked hard to exploit the one thing we had that terrestrial TV didn't – time. Sky had hours of programming to fill and we used that for something that had previously rarely been applied to football, tactical analysis.

In the summer of 1991 Andy Melvin came to me with a proposal for a new show. What had happened was that two years previously in the early days of BSB we'd been up in Scotland doing a game. Afterwards we went to the pub, as we usually did, and we were talking about what had gone on in the match. At some point Andy had asked me a question about the systems the two teams had been playing. We were sitting at a big table and I'd have to say there were a fair few bottles on it. So I said, 'Right, the best way is to show you.' I cleared a space and, using the bottles as players, outlined the different formations the sides had used and shifted a few things around to illustrate how you overcome them, their various weak points and so on. I rabbitted on for about ten minutes or so and afterwards thought no more about it. But Andy – the producer

– had obviously taken it all on board and stored it away with half an idea that we could maybe one day use it.

Sure enough it became the Boot Room, which was Andy's idea for the name of the show. We had the little dressing room set, a Subbuteo board and a guest in each week to talk about and explain tactics. It was a simple idea, but it was also a revolutionary one. Because amazingly nobody before that had ever sat on television and explained what a flat back four or a sweeper system actually was, or what it did.

Sometimes coaches talk about football in a language that is much too elevated and it confuses people. Football isn't rocket science. It's a simple game that too often is made difficult to understand. I think if you can explain verbally and at the same time back up your words with images or pictures then you have a strong chance of getting your point across. So on the show I tried to talk about the game in a no-nonsense way and illustrate what I was saying with video clips. The response from viewers was phenomenal.

I was very careful about the guests we got in. Right from the start I made it clear I didn't want Premiership managers coming on the show. My reasoning was that they wouldn't say anything. They'd be too canny for that. If I get the manager of, say, Arsenal into the studio he's not going to sit there and explain how you should set about playing Manchester United, is he? So instead we got people who would: coaches from the First and Second Divisions and people who were retired from the game like the late Bobby Moore, who was excellent, Frank McLintock and Ray Clemence.

Glenn Hoddle, then player-manager of Swindon, was also great when he came on. Glenn reminded us that playing a sweeper isn't just a defensive measure. For the Robins he'd been playing himself in that position, using his vision and range of long passes to switch defence into attack as quickly as possible in the way that Ronald Koeman did for Holland. Glenn was very influenced by his time playing in France. He'd been at Monaco and he'd learned a lot there, playing under a Frenchman who just about nobody in England had heard of at that time – Arsene Wenger.

On the last Boot Room we ever did we had Eric Cantona as the guest. The producer of the Boot Room was a young lad named Jason Ferguson, which clearly helped us to get the Frenchman. We went up to Old Trafford, took all the gear and filmed it up there. Eric was terrific. He was huge fan of Fabio Capello's Milan. He showed us how they played, the pressing game, the way the midfield hunted for the ball in a pack and then scattered when they were in possession. He also told us he believed that Manchester United could never win the Champions' League playing as they did at that time with two out-and-out wingers. 'It is impossible,' he said, 'wide midfielders, yes. But wingers, non.'

Obviously with a Scot and a Frenchman in conversation there were bound to be one or two moments that were lost in the sub-titles. At one point I asked Eric, 'Would eleven Cantonas make a good football team?' And he looked at me as if I was mad and said, 'Eleven Eric Cantonas. It is impossible.' So I thought quickly and rephrased the question. I said 'Do you think a team of eleven players like Eric Cantona, with your ability and attitude, would make a good team?' And Eric smiled slightly and said, 'But of course.'

We had some really good people on the show. And we had some incredibly bad ones, too. One First Division manager, who I won't name to save him from humiliation, stands out in particular. The show started and he came onto the set. I had my board arranged and was looking forward to an hour of informative chat. We sat down and I said to him, 'Let's talk a bit about your ideas and theories of the game. How do you approach a match tactically?' He looked me straight in the eye and said, 'Well, it's very simple. If we play against a team that uses the long ball then we use the long ball and if we play against a team that passes the ball then we pass the ball.' And in my ear I heard the producer go, 'Oh, shit!' I had another fifty-seven minutes talking tactics with a guy who basically had no tactics. When I finished I had to wring the sweat out of my clothing.

I worked really hard on the Boot Room, and not just on that occasion. There were two days of preparation for the show, finding the tapes I wanted, preparing the questions. And it got harder as time went on. Because there's only so much to cover before you start to repeat yourself. But Andy Melvin was convinced that it didn't really matter because he said Sky was building an audience and we were getting new viewers all the time, so that although it wasn't fresh for us it would be fresh for them. It was supposed to run for one year and ended up running for three. I learned a lot from it, not just about television, but also about the game itself.

When I was a player I think it's fair to say that I never analysed the game at all. That isn't unusual. There are guys who spend twenty years at the highest level and never give the tactical or technical sides of football a second thought. I remember Ian Wright once saying to me that he never wanted to be invited onto the Boot Room. I asked him why and he said, 'Because I don't know anything about the game. I just play it.' And that was pretty much my attitude. So ironically in some ways I've learned more about the game since I left it.

The really extraordinary thing about the Boot Room is that even now, ten years later, people still remember it and ask me about it as if it's still running. And there's no doubt in my mind that it changed the way other channels cover football. There's a much more analytical approach to the way television looks at the game these days – on all channels – and I believe the Boot Room is responsible for that.

Technology was another area in which Sky led the way. Now the use of something like the telestrator, the pen you can circle and indicate things with on the screen, has become commonplace, but again we were the ones who first used it.

That was something that kept me on my toes, because with new gadgets at Sky it's a case of learning on the hoof. When we stopped doing the Boot Room Andy Melvin moved me to *Monday Night Football*. He wanted me to analyse the games and he wanted me to operate all the machinery myself. We could easily have dummied it up, but Andy wanted it to look real. Ironically, of course, everybody thought it was fake anyway. But it wasn't.

I had a whole bank of video machinery and computers and didn't get a single lesson in how to use any of it. Andy would phone me on a Friday and say, 'Get in early on Monday. We've got a new machine to try out and you need to have a go on it before we're on air.' I'd say to him. 'What if I mess up with it when we're live?' And Andy would say, 'If you do it'll be good. It'll prove you're actually operating it.'

The technology has got better and slicker as time has gone on. The huge great touch screen we used on *Monday Night*

Football that drew and highlighted everything was a fantastic device. My basic experience with that machine was that I walked in on Monday at 2 o'clock, the producer said, 'That's it. We're using it tonight,' and I had an hour fiddling about with it before I was using it in front of millions of viewers. And in a way that's what's great about working for Sky. I don't get six weeks to rehearse and plan. It's all live and on the edge, and if you make a mistake you just forget about it and move on.

Martin and I are much the same. We've fallen into a sort of conversational style of commentary. We have some stuff that has to be rigid and disciplined but basically we are chatting to one another about what we're seeing.

When we're doing a match commentary on a Saturday I'm not involved in the studio so I usually hang around inside the players' entrance with Martin Tyler and the crew. It gives us a chance to chat to the managers and the teams as they arrive and check on any news about injuries and fitness tests. I enjoy a bit of banter with the players and Martin gets to pass on the information that if so and so scores today he'll be the twenty-seventh red-headed player to get a goal on a live game when there's an R in the month.

About half an hour before kick-off we go up to the gantry. People talk about a commentary box, but there's nothing enclosed about it. Unlike Richard, Martin and I don't get to spend all our time in a cosy studio, we're exposed to the elements. We have all our equipment close at hand, touch screens and the like, and Martin has his stopwatch to keep track of the timing of incidents. There's plenty of room up there even with the two cameras but we tend to sit shoulder to shoulder, partly so they can get us both in when we do our pieces to camera, but also because it makes it easier for us to communicate during the game if the crowd gets noisy. After we've done our pre-match chat to camera we get ourselves ready. We always have a bet on the result. You win a £1 if you get the result right and £2 if you get the correct score. Then just before we go live we shake hands, a little ritual we've got into, and away we go.

We know where all the cameras are around the ground, so we can call up angles for the replays. Replays are a thing that to my mind you have to use right. There's no point in just bombarding the viewer with endless shots from every available angle. You're looking to paint a picture for the viewer that shows them how things have happened and to do that you have to select carefully. I believe that every replay should tell us something we didn't already know and it must illustrate the point Martin and I are trying to make.

Andy Melvin had a motto, 'Tell me something I don't know.' And that is what we set out to do. One of the things that I was concerned with from very early on was the camera angles. If I was going to give analysis I needed pictures that I could work with. For example, traditionally the camera on the eighteen-yard line was used to go in tight on the player with the ball and show close-ups. That's good for detail, but because it doesn't show the width of the pitch it's useless if you want to illustrate the way that another attacker has dragged a defender out of position to create the opening. So one of the things we did early on was have our eighteen-yard cameramen go wide on the action. We got other cameras on the gantry to shoot wider too and using them together we got a series of images that literally showed the bigger picture. So the viewer didn't just see the goal, but how that goal was created and what the defence could or should have done to stop it.

On air Martin and I chat away in much the same way we do off it, only with a bit less swearing. In fact, one of my recurring nightmares used to be that at some game I'd get so carried away I'd forget where I was and really let fly. I used to worry about it all the time. I'm not the only one. My mate Alan Brazil, who worked at Sky and is now with Talksport, was so worried that he'd do something similar he actually stopped swearing altogether.

I never went that far. Like most men my language can be choice at times and people who know me can't believe I've gone twelve years without swearing on TV. The nearest I came to it was when Richard and I were doing *Monday Night Football*. We used to get in early and discuss what was going to go into the show. One time Keysie was talking about one of the sides we were featuring and he said, 'They're a real fiddly-fanny outfit.' It stuck in my mind for some reason. So that night we're live on air and we're sitting talking about this team and I say, 'There's a school of thought, Richard, that they are a fiddle . . .' and as the words are coming out of my mouth I realize with horror where they are leading me. I look across at Keysie and he's just sitting there smirking at me as if to say, 'Come on, then.' And I say, 'a fiddle, a fiddle, a fiddle-farty outfit.' Which, thanks to my accent, just about got me out of it.

The heavyweight boxer Gary Mason wasn't so lucky. He was doing a boxing show on Sky with Paul Dempsey. Earlier in the day Gary had loaned his tie to someone and then forgotten all about it. The titles and the music for the show rolled, the cameras went live. Paul welcomed viewers and then turned to Gary and said, 'So, Gary, Lennox Lewis you've boxed him . . .' At which point Gary Mason caught sight of himself on the monitor and blurted out, 'Where the f***s my tie gone?' Paul said, 'Never mind your tie, Gary, what about Lennox Lewis?' At which point Gary did the worst thing you possibly can in that situation; he said, 'What, we're not on air, are we? Oh no! Oh Christ. I'm really sorry.'

One of the best stories about on-air swearing involved the former Manchester City boss Malcolm Allison. Big Mal was living up on Teesside and working as a summarizer on local radio. In one important game something had happened that had made him lose his temper and he'd let fly with a real mouthful. He might have been sacked but because he was popular with fans the producers hit on another idea. They gave Mal a device with a button on it. He had to press the button to make his microphone go live. They hoped that would cut out any swearing. Unfortunately when Mal wanted to chip in with something his mouth tended to start working before his button finger. As a result as far as listeners were concerned most of his sentences started in the middle. Eventually Big Mal came up with a simple solution to this problem – he sat on the button. The result was a tirade they still talk about to this day in the North-East. Believe me it can happen to anyone but, touch wood, it's never yet happened to me.

There's always the problem with gaffes, of course. All commentators make them and I've contributed a few in my time. 'Leeds have only had one shot on target, which may well have been the goal,' was one outstanding moment. Another was my comment, 'That's bread and butter straight down the goalie's throat.' But I think my best effort was probably informing viewers that, 'The most vulnerable area for goalies is between their legs.' Even Martin Tyler has had these moments. I remember during a game at Anfield the Voice saying, 'And tonight we have the added ingredient of Kenny Dalglish not being here.'

And then there was the classic a few years back when Lee Bowyer played for West Ham at the Valley and Jeff Stelling said the former Charlton man had 'returned to his old stamping ground'.

Jeff's another big part of the Sky team. He was brought in to do the Saturday show, which was another excellent appointment. Jeff's very calm. He handles the panel and the results brilliantly. Contrary to rumour he isn't fed all the statistics he trots out by a team of researchers talking to him through the ear-piece. He actually sits down and learns them. He's got one lad, a Colchester fan, who helps him out digging stuff up, but apart from that it's all his own work. Jeff prides himself on the fact that at any point in the season he can name the top scorers at all ninety-two League clubs. Just like that.

Another guy who does a fantastic amount is our man on the touchline, Geoff Shreeves. Geoff's a great guy and a hell of a character. During the London property boom in the 1980s Shreevsie had a massively successful estate agency. He got out of that and moved into the media. He was with us at BSB pretty much from the start. He began at the bottom, worked really hard, built up the best contacts book in the business and became a terrific reporter. Geoff was the guy who literally got the ball rolling on live Premiership football, because it was him who gave the thumbs-up to the referee to blow his whistle for kick-off on that memorable Sunday afternoon at the City Ground.

I cover about a hundred matches a year, sixty-six in the Premiership. Apart from the games I'm actually covering I tend to shy away from live matches. I think there's a danger of getting the equivalent of word blindness if you don't. So I keep up to speed via the newspapers and Sky Sports News. If the game Martin and I are doing is a brilliant contest then it's an easy job. If it isn't, if nothing much happens, then that's when the pair of us feel we really have to earn our money. In the end it's the great games that make the poor games palatable.

I've been lucky enough to be commentator on a lot of great games. If I had to pick a top five I think Deportivo La Coruna's game against Milan on 7 April 2004 would have to be in there. I was out in Spain for that one. To many the result was a foregone conclusion. Milan were Champions' League holders, top of Serie A, defending what seemed an unassailable lead from the first leg. Yet despite the fact that the Italians are a tight unit I always felt that there was still a chance for the Spaniards. Because you knew with them that they could get goals. The crowd thought so, too. The atmosphere in the Riazor Stadium was unbelievable. And the moment Pandiani popped in their first you could sense that it was going to be special. By half-time with Depor 3–0 up the place was jumping. Milan had a terrible night, admittedly, but you can't take anything away from La Coruna. They played some fantastic stuff; it was the biggest comeback in Champions' League history and it came against a really good side.

Next I'd have to select the last-ever FA Cup semi-final replay, Manchester United versus Arsenal at Villa Park on 14 April 1999. People will remember that for Ryan Giggs' extraordinary solo run for the winning goal, but that was just the grand finale of a really fabulous game. Roy Keane was sent off. United are down to ten men. Arsenal get a penalty and with the last kick of normal time Dennis Bergkamp has the chance to end Fergie's charge for the treble. Peter Schmeichel saves the kick. We go into extra time and the ten men win it with a goal of absolutely outstanding quality. Packed with skill, passion and drama, it was just the sort of match you'd want to remember the FA Cup by.

Although I'm a Scot I'd also have to pick England's 5–1 win in Munich, 1 September 2001. To travel to Germany and come away with a scoreline like that was barely believable. I think a lot of people thought England could get a result. It wasn't the strongest German side. But to turn them over in their own backyard like that was incredible. The other thing to remember is that before they scored England could easily have been 3–0 down. The Germans got their goal and missed a couple of good chances. So for England to rally from that was exceptional. They created about six chances, scored five of them and by the end they were playing keep ball. Certainly none of the English people I work with could remember seeing anything like it. And they may never again.

To balance that for my final selection I'd have to go for the last-ever game between England and Scotland at Wembley in the play-off for the 2000 European Championships on 17 November 1999. The Scots' performance that night made me really proud. We'd lost the first leg 2–0 at Hampden and everybody was talking about it as a walkover. But the boys came out and put on a superb display. Don Hutchison got a great goal and but for an unbelievable save by David Seaman from Christian Dailly's header we would have taken it into extra time and in all likelihood won it. So although we went out, we went out with all guns blazing.

Finally there is what I think everyone who works on Sky would agree is the best live game we've ever shown – Liverpool v Kevin Keegan's Newcastle at Anfield on 3 April 1996. The only bad thing about the game was the referee blowing the final whistle. It had everything – a goal in the first minute, a winner in stoppage time and five other goals in between and a stack of other chances, too. In my piece to camera at the end I just said, 'Well, it has been a privilege to be here and see that.' I couldn't think of any better way to sum it up and I still can't.

Not all games are like that one. Of course they're not. And people sometimes have a pop at me because they claim that I'm never critical if it's a poor match. They say that I'm always selling the product and that I make a throw-in sound exciting. I resent that. I feel that I genuinely do say if it's a bad game, because fans have more intelligence than they're given credit for and they can see for themselves if something is poor. But what I don't do is just sit there slagging it off and giving abuse to everyone. I try to offer a reason why it's poor. If the ball is fired across the edge of the six-yard area and a striker fails to bury it people will say, 'That's an easy chance,' or 'He's missed a sitter.' But I've been in that situation and I know that there are all sorts of factors determining whether a player finishes well or doesn't. I see my job as explaining that.

Let's face it, it's easy to be negative. Anyone can do it. I try to be constructive. My view is that no matter how hopeless and dull a game is it always offers the potential to excite you with a great bit of skill, a lovely pass, a good save. And I'm sitting waiting for that to happen.

I'd always rather accentuate the positive. When a goal is scored I always try and focus on what the attackers have done right rather than picking over the bones of the defending. Because the fact is that you could stop every goal that has ever been scored, if the defence was perfect.

A few seasons ago I got into a row with the BBC's Alan Green about this. I was in the car driving home listening to Five Live. It was the semi-final of the FA Cup, Aston Villa versus

Bolton, and Alan Green was saying things like 'Oh, please blow your whistle, referee. Not another thirty minutes of this. I'm going to miss my plane.' I couldn't believe it. I don't want to listen to that and I'm sure most football fans don't.

To me part of the problem is that someone like Alan Green has never played the game at a high level. I'm not saying that means he's not entitled to his opinion. I never would say that. But what I will say is that because he's never been there he doesn't know what it's like, how hard it is and the conditions that bring that about. These were two teams who haven't exactly had a lot of success over the past couple of decades and to me it was obvious that both sets of players would be desperate to win. So they plainly weren't going to throw everything into attack and risk losing 5–3. It's just not going to happen and it's pointless complaining about that. In football teams make life difficult for one another. Defending, smothering the opposition, that's part of the game. If it wasn't every match would end in a basketball score.

So I made my feelings plain about that sort of scathing, negative, opinionated style of commentary. And Alan Green had a little pop back at me. That's his entitlement. Though frankly his opinion on anything has never interested me in the slightest.

At Sky we are encouraged to be positive about the game, but I can honestly say that no one in management has ever come up to me and told me I have to sell a match no matter how bad it is. My enthusiasm is genuine. I love football. It has every emotion that you experience in life – excitement, joy, despair, anger and frustration, it has the lot. Whether you're a manager, player, coach or fan you experience all these feelings and more during a season, sometimes even during a match. To me being involved with something that produces all those feelings is fantastic. And my commentary style reflects it.

I don't think there's anything wrong with that. I've never heard Richie Benaud at Lord's saying, 'Oh, jeez is there still an hour till the tea interval? I'm bored to death. Can't we watch a film instead?' I've never heard Peter Alliss rubbish golf, or Murray Walker telling viewers that a Grand Prix is really dull because Michael Schumacher's in the lead again. They love their sports and they sell them. That's nothing to apologize for.

When the Premiership started up we were doing games on Sunday and Monday. On Sundays we did this massive six-hour show – two hours at the front, two hours at the back, with two hours of football sandwiched in between. It was ridiculous, really. But it was trial and error.

Nowadays on a typical *Super Sunday* I get to the ground at about 10.30. I go up to the studio we have set up there and watch Keysie rehearse. I like to see what's going into the show pre-game in case I can pick up anything from that for the commentary. I then sit down and watch Saturday's games to pick out the bits I want to talk about in the first half hour of the show and select which games we're going to show highlights from. When we've done that at about 11.45 I sit and watch the Premiership goals from Saturday. Richard, the producer, and I then go through all the Sunday papers to see if there's anything there that has to be discussed. We have a guest on the show, so quite often we'll try and shape what we're going to talk about to fit in with them. If, say, it's Sam Allardyce, then we might look at some incidents from Bolton's game the previous day.

The guest situation has got a lot better in recent years because managers and players have got much more used to the cameras. A decade ago when a TV crew turned up and stuck a microphone in their face a lot of players and coaches became paralysed. They were like rabbits trapped in the headlights. Quite often you couldn't squeeze a word out of them. These days television cameras are so much an everyday feature in the game that the vast majority of football people are very relaxed and comfortable in front of them, which makes things a lot easier for everybody.

We break for lunch for an hour and after that Sky usually broadcast a Premiership Plus pay-per-view game so I like to go up to the studio and watch that as it comes through. We go on air at three o'clock. I do the first twenty minutes or so and then at the first break I go up and join Martin on the gantry.

After the game I go back down to the studio and watch the discussion down there until we wrap up the show at 6.30. I'm on air for a fairly large chunk of the three and a half hours. That's quite a long time because you have to be 'up' all the time. You can't afford to flag or drift, because that transmits itself to the viewers. Sometimes if it's a poor game with nothing to excite you, maintaining that can be quite hard. But all in all it's great. In fact the only real moan I have is about getting to and from the stadium because the roads in this country on a Sunday are a total joke.

At most grounds the people know who we are, they know the game is live and they let us get on with it. The only exception to that has been at Anfield. I don't recall any problems there when we first started, but in April 2001 I turned up as usual at eleven o'clock in the morning only for a guy at the main gate to stop me from coming in because I didn't have a pass. I phoned one of the boys and got him to bring a pass down for me and up I went to the studio. Then a while later as Richard and I were beginning rehearsals in came another Liverpool official to check that we all had the right documentation. He held everything up while he checked the crew, which understandably did not go down too well. There'd been a bomb outside the BBC a few weeks before, so we understood the need for security, but this was a little, shall we say, over the top. To cap it all, a few minutes after that we got a call from our studio guest Kenny Dalglish saying that security wouldn't let him into the stand because he didn't have the correct pass. Kenny Dalglish! We were a bit annoyed. So the next time we covered a game at Liverpool I got the lads to give me their passes. I had about a dozen of them and I stuck them all over myself, on my head, my face, my arms, and I walked around the whole afternoon like that. I think I made my point. We had a bit of a joke with the stewards about it and the situation calmed down after that. But we don't go to Liverpool without our passes any more.

Originally on Mondays I'd done the match commentary with Ian Darke, but after a few years Andy Melvin came up with the idea of incorporating elements from the Boot Room into the show and taking me off the commentary and putting me into the studio with Richard instead. As I say, what Andy wanted me to do was select and run all my own tapes. So I'd spend the first hour of the show analysing football, sticking in my videos and pressing fast forward when I meant to press rewind, and so on. Then I'd spend the rest of the evening with Keysie. That was how the Monday night show evolved. And that was how I came to witness one of the most famous incidents in Sky Sports history.

I was in the studio that night with Richard. We didn't usually have guests on Monday night because of all the analysis, but this night we had Barry Venison on with us. It had been a good season for us, probably the best we'd had since Blackburn, and Manchester United were going for the title on the last day. That had drama to the final whistle. This one had great football, including that unbelievable Liverpool Newcastle game.

The game that Monday also featured Newcastle; they were away to Nottingham Forest and Forest won it. Newcastle had fallen away dramatically after the Liverpool game and this loss meant they could no longer win the title unless United slipped up in the final game at Middlesbrough, which seemed highly unlikely.

After the game Kevin Keegan came on through the link from down by the dressing rooms and you could tell right away that he was emotional. There'd been a bit of nip and tuck in the press involving Alex Ferguson and Kevin had taken exception to one or two things the United boss had said.

Fergie had criticized Leeds United because they'd gone to Old Trafford and to his eyes put in an exceptional display, working their socks off. He'd suggested that teams were deliberately trying harder against his side than they were against Newcastle because they didn't want Man United to win the title. He went on to say that he would be interested to watch Forest's game against Newcastle because Keegan's team had agreed to play in Stuart Pearce's testimonial and maybe they might be keen to repay that favour. Rubbish, clearly, but it was Alex's way of sharpening things up a bit.

When Richard and I did Monday nights it was me who asked the football questions while Richard acted as the journalist. If a story came up during the interview I would back off and let Richard go for it. So we asked Kevin about the game, talked a bit about the disappointment of the defeat, and so on. Then Kevin mentioned the things Alex had said about the testimonial. At this point I think Keysie realized that he was on to something because he said in a sort of off-hand way, 'Well, you've got to expect that, haven't you? It's all part and parcel of the game, after all.'

And that just made Kevin flip. He said 'No,' and then he really went off on one. I was open mouthed. My initial reaction was to jump in, cut him off and tell him not to worry about it. I wanted to stop him talking because I really thought he was going to start to cry. But I couldn't because I knew this was a big story. Richard, of course, knew that too, so he kept it going. It was great television and it became one of the most famous interviews in football history. As Keysie said later, when Kevin dies they'll probably carve the words 'I would love it, really love it' on his gravestone.

Coaching was an option I'd strongly considered when my playing career was coming to an end. After I left Rangers I'd had preliminary talks with the chairman of Hibernian about taking charge at Easter Road and I'd also had that spell as Big Ron's assistant at Villa. The closest I ever came to becoming a football manager, though, was in the summer of 1997, when for a brief while it seemed likely I would succeed Joe Royle at Goodison Park. That period generated a fair amount of controversy amongst fans and a lot of speculation and guesswork in the press. From my perspective this is what really happened.

After Joe departed in April Everton were without a manager for several months. The big centre back Dave Watson was put in temporary charge until the end of the season, but when it came to the permanent role all sorts of names were being bandied about, including Bobby Robson and even the former Spurs and Germany striker Jurgen Klinsmann. I'd been covering games for Sky around the country and every time the vacancy at Goodison Park came up people would say, 'Well, what about you? Aren't you going to go for it?' And I guess that was what put the idea in my head.

Eventually I got into conversation with a journalist from a

terrestrial broadcaster who knew people at Everton. He suggested that maybe they'd be interested in talking to me. There didn't seem any harm in that. I told him I would be happy to hear from them. So this guy put the wheels in motion and a little while later I got a call from the Everton chairman Peter Johnson. This was in early June. Peter invited me up to Merseyside to meet him and some of the other directors and have an informal chat about the position.

As I travelled up the motorway my head was whirring. At that moment I was absolutely clear in my mind – if I was offered the job, then I'd leave Sky and take it.

I went to the Wirral to Peter Johnson's Park Foods factory and met Peter and two other members of the Everton board. We sat around a table for two or three hours discussing the club, the plight it was in and what, hypothetically – a word that was stressed to me over and over – I would do if I took charge: who I would buy, who I would bring in staff-wise and how much that would all cost.

Now, after two and a half hours of outlining my plans, I fully expected that if Everton were serious about wanting me to take the job they'd make some commitment there and then, because I was flying out to Spain the next day for a week and they were aware of the fact.

But Peter Johnson didn't come up with anything. He never mentioned a contract, terms or wages. Nothing. He just said, 'Thanks very much for coming, Andy, and I know you'll appreciate that none of this conversation is to go outside these four walls.' I said I understood that and off I went.

I drove home thinking that maybe they'd call me that evening. After all, Everton had been without a manager for three months. If there were other candidates for the post they'd surely have talked to them all by this stage. Time was running out. It was the close season and whoever was going to take over was going to need to do deals to sign players and staff and sort things out. A quick decision was needed.

But I heard nothing at all and the next day I flew off to Spain for an ex-players golf week that takes place each year in La Manga. Dozens of former pros come to it, people like Frank McLintock, Glenn Hoddle, Liam Brady, Phil Parkes and Pat Jennings, and we have a great time. Naturally there was a lot of talk that week about the Everton job, because it was no secret that I'd been linked with it. And the question I kept getting asked by these boys was 'Why?' Why would I leave the job I was doing at Sky – well paid, secure, limited pressure – and take over at Goodison? There was a low opinion amongst the guys of the club, its situation and, I have to say, of Peter Johnson, who'd been chairman of Tranmere Rovers and a Liverpool shareholder before outbidding Bill Kenwright to take over Everton when the Moores family sold its interest in the club in 1993.

And there was someone else I hadn't given any thought to when my head was spinning at the thought of taking over at Goodison – my youngest daughter Sophie. Since her mother Jacqui and I split up I've had her over on alternate weekends, which means I pick her up on Friday after school and spend Saturday and Sunday with her. My relationship with my other kids had drifted over the years and I was determined that wouldn't happen with Sophie. But if I was manager of Everton I wouldn't be able to see her. Managing a football club is a twenty-four-hour-a-day job and it wouldn't leave time for much else. So that also became a factor.

The other big thing was that I hadn't yet spoken to my

employers, Sky. When I'd first got out to Spain I'd had a call from my boss Sam Chisholm. He said, 'I know what's going on Andy. I need to talk to you when you get back.' I was coming back on Saturday morning, so a meeting was arranged with Sam for that afternoon at his apartment in St John's Wood.

On the Thursday I got a call from Peter Johnson. He told me that they had had a board meeting at Goodison about my appointment and that it had gone very favourably for me. There was just one dissenting voice and that was Bill Kenwright, who wanted Howard Kendall to come back for his third spell at the club. And that was as far as that conversation went. Again, there was no firm job offer.

When I'd first gone up to Merseyside my heart had been ruling my head. Now, after speaking to the boys out in Spain and Sam Chisholm, and thinking about what it would mean to my relationship with Sophie, my head had started to take control. And I began to wonder if taking on Everton was really such a great idea.

Another thing that contributed to my change of mood was that while I was out in Spain stories had started to appear in the newspapers in England. Every day it seemed there was something new about me and my plans for Everton. They weren't just wild speculation, either. They were very specific. There were quotes, details of my vision for the club. They even mentioned the names of staff I was proposing to bring in – some of whom, incidentally, were still working for other clubs. It was embarrassing.

A lot of what was printed was rubbish, but there was enough that was true to make me suspicious. These were things we'd discussed that afternoon in Peter Johnson's factory. Things I'd been told were confidential. Only four people had been there.

Three of them were Everton employees and the other one was me. And I hadn't spoken about what went on at that meeting with anybody. So the stories had to have come from someone at the club.

My feeling is that it was a deliberate and concerted effort. Everton had been getting stick from the press and from supporters about the fact that they hadn't yet filled the vacancy and this was their way of showing that they were doing something about it. They were drip-feeding Everton fans hope on a daily basis confident that when I came back I would say yes.

Somebody was presenting the whole thing as signed and sealed, yet we hadn't even discussed terms. For all anybody knew Everton might offer me a contract that was worth nothing and I'd say, 'No, thanks,' and walk away. They might not have been able to provide the transfer fund I required. In which case, again, I wouldn't have taken the job.

Everything was working to change my mind about taking over at Everton, but the single biggest factor was undoubtedly my meeting with Sam Chisholm. I walked into his apartment that afternoon feeling that I was in control of things and knew what I was doing and within five minutes Sam had turned me into a gibbering idiot.

He made it clear straightaway that there was no way Sky were going to let me go. They'd fight tooth and nail to keep me. I had four years left on my contract and they would force me to honour that through the courts if necessary. They'd sue Everton and spin the whole thing out for as long as it took.

Sam then produced another contract. He said this was a new offer he was prepared to make me to stay on at Sky. I took a look at it. It was very generous. I told Sam I'd like to take some time to think about it. Sam said, 'You haven't got any.'

I said 'What?' He said, 'You haven't got any time to think about it. This is a one-off. Sign it now, or I'll tear it up and you can forget about it.' Now, that's hard bargaining.

Since then a lot has been said about the value of the contract Sky used to keep me. As I say, it was very generous, no doubt about that. But as I've emphasized before, money has never been my prime motivation in life. And if I'd been certain that I wanted to take the job at Goodison there would have been no sum of cash Sam Chisholm or anyone else could have waved at me that would have changed my mind. As it was by this stage I had plenty of doubts. So after a couple of hours of discussion I signed the contract with Sam and right away telephoned Everton and told them that I no longer wished to be considered for the post of manager.

I received a massive amount of flack from the club for that decision. Peter Johnson claimed that I'd turned my back on them and totally let the supporters down. He said that I'd promised them this and I'd promised them that. All of it was absolute nonsense. Regardless of all the ins and outs of the affair the plain truth is that I didn't reject the Everton job. How could I when I was never formerly offered it?

Though the chairman had never discussed my salary or the terms of my employment with me, or even told me the position of manager was mine if I wanted it, he still made out that I'd betrayed him and the fans. The latter really hurt and angered me, because I'd had a great relationship with the supporters at Goodison as a player and now Peter Johnson was trying to destroy that just to cover his own backside.

In actual fact I don't think he could have met my financial demands and I think he knew it. I don't mean for me personally – although I'd guess my salary and the compensation they'd have had to pay Sky might also have been a problem – I mean the money I would have wanted to return Everton to being a great club again. That was my intention. I wanted Everton to be the best. I wasn't interested in keeping them ticking along in mid-table and making a small profit.

When I met Johnson that day on the Wirral he asked me how much I thought I'd need to spend on players. I told him that in the first year we might be looking at an outlay of £20 million on three or four signings. He nearly choked on his tea. I'm not sure Everton spent that sort of money in all the years Johnson was chairman, never mind in a single season.

In the end Howard Kendall resigned from Sheffield United and returned to Goodison Park for a second time as manager. I know why he did it. The temptation to go back to a club where you've had good times is hard to resist. That was part of the reason I'd been tempted. But as with my return to Villa Park it proved a mistake. Howard had won two championships, the FA Cup and the Cup Winners' Cup, during his first spell in charge of Everton. This time he won nothing and never looked likely to. In many ways it soured what he'd achieved before. That was a real pity because Howard's achievements with Everton in the 1980s should never be underestimated.

I should say here that though there was a lot of speculation at the time, I hadn't asked Peter Johnson for Howard as my assistant. That may have been Everton's idea of a dream ticket but I had never suggested it. Nor was it something Everton had proposed and I'd objected to. Although I hadn't liked the decision to sell me, I hadn't fallen out with anyone over it either. I didn't agree with his decision but I understood why he'd made it. I was realistic. It was business. Despite all the rumours Howard was not a factor in my decision.

Do I regret the fact that I didn't take over at Goodison? No, I don't. I still believe I made the correct decision. Everton was the right club, but it was the wrong time. And I think if you look at what happened at the club subsequently under Peter Johnson's stewardship you'll agree with me. I certainly think the Everton fans have come to see it that way, because despite a sticky patch directly after this business was over my relationship with them today is as good as it ever was.

Of course I'd love to have tested myself in management. It was something I always thought I would do one day. I'd learned an immense amount under Big Ron and I'd been piling up tactical knowledge through my work on the Boot Room. It would have been great to have had the chance to test that in action.

Being a manager these days is more complicated than it was even that short while ago. You need a lot of certificates and diplomas – as if having played the game for twenty years counts for nothing. Qualifying for management is a huge test. But I sometimes wonder what the diplomas prove. Howard Wilkinson and Steve Cotterill – the two most highly qualified coaches in England – worked together at Sunderland and the team got relegated. Meanwhile Sir Alex Ferguson, who hasn't passed any FA exams, is the most successful manager in the history of the Premiership.

There's no doubt either that the manager's job has changed immensely over the last decade. The proof of that is that with the exception of Bobby Robson and Alex Ferguson no pre-Premiership managers have survived at the top level. Increased player wages, the influence of agents and the Bosman ruling that allows players to leave for free when their contract ends mean that the balance of power between footballer and club has shifted. It's hard to imagine that many of today's stars would put up with the kind of treatment Brian Clough meted out to his team. The first punch in the stomach or clip around the ear and they'd be straight on the mobile to their representative.

It used to be possible to motivate and control players with money. When I was playing win bonuses and club fines really mattered. That's no longer the case any more. I heard recently of a player who wanted to take a midweek trip to Paris against the club's wishes. 'If I go what will happen?' he asked his manager. 'You'll be fined ten grand,' the manager replied. So the player took out his cheque book, wrote a cheque for £10,000, handed it to his boss and waved goodbye.

With great players motivation comes from within. Winning is what counts to them, not money. You can see that because even though the big stars are set up for life they carry on playing. If it was about money somebody like Zinedine Zidane could have packed in years ago. So could David Beckham.

It may no longer frighten players, but in the game at large money has a bigger influence than it ever did. And I see the gap between the mighty and the rest widening with every passing year. It's hard to see a provincial side like Nottingham Forest coming through to take the title. Even teams like Everton are miles away financially. That's disappointing. Because we've seen the Premiership dominated by two teams. Clubs have invested heavily in their youth systems over the past decade, so there is a possibility that somebody might pull up a crop of youngsters like Alex Ferguson did at United. The problem then, though, is holding on to them. In the modern game that's not easy.

On the other hand there's maybe a few signs that the game

has reached its financial peak. Clubs are cutting their cloth to suit. Transfer fees have certainly come down. What happened at Leeds has frightened everybody. They've lumbered themselves with players on vast salaries that can't be got rid of. If they don't want to play and they don't want to move they can just sit in the stands and pick up thirty grand a week.

For managers nowadays there's no need to go out and blow £9 million or £10 million on a player. There are so many good players available on Bosman deals these days that the whole nature of the transfer market has changed. They have to keep tabs on who is going out of contract and spend time working on putting wage deals together to bring these guys in, not on haggling over transfer fees. Sam Allardyce has shown that. Ten years ago who'd have thought of people like Jay Jay Okocha and Youri Djorkaeff playing for somebody like Bolton, or Gaizka Mendieta turning out for Middlesbrough or Christophe Dugarry at St Andrews? These are world-class players who cost nothing.

Since the talks with Everton my name has been linked with various clubs. It's inevitable, I suppose, that when a vacancy comes up at Villa Park or Molineux the newspapers will speculate that I am in the frame for the job. The truth is that no other offers have come my way. I would love to have given it a shot but, though it would be wrong to rule anything out, as the years go by that seems less and less likely to happen.

Football is a game of strong emotions the fans are caught up in it and commentating on the number of games I do I am more or less bound to offend somebody. The funny thing is that most times when fans have actually approached me to have a go over something I've said it's turned out to be something I didn't say at all. I can't count the times people have come up and said, 'I totally disagreed with what you said about so and so,' and it's turned out to be a game they watched on ITV or BBC.

Three years ago a Birmingham City fan strode up to me and said, 'You're typical Villa, you. You hate the Blues. You never have a good word to say about City, you don't.'

I said, 'Hang on a minute. What division do Birmingham City play in?' He said, 'The First.'

I said, 'I work for Sky. Do Sky cover Division One matches?' He looked at me for a few seconds and then said, 'They don't, do they? Hey, I'm really sorry, Andy. I must be thinking of someone else,' and off he went.

My view is that I am neutral and it's actually the fans who are biased. Of course they are, they love their club. Over the years I've been accused of hating Chelsea by Chelsea fans and loving Chelsea by Spurs fans and the same goes for just about every combination of Premiership clubs and their supporters you can think of. Which I guess shows that I must be just about getting the balance right.

The fans aren't the only ones who can occasionally over-react. We've had our fair share of run-ins with the clubs down the years, too.

I fell out with Alex Ferguson after United played an FA Cup tie against Barnsley at Old Trafford in 1998. I felt the Tykes should have been awarded a penalty and said so, suggesting that if the same incident had occurred at the other end of the field the ref would have pointed to the spot. I doubt I'm the only person ever to have expressed that view. After the game Fergie was absolutely livid. He produced this big list of statistics from somewhere that apparently detailed every penalty shout United had ever had turned down on home turf. 'Andy Gray is talking rubbish,' he said.

A while later we had another dust-up over a newspaper article I'd written. Andy Melvin had known Alex since his Aberdeen days so I asked him how I should set about patching things up with the United boss. He told me that the best thing to do was to phone and talk to him. I called Fergie up fearing the worst. Instead he was as friendly as could be, 'When you get two guys who're as passionate about the game as we are there are bound to be bust-ups,' he said. That's Alex. He's quick to anger but he doesn't bear grudges over small things.

Arsenal fell out with us in 2003 because they held us responsible for highlighting too many disciplinary incidents involving their players. It wasn't the first time they'd done that. I've had arguments with David Dein in the past and a few years ago at Villa Park, Pat Rice, Arsene Wenger's assistant, accused me of being 'anti-Arsenal'.

That was rubbish. What I would say, however, is that maybe the fact that the Gunners' manager consistently fails to see any serious offence involving his own players while never missing a single trick the opposition get up to has worn a bit thin with a lot a people. And the thing is that in many ways by claiming that he hasn't witnessed any offence he's made things much worse for himself and his team. He's brought the spotlight onto them more. Because what's happening is that Arsene Wenger is saying, 'I wasn't looking. I don't know what went on,' and so we're responding, 'Well, here it is for you then, Arsene. And now here it is again, this time in slow motion from another angle.' It annoys him, but whose fault is it? Who has created the situation?

I pointed that out to Pat. I also told him that there have been loads of times when the producer has brought footage of incidents to my attention that everybody else – the press, the radio and the supporters – has missed. When that happens I don't use it, because in my view we are not there to create the headlines. We are there to report the headlines. And a lot of players, including a few from Arsenal, have benefited from that approach.

In my view if a player is lying on the ground bleeding and everybody is asking 'What happened to him?' it is then our duty, if possible, to answer that question. We try to do that.

I'll give you an example of what I mean – in this case one that ended with me having to be accompanied around the football grounds of Britain by a couple of eighteen-stone body-guards. It was a Monday night game between West Ham and Manchester United and I was in the studio with Richard.

In the second half the Hammers defender Julian Dicks went flying in on Andy Cole. Nothing unusual in that. Dicks had done a few players in his time. He liked to rattle people. That was his style. What was out of the ordinary was Cole's reaction. He went absolutely crazy, running after Dicks, yelling and pointing at him. He was so upset that in the end Fergie substituted him just to stop it bubbling over. Naturally everybody wanted to know what had provoked Cole's extraordinary reaction.

Trevor Francis was the co-commentator on the game and if he'd seen the incident properly he might have been able to explain it there and then. As it was he didn't, so Andy Melvin asked me if I knew what had gone on. As it happened I did. I asked Andy to get me the footage from the high-angle camera behind the goal. When you looked at the tackle from that angle you could see what Cole was so upset about. He'd managed to lift his foot off the ground a split second before Dicks' challenge came in. If he hadn't done that there was a fair probability he would have ended up with a broken leg. It was a horrendous challenge.

Our producer decided that we needed to run the footage to show what had provoked Cole and I commented on it saying that I thought it was a leg-breaking tackle. That created a storm. The papers went ballistic, with Julian acting as if butter wouldn't melt in his mouth, and my old Villa teammate Dennis Mortimer came out and denounced me as a hypocrite. Dennis and I go back a long way. He arrived at Villa Park shortly after I came in from Dundee United. He was a good player and a terrific captain but I never got on with him. I always thought he was too close to Ron Saunders. He was the manager's eyes and ears in the dressing room and if anything got said Saunders soon heard about it. Dennis and I clashed a few times in training at Villa. Then when I was at Wolves I was sent off for having a go at him in a derby match at Villa Park. I make no excuses for that. It was a bad challenge. But it didn't connect and it was a one-off. I didn't make a habit of that sort of thing. I'm not sure you could say the same about Julian Dicks.

The result of all the hysteria was a sack of hate mail and a load of death threats from alleged West Ham fans. Personally I took these pretty lightly. But for insurance purposes Sky felt they had to take extra precautions so they hired a couple of hefty security operatives to protect me at games. No disrespect to the two lads involved, who were thoroughly professional, but the situation was farcical. I'd arrive at the ground at eleven in the morning and I'd be walking up to the gantry in a totally empty stand with this pair standing on either side of me protecting me from absolutely nobody. In the end I had to ask them if they'd walk ten yards behind me to save me from embarrassment. They obliged and luckily after a couple of months things went back to normal.

I stand by everything I said about Dicks' challenge on Andy Cole and our right as a broadcaster to highlight it. We can't ignore things like that. Which brings us back to Arsenal. When they played Manchester United at Old Trafford in 2003 what were we supposed to do about the closing moments of the match? We were showing a live game. When Martin Keown began pulling faces and jumping all over Ruud van Nistelrooy did David Dein really expect us to turn the cameras off? And does he genuinely believe that if we had ignored it the 200 journalists who were there would have followed our lead and not written about it?

A few weeks later Martin Tyler and I were doing the Arsenal versus Liverpool game. To get to the commentary position we have to walk through the Arsenal supporters. That's never bothered us. We do it at every ground. We have a bit of chatter with the fans and it's great. But on this day we start getting a load of abuse. Why? Because Arsenal players behaved badly live on the TV station we work for. How is that our responsibility, or the responsibility of Sky Television?

I understand Wenger's annoyance at the hype that came to surround the incident. The newspapers went overboard on it and they ran with it all week. But that had nothing to do with Sky.

I do think that Arsenal have been unlucky at times. I've been there when Arsenal players have been sent off when they shouldn't have been. On the other hand if over a two-year period you've had nearly twice as many players red carded as your nearest rivals, then I don't think that's all down to misfortune. I believe Arsenal have developed a tendency to overreact to things on the field. I'm sure part of the reason for that is the Arsene's reluctance to condemn his players for their actions. By constantly giving out the idea that his team have been unjustly treated he's added to the problem, because whenever things go against them his team tend to behave as if they've been hard done by *yet again*.

Martin Keown is an incredibly good defender, but he's also a very intense guy who's always likely to erupt. I've known him since my second spell at Villa and though I didn't have much time for him then, as I said I've come to admire him since. He's a difficult opponent. He marks tight and gets right up your nose. On the other hand he's always likely to react, and players that come up against him know that and they act accordingly.

His reaction to everything that went on around him that afternoon at Old Trafford was bizarre and extraordinary and I'm sure when he looked at it next day he must have realized he'd gone too far. In a way the incident perhaps did Arsenal a favour. The FA cracked down on them and for the rest of the season barring the odd individual incident their disciplinary record was much better.

Football and Sky is a two-way street. The certainty is that Sky would not be in the position it is without football, but financially football wouldn't be in its current shape without Sky.

Looking back it's plain that getting the Premiership was a massive moment for Sky. Without it it's hard to see what would have happened to the channel. We've got eight million subscribers now, but without the Premiership how many of those would we have? I think its fair to say that Sky's past, present and future rest on the Premiership. We need football and football needs us.

People may feel that the bond between the Premiership and Sky is a very close one. I'm not sure that it's actually as strong as it should be. My feeling is that there is still an attitude from some people within football that 'If it wasn't Sky it would be somebody else'. But I honestly don't think that anyone else would make the kind of investment we do.

I'm also certain that we don't make the kinds of demands of the clubs we might feel entitled to given the money we've paid for the rights. In the US, for example, access to players and coaches is not something TV asks for, but something it demands. The US broadcasters are guaranteed to get interviews with whichever players they want because that helps promote the game. It's not the same here. We're constantly denied permission to speak to players. Sometimes that is as retribution for something that's been said or done that has upset the club. Quite often that has little to do with the sports arm of Sky. At the start of the 2003–4 season, for instance, we were banned by Sir Alex Ferguson because a reporter from Sky News had approached him while he was on holiday in France, stuck a microphone in his face and asked him about Beckham. I can understand why Alex was annoyed about it. It's unacceptable behaviour. But it had nothing to do with Sky Sports. However, we were the ones who suffered most as a consequence of it. Oddly enough, within a few weeks Arsenal were also threatening to ban us for what they claimed was our 'Pro-United bias' over the Martin Keown business.

In some ways it's maybe not surprising that our major clashes have been with United and Arsenal. They've been the Premiership's two dominant clubs and so the pressure is greatest on them. The rivalry between Arsene Wenger and Sir Alex Ferguson has been great for us. United would have carried all before them if it hadn't been for the arrival of the Frenchman. Since he came in Arsenal have really gone toe to toe and slugged it out with Fergie's team.

The contrast in the personalities of the two managers has been fascinating. It's been the old professor versus the mad Scot. I think they're both passionate about football, both determined to be the best, but the way they set about it is totally different and it makes for great viewing.

Sir Alex is an expert at taking the pressure off his own team and dumping it onto the shoulders of his rivals. People talk about mind games but that's what it amounts to. And the only one who has really stood up to it is Arsene Wenger, who's tended to deflect it by acting as if it was all a bit of a joke. Unlike Kevin Keegan he's always handled it well. The only time he's come close to cracking was towards the end of the 2002–3 season.

When it comes down to that stage a manager has to hold things together. And that's not easy. Even somebody like Arsene Wenger, a very calm, cerebral kind of guy, sometimes finds it hard. I think that was maybe what cost Arsenal the Premiership that year. The Gunners had a decent lead over United but for the first time Arsene seemed to be struggling to keep it steady. I watched him all season getting gradually more and more agitated on the touchline. The day they drew at Bolton he was more demonstrative than I'd ever seen him. And that edginess has a way of transmitting itself to the players. The manager has to be a bit like a swan. It doesn't matter how much his emotions are churning away below the surface, above the surface he has to appear calm and serene. Alex Ferguson has learned that. It's taken him years to control the tension, to keep it under the surface, but now he's the master of it. And in fairness to Arsene he came back last year and was back to his cool, thoughtful self again.

Just as I've been accused of being biased against certain clubs I've also had the finger pointed at me as somebody who is anti-ref. That's not the case. I just want games to be decided by the actions of the players not by the decisions of the match officials. It's a tough job. I know it is. And it's got tougher, because the game has got faster, so much so that it's hard to keep up with it at times. I think most referees understand that my criticism is aimed at making the game better. The game has to improve and they have to improve with it. Simple as that.

Most of the match officials take it in good spirit. I don't hide away in the studio and avoid them. I have a chat with them before matches and I've even been to one of their seminars to talk about developments and changes within the game. Where they have a go at me is because they think I use all sorts of technology to show when they're wrong. That's not entirely true. Nine times out of ten I try to call it as I see it when it happens just the same as they do. They will trot out the party line that they get 99 per cent of all their decisions right. That's true. But then again I could get 99 per cent of their decisions right, too – most of them are dead easy.

I'm only really critical of referees when they get the big decisions wrong, the ones that influence games. I can understand why they get touchy, but if you're making errors that affect people's futures you have to expect that.

I think we've got some good referees in this country, but the inconsistency is as bad as it's ever been. Players don't know what they're getting booked for, or if they're going to get booked. Things have improved in some ways. I thought the old regime under Philip Don was terrible. It was too regimented, too straight-laced. I always felt it was dangerous to have so much power resting in the hands of one man, especially a man like Philip Don. This, after all, was a guy who had the arrogance to accuse Pierluigi Collina of handling the Turkey versus England game in Istanbul badly. Like most observers I thought the Italian did a brilliant job. Given the tension before the game and the trouble between the two sets of players, just preventing things kicking off into a full-scale riot was a major achievement.

I suppose Don was just trying to make a point. Collina is held up as an example to referees of how to do their job and perhaps some of them resent that. If that's the case then I don't think they should. The Italian is an example of what can be achieved. His demeanour is so much better than that of our referees. He commands respect by force of personality, not by flashing cards around unnecessarily. Every time I've watched him I've thought he was excellent. I'm not saying he gets everything right. Of course, he doesn't. Nobody does. But he gets most things right. And that's the way you judge referees.

Now Philip Don has gone things are more flexible and the referees feel they have a bit more latitude to make their own judgements. The fear that there's somebody up in the stand who is going to mark them down for not sending a player off for a mistimed tackle has been removed. But I still feel the answer to a lot of the problems is to put the things in the hands of a committee made up of referees, retired pros and former managers. That way you get a spread of opinions and knowledge. I don't feel we use the available experience enough in football. The fact that there's no place in the game for somebody like Howard Kendall these days, to me that is staggering.

The way we play the game in this country is different from the way its played in the rest of the world. It's faster and more physical and offences need to be seen in that context. To me it's a referee's duty to try and keep twenty-two players on the pitch, and too often they are too quick to send people off. I understand that it's a hard balance to strike. We don't want a situation like the one that has developed in Brazil. A player can't buy a red card in the first half over there because the Brazilian FA have practically forbidden the refs from sending anyone off in the first half. As a result you end up with a bloodbath for forty-five minutes.

Our referees will point the finger at FIFA and blame them for forcing their hand. They make out that if they don't follow all the directives and enforce the codes they are going to get in big trouble. That plainly isn't the case. Just look at the Brazilian situation. So if we want to interpret the laws slightly differently to accommodate the way we play the game, then let's do it.

The tension between those who play or manage and those

who officiate isn't helped by the fact that in some ways the referees have become bigger than they should be. Nowadays they are full-time. They have agents. I see them doing after-dinner speeches and appearing on talk shows. I'm not saying they shouldn't, but it's difficult for managers. When they see some guy on TV laughing and joking a few hours after he's wrongly given a penalty that's maybe contributed to somebody losing their job what are they supposed to think? The referees are getting paid good money. It's not like they need to find extra sources of income. If they want to it's up to them, but maybe they should think about how things look to the rest of football. Referees are an important part of the game, but they shouldn't run the game. And there have been times recently when it looked like we were in danger of that happening.

When I was playing my favourite ref was the Welshman Clive Thomas. That will surprise a lot of people because Clive has a reputation for being a bit whistle happy. He was nick-named Clive the Book. I guess he'll always remain famous, or perhaps infamous, for blowing up seconds before the ball crossed the line in a World Cup match involving Brazil. To me, though, Clive was just the right mix of authority and common sense. He wanted to enforce discipline, but not by waving cards around for the sake of it.

I recall once when I was playing for Villa running towards him waving my arms about and yelling in protest over some decision that had gone against us. A lot of refs would have booked me there and then, but Clive just looked at me and said, 'For Christ's sake, Andy, stop waving your arms about, will you? Don't you realize that when you do that the whole ground can see you're having a go at me? It looks bad. They're waiting to see how I react and if I don't do anything they'll think I'm soft. So if you've got any complaints shout, but keep your arms by your side otherwise I'll take action.' Great advice. After that I always made sure I had my hands down when I launched a volley of abuse at the officials.

When I was playing that kind of approach was fairly typical. Men like Clive, Jack Taylor, Gordon Hill and Pat Partridge had their own personalities and they were allowed to use them in a positive way. I'd like to see a return to that sort of approach.

Sky winning the rights to screen the Champions' League was terrific for us. We've done the same competitions for a decade now and this is something different. After twelve years we have something new to keep us on our toes. The only objection I have to the competition is the way the qualification process and the sums of money involved for it have affected English football. It has eased the pressure on managers and players considerably. When I was playing, finishing third or fourth meant nothing. Now it's more important than winning the Cup. The Champions' League has allowed clubs to succeed by failing.

Apart from that it's a very exciting competition because the standard is high across the board. By the time you get down to the last sixteen there are very few weak teams left. Any of the quarter-finalists could win it, as we saw last season with Real Madrid, Arsenal and Milan all getting knocked out at that stage.

Showing every game of that competition is a huge invest-ment. The coverage is extraordinary, certainly the most com-prehensive there has ever been. On Tuesday nights now you can sit at Sky Sports and watch six live games simultaneously.

Richard and I have been moved off the Monday football show so we can be involved in that. I miss doing the Monday night football and I know Keysie feels the same. I thought that was a good show. I particularly enjoyed the first hour. We really got our teeth into the analysis. In a perfect world I'd probably like to still be doing that, but it becomes difficult when you're doing Saturday and Sunday to do Monday and then also Tuesday and Wednesday. So we had to give it up. Monday's a completely different show now. It would have been totally impossible for anybody else to come in and do what Richard and I did because I think it was quite unique.

On the Champions' League show I'm basically working from 5 p.m. until 11 p.m. It's mentally taxing. Like most ex-footballers I get kind of impatient if I have to sit around for too long. When we bring players in for the first time that's one of the things you notice – that footballers find it hard to sit still and concentrate for blocks of time. They're used to action.

For me the new show has involved a bit more homework because clearly I'm not seeing the European teams week in and week out. But that's been good because it's given me something else to work on and that helps you to keep focused in other areas. I think whatever field you work in, whether it's playing football or anything else, you need fresh challenges or you end up coasting.

One thing that's been interesting for me in particular is analysing the foreign teams. We've been brought up to believe that tactically the Continentals play in a very different way from us. But when you actually watch them and break down what they're doing you see that in fact the differences are generally pretty minimal. You watch a team like, for example, Stuttgart, who played Manchester United and Chelsea last season, and you'll see they've got a solid block of four at the back, four midfielders who are not spectacular but really, really graft, and a couple of front players with good movement and a bit of pace and power – just the sort of formation and style of player that wouldn't look out of place in the Premiership.

As I've said before, there are a lot of people around who'd like you to think that to understand football you need the brain of an Albert Einstein, but that's not the case. If you look at Juventus, Milan, Real Madrid or Manchester United, you see they're all basically playing with slight variations on 4–4–2, maybe with a little added flexibility. If Real Madrid beat you it's not because of some revolutionary strategy. It's because they have better players. That's why they win games.

Because we have been adjusting to the new European coverage we held back on technical innovations last season. In the end you have to accept that you can't reinvent the wheel. It may be that at the moment we have pushed the boundaries as far as they can go, but I'm sure that won't last.

Whatever comes up next the great thing for me is that I've been here since day one. I've watched the thing grow into something nobody, not even the top executives at Sky, could have imagined. And I can look back from the position we're in now to those early days when things were a lot less slick and we had to improvise a bit more. I can recall times like the one when I was leaving the studio to go home, walking across the car park and hearing the producer yelling after me, 'Andy, Andy, come back. Nicky Horne's sick. We need you to present the American Football.' And I turned around and went back in and did four hours of coverage of the Dallas Cowboys versus the Philadelphia Eagles.

I don't think there's any doubt that for overall coverage in those fourteen years we have set the standards. The most difficult task we have now is maintaining them. We're very pleased with what we've achieved, but we're not sitting back and getting the cigars out. We know we're nothing without the product. And the product is football.

Like Sky I intend to be involved with the game for a good few years yet. In between matches I have plenty to keep me happy. My daughters Amy, Katie and Sophie, of course, and my partner Suzanne Dando. I've known Suzanne for about twenty years. We shared the same agent and we used to bump into one another at parties and functions. For the past ten years Suzanne has been working at Sky doing the basketball coverage. Our relationship began about four years ago. We'd both broken up with our partners and used to bump into each other in the Sky offices and joke about how we really ought to get together. Eventually I asked Suzanne to have dinner with me, we got on great and we've more or less been together ever since. Suzie's a former Olympic gymnast and I guess because we were both involved in top-level sport we have the same drive and outlook. We bought the house, a converted sixteenth-century barn in Warwickshire, together in 2000. We have two dogs, Teddy and Rocky, we got from a rescue centre, two cats, Ozzy and Pom and a horse named Lulu and a big garden we're gradually getting to grips with.

I've got my golf, too. I play a lot off an iffy nine handicap. It's one of the things that as an ex-sportsman of forty-eight you can still do to test yourself. It gets the competitive juices flowing when not much else can any more. It takes you to some great places and lovely courses, and you get to meet some great people. I do loads of pro-ams and celeb-ams, and I'm pleased to say a fair bit of silverware has found it's way back into the house. I still like competing. I still don't like losing.

I get to hang out with some of the pros and play with them, too. I've got to know people like Padraig Harrington, Ian

Woosnam, Colin Montogomerie and Darren Clarke. Most of them are mad keen football fans and they like to get a bit of inside gen. They're not that different from footballers in a lot of ways. It's a different sport, and a much harder one, too, with incredibly small margins of error. The competition is very high, the line between winning and losing is very fine and it's very tough for them. But like most sportspeople they like to let their hair down and have a few beers. I've never met any golfers I didn't like. And that says something.

Miraculously, given the predictions of John Bond and others, I can get around the course without the need for a golf cart. Although I spent a lot of time on the treatment table during my playing days compared to some of my teammates I was very fortunate. Guys like Gary Shaw, Ian Durrant, Brian Little and Mark Higgins had their careers brought to an abrupt end by injury. I was the player my teammates at Goodison called the Iceman because of the amount of times they saw me with my leg in freezing water, but I went on playing until I was thirty-two, far longer than many people, including myself, thought was likely when I started out.

When it came to long-term damage I was lucky, too. Although my knee stiffens up if I sit still for too long I can still get about without any problems. Not all ex-pros can say that. A few years ago Derek Dougan said that there are three questions old players always ask each other when they meet up: 'Are you still with the wife?' 'Have you got any grandchildren yet?' and 'How's the knee?' When you look at somebody like the late Bobby Murdoch of Celtic, a fantastic midfield player who could hardly walk by the time he was fifty, you see how bad it can be.

Some people undoubtedly are lucky. It's often been said

about me. My friends tell me that things always seem to drop into my lap or fall just right. I'd have to say that when I look back over my life and what I have around me now, my family, my home and my job, I'd go along with that. Look at how Everton came in for me when my career was heading down a blind alley and they really wanted a Brazilian; how injuries to Ally McCoist and Billy Drinkell gave me the chance to play for Rangers; and how when that all finished BSB turned up right on cue. Yes, I've worked hard. But so have millions of other people and they haven't ended up with all that I have. There's no doubt about it, I am a very lucky guy.

INDEX

Aberdeen (football club) 89, 114, 118, 177, 178, 179

Adams, Tony 141

Advocaat, Dick 170

African Cup of Nations 117

Albany Hotel, Glasgow 22

Albion Rovers 122

Albiston, Arthur 149

Algarve, Portugal 150

Ali, Muhammad 14

Allardyce, Sam 53, 132, 142, 232, 246

Allback, Marcus 201

Allen, Clive 133

Allison, Malcolm 48, 57, 226

Alliss, Peter 232

American Football 261
  see also National Football League (NFL)

Anderson, Viv 53

Anfield 73, 85, 94, 114, 143, 167, 169, 172, 205, 226, 229, 233–4

Angel, Juan Pablo 201

Anglo-Scots 131

Anglo-Scottish Cup 159–60

Anniesland, Glasgow 161

Archibald, Steve 126, 130

Ardiles, Ossie 62, 93

Argentina 115, 118, 119

Argentina (football team) 121

Arnold, Jim 80, 92

Arsenal 13, 40, 48, 56, 63, 75, 94, 107, 108, 109–10, 124, 143, 149, 159, 219, 228–9, 248–9, 251–3, 254–5, 259
  see also Highbury

Aston Villa vi, 6, 24, 25–46, 47–8, 50–1, 52, 53, 54, 61, 64, 66, 71, 75, 111, 113, 116–17, 118, 130, 134, 137–8, 139–40, 142–4, 146–8, 149, 150, 158–9, 161, 177, 181, 186, 192, 193–207, 209, 210, 212–13, 230–1, 247, 250–1, 252
  see also Villa Park

Athletic Bilbao (football club) 42, 110

Atkinson, Dalian 204, 205

Atkinson, Ron 64–5, 111, 118, 138, 148–9, 150–1, 152, 153, 164, 168, 192, 193, 194, 195–6, 198–9, 202–8, 209, 212–13, 237, 244

Augenthaler, Klaus 101

Australia 196

Australia (football team) 127, 130

Austria (football team) 119, 121

Ayr United 119

Ayresome Park, Middlesbrough 30

INDEX

Back, Isle of Lewis 156, 157–9
Bailey, John ('Gnasher') 75, 91–2
Baker, Joe 22
Balaban, Bosco 201
Ball, Alan 89
Banks, Gordon 71
Barcelona (football club) 42, 113
Barker, Richie 61–2
Barker, Sue 93
Barnes, John 19, 85
Barnsley (football club) 248
Barnwell, John 47, 48–50, 53–4, 56–7, 60–1, 63
Barron, Jim 195
Bates, Ken 211
Batson, Brendan 148
Bauld, Willie 10
Baxter, 'Slim Jim' 159, 179
Bayern Munich 8, 100–2, 103, 126, 135
Beasant, Dave 208
Beckham, David v, vii, 21, 108, 116, 132, 245, 254
Belgium 171
Bellamy, Craig 31
Bellefield 75, 110–11
Benaud, Richie 232
Bendall, Ron 45, 64
Bergkamp, Dennis 228
Bertschin, Keith 148
Best, George 9, 177
Bhatti brothers 65
Birmingham City 27, 30, 43, 46, 74, 76, 88, 138, 143, 145, 150, 202, 247
    see also St Andrews
Birmingham Five 88, 149
Black Sabbath 44
Blackburn (football club) 28, 160, 209, 235
Blake, Noel 149
Blatter, Sepp 52–3

Blyth Spartans 69
Bodymoor 137
Boer, Ronald de 169
Bolton Wanderers 53, 60, 63, 142, 230–1, 232, 246
Bond, John 11, 263
Bonds, Billy 'Bonzo' 143
Boot Room 219, 220–2, 234, 244
Bosman contracts 25, 244–5, 246
Bosnich, Mark 196–8
Bowyer, Lee 227
Bracewell, Paul 68, 87–8, 97, 108, 109
Bradford Park Avenue 71
Bradford (stadium) 59, 162
Bradshaw, Paul 55–6
Brady, Liam 239
Bramall Lane 80
Brazil 257
Brazil (football team) 7, 135, 258
Brazil, Alan 225
Brazilian Football Association 257
Breakfast AM (radio programme) 185
Bremner, Billy 120, 121
Briggs, Neville 25, 26
British Broadcasting Corporation (BBC)
    19, 25, 126, 157, 183, 193, 230, 234, 247
British Sky Broadcasting (BSB) 133, 183–4, 185, 187, 189, 194–5, 209–10, 211, 217, 218, 227, 264
    see also BSkyB
Brock, Kevin 76
Broughty Ferry 4
Brown, Craig 131
BSkyB 209–12
    see also British Sky Broadcasting
Bundesliga 23
Burnley (football club) 60, 85
Burns, Kenny 145–6
Burridge, Janet 29

INDEX

Burridge, John 28–30, 68–71, 80
Burrows, David 149
Busby, Sir Matt 122, 207
Butcher, Terry 167–8, 170
Butler, Geezer 44
Butt, Nicky 36

Cambridge United 62
Camp Nou 42
Canada (football team) 127
Cantona, Eric 86, 134, 220
Capello, Fabio 220
Cardiff (football team) 66
Carr, Willie 50, 54, 56
Carrodus, Frank 36
Carter, Philip 75
Case, Jimmy 143–4
Celtic 3, 12–14, 15, 22, 24, 49, 104,
    120, 122, 123, 131, 132, 146, 147,
    154, 163, 165–6, 169, 170, 171,
    263
    see also Old Firm
Celtic Park 122
Central TV 198
Champion studios, West London 185,
    191
Champions' Cup 18, 23, 110, 113, 146
Champions' League vi, 101, 108, 132–3,
    135, 171, 175, 186, 190, 201, 202,
    220, 228, 259, 260–1
Chapman, Lee 31
Charity Shield 89
Charles, John 21
Charlton (football club) 26, 68, 227
Charlton, Bobby 141
Charlton, Jack 141
Chelmsford (football club) 66
Chelsea (football club) 49, 51, 95, 142,
    143, 197, 211, 247, 260
Cheltenham Town (football club) 141,
    195

Chesterfield (football club) 73
Chinn, Buck 201–2
Chisholm, Sam 240, 241–2
City of Manchester Stadium 58
Clarke, Darren 263
Clarke, Wayne 67
Clemence, Ray 97–8, 219
Clough, Brian 1, 53, 164, 214, 215,
    245
Clydebank Strollers 1, 2, 3, 154,
    155–6
Coates, Ralph 85
Colchester (football club) 227
Cole, Andy 31, 172, 249–50, 251
Coleman, David 93
Collina, Pierluigi 256–7
Collymore, Stan 201
Connaghan, Dennis 13
Cooke, Charlie 7
Cooper, Davie 129, 177
Cooper, Neale 140, 141, 163–4
Copenhagen 121
Copland, Jacky 7, 9, 24, 160
Corinthian Casuals 190
Coton, Tony 149
Cotterill, Steve 244
County Ground 141
Coventry City 31, 49, 79, 127, 170, 185,
    207–8
Cowan, Tom 170
Cowgill, Brian 183–4, 185, 191
Crerand, Paddy 119
Crooks, Garth 93
Cropley, Alex 31
Crouch, Peter 201
Cruyff, Johan 42, 120
Crystal Palace (football club) 47, 211
Cullis, Stan 56, 57
Cunningham, Laurie 148
Cup Winners' Cup 98, 103, 104, 106,
    112, 126, 243

INDEX

Curran, Terry 80, 99
Czechoslovakia (football team) 115–16

Dailly, Christian 229
Daley, Steve 48, 57
Daley, Tony 205–6
Dalglish, Kenny 12, 115, 118, 121,
    125–6, 130, 141, 160, 166, 178,
    226, 234
Dallas Cowboys 261
Dando, Suzanne 262
Daniel, Peter 54–5
Darke, Ian 234
Darlington (football club) 58
Darracott, Terry 92–3
Davies, Barry 189
Davies, Wyn 159
Dean, Dixie 79
Deehan, John 41
Deepdale 76, 81
Dein, David 248, 251
Dell, Southampton 60, 217
Dempsey, Paul 225–6
Dens Park, Dundee 7, 179
Depor 228
Deportivo La Coruna 228
Derby County 40, 146
Dettori, Frankie 93
Dicks, Julian 249–50, 251
Djorkaeff, Youri 246
Docherty, Tommy 198
Dodd, Alan 67
Dodds, Jason 207
Don, Philip 256–7
Dougan, Derek 33–5, 59, 65–6, 159,
    263
Draper, Mark 201
Drinkell, Kevin ('Billy') 152, 176–7, 264
Droy, Mick 143
Drumchapel vii, 24, 123, 153, 158
Dugarry, Christophe 246

Dumbarton (football team) 10, 89
Dundee United vi, 1, 2, 3, 4–6, 7–14,
    15–17, 21, 24–6, 27, 30, 32, 40, 52,
    53, 120, 126, 144–5, 156, 159–60,
    161, 172, 174–5, 201, 250
Dunfermline Athletic 12, 122, 164, 170
Durrant, Ian 163–4, 178–9, 263
Duvall, Robert 175–6
Dyke, Greg 183

East Fife (football club) 9
Easter Road 237
Eder 102
Edwards, Martin 75
Ehiogu, Ugo 195
Elland Road 57, 60, 63, 122
Ellis, Doug 45, 64, 198–202, 203, 210,
    212
Ellis, Simon 199
England (football team) 3, 32, 59, 117,
    125, 126–7, 132, 133, 135–6,
    138–9, 184, 205, 229, 256
    B team 91–2
England, Mike 127
Eriksson, Sven Goran 132, 135
Euro 96 132
Euro 2000 125
European Championship
    1976 104–5
    2000 229
European Cup 46, 53, 61, 110, 139, 169
European Footballer of the Year 23
European League 171
Evans, Allan 139
Everton (football club) vi, 5, 10, 11, 26,
    32–3, 40, 52, 56, 71–2, 73–86,
    87–113, 126–7, 128, 130, 132, 139,
    140, 141, 149, 167, 168, 209,
    237–44, 245, 246, 264
    A Team 109
    B Team 109

INDEX

Everton (football club) (*cont.*)
　see also Goodison Park
Eves, Mel 67, 71

FA Cup 53, 56, 62, 76, 81, 89, 91, 95, 98,
　　103, 106, 108, 112, 138, 149, 164,
　　184, 202, 205, 206, 228–9, 230–1,
　　243, 248
Falco, Mark 98
Far East 135
Fenerbahce (football club) 42
Ferdinand, Rio 28, 108
Ferguson, Alex 7, 10, 18, 19, 75, 107–8,
　　114, 123, 128, 130, 134, 141,
　　192–3, 196, 197, 207, 228, 235–6,
　　244, 246, 248, 250, 254, 255
Ferguson, Duncan 5
Ferguson, Ian 170, 179
Ferguson, Jason 220
FIFA 117, 124, 170–1, 257
Filbert Street 96
Findlay (goalkeeper) 92
Finland (football team) 115
First Division 27, 68, 79, 100, 131, 142,
　　144, 210–11, 247
　see also Premiership; Scottish First
　　Division
Five Live 230–1
Fletcher, Darren 132
Football Association (FA) 37, 124, 127,
　　196, 253
　see also FA Cup
Formby, Lancashire 110, 111
Forsyth, Allan 11
Forsyth, Bruce 68
Fortuna Sittard 98–9, 100
Fourth Division 138
Fox 217
France 132–4, 220
Francis, Trevor 53, 100, 250
Free Church of Scotland 153

Friel, Maurice 1, 2, 156
Froggatt, Steve 205, 206

G14 171
Gallagher, Joe 27–8, 143
Gardner, Pat 7, 8, 9
Gascoigne, Paul 178
Gay Meadow 141
Gelsenkirchen 21
Gemmill, Archie 115, 125, 163
Germany 132, 192, 193, 229
Germany (football team) 135, 136, 229,
　　237
Gerrard, Steven 132
Gidman, John 45, 46
Giggs, Ryan 36, 228
Gillingham (football club) 81–2, 90–1
Gilzean, Alan 7, 159
Glasgow Boys 155, 164
Glasgow Cup 14
Glasgow Rangers vi,, 3, 7, 8, 21, 93, 108,
　　118, 129, 141, 146, 152–3, 159,
　　160–2, 163–80, 181, 182, 237, 264
　see also Ibrox; Old Firm
Goal Post pub, Wolverhampton 71
Goodison Park 10, 52, 56, 72, 73, 74, 77,
　　79, 80, 81, 86, 89, 94, 97, 98–9,
　　101, 103, 105, 110, 111, 113, 209,
　　237, 239, 240, 242, 243–4, 263
Goodman, Don 149
Gornik (football club) 42
Gough, Richard 128, 168
Govan 159
Graham, George 142
Gray, Amy (Andy's daughter) 262

Gray, Andy
Aston Villa career 6–7, 24, 25–46, 52, 54,
　　116–17, 118, 130, 150, 158–9, 161,
　　181, 250

Gray, Andy (*cont.*)

assistant to Ron Atkinson 192, 193–207, 209, 210, 212–13, 237

clashes with Saunders 32–5, 36–7, 39, 40, 41–3, 44–6, 47–8, 49, 52, 116–17, 134

debut 30

final game 43

first season 30–2

leaves for Wolverhampton 44–6

money matters 25, 39–40, 46

second season 32–3

second spell 50–1, 111, 113, 137–8, 139–40, 142–4, 146–8

as Britain's most expensive footballer vi, 47, 51–2

broadcasting career vii, 132–6, 139, 182–91, 194–5, 207–8, 209–13, 214–36, 248–62, 264

appearances on *A Question of Sport* 93–4, 175

Boot Room 219, 220–2, 234

camera knowledge 224

Champions' League show 259, 260–1

commentary techniques 223–4, 225

enthusiasm 231–2

gaffes 226–7

memorable matches 228–30

Monday Night Football 207–8, 222–3, 225

neutrality 247–8

on-air swearing 225–6

on poor games 230–1

receives death threats 251

on referees 255–8

on replays 224

skirmishes with footballing professionals 248–55

stars in *Shot at Glory* (film) 175–6

stars on *Who Wants to Be A Millionaire* 187–9

on technology 222–3

thinks of leaving 238, 239, 240, 241–3

Cheltenham career 141, 195

childhood 153–8, 160–2

on club/country conflicts 116–18

Clydebank Strollers career 1, 2, 3, 155–6

on coaches 140–1

competitive streak 14–15, 262–3

on dedication 5–7

diet 9, 27, 120

drinking 9, 16–17, 120

Dundee United career 3–6, 7–14, 15–16, 21, 24–6, 32, 52, 120, 144–5, 156, 159–60, 161, 172

back-stick player 27

crowd sizes 30

first goal 9

first season 3–6, 7–14, 15–16

leaves for Aston Villa 17, 24–6

media speculation regarding 10

Player of the Year 15, 17

second season 16, 17

trials 1, 2, 3–4

wages 3–4, 15–16

end of his playing career 181–5

on European football 99–100

Everton career 5, 73–86, 87–113, 139, 140, 149, 264

and Andy's international career 126–7

first game 75

leaves for Aston Villa 110–13

management opportunity 237–44, 246

money matters 73

signed 71–2, 73–4

on fame 36–40, 187, 197–8

on fans 179–80

fearless playing style 11

on football disasters 161–2

INDEX

Gray, Andy (*cont.*)
on football's hard men 143–5
on football's transformation vi, 28, 117
on foreign players in the Scottish League
    168–71
on forwards 105
on fouling 27–8, 100
scores Goal of the Season (Scotland) 115
on goalkeepers 69–70
love of golf 14, 262–3
grandparents *see* Murrays
heroes 8–9
home life 262
on hooliganism 59, 133–4
on the importance of watching other
    players 8–9
injuries 263
    ankle injury 33–4
    broken foot 91
    knee injuries vii, 11–12, 32, 43, 44,
        48–9, 71–2, 73, 114, 263
    ligament damage 40
    thigh injury 42–3
    working through 43
on the joy of scoring 30
love of the game vii
luck 263–4
on managers 244–5
    divisional management 141–2
    player–manager relations 134–5
    qualifications 244
on money and football 245–6
opens nightclub Holy City Zoo 44, 47
on overplay 156
on partying 16–17, 38
voted PFA Young Player of the Year/
    Player of the Year vi, 33–5
playing philosophy 96–7
on the privileged lifestyle of professional
    footballers 181–2
PSV Eindhoven bid for 23

Rangers career 152–3, 163–9, 171–80,
    181, 182, 264
on referees 52–3, 255–9
Schalke bid for 21, 22–3, 24
school football 14–15, 155
and the Scotland squad 114–32
Scottish Professional Youth career 2–3
send offs 52–3, 115–16
on stamina 106–8
superstitious nature 95–6, 152
West Bromwich Albion career 148–51,
    152, 173, 182, 194
Wolverhampton Wanderers career vi, 34,
    47–58, 60–72, 74, 121, 124, 125,
    140, 143, 158–9, 195, 250–1
    coaching 61–2
    highpoint 56
    leaves for Everton 71–2
    money matters 47
    second season 60
    signing 47–50

Gray, Margaret (Andy's mother) 24, 153,
    154–5, 156, 157, 158, 161–2
Gray, Duncan (Andy's brother) 153, 161
Gray, Eddie 115
Gray, Frank 53, 121, 125
Gray, James (Andy's brother) 4, 153, 154,
    155, 156, 161
Gray, Katie (Andy's daughter) 262
Gray, Sophie (Andy's daughter) v, 23,
    159, 239, 240, 262
Gray, William (Andy's father) 153, 160–1
Gray, Willie (Andy's brother) 3–4, 23,
    153, 155, 159, 161
Greaves, Ian 63–5
Greaves, Jimmy 22, 130, 198–9
Green, Alan 230–1
Gregory, John 201
Greig, John 159
Grimsby (football club) 110

INDEX

Haaland, Alf-Inge 37
Haffey, Frank 154
Hamburg 193–4
Hamilton Academicals 164
Hampden Park 115, 123, 124, 125, 127, 163, 165, 229
Hansen, Alan 130, 146
Harford, Mick 149
Harper, Joe 118
Harrington, Padraig 262–3
Harris, Ron 'Chopper' 143
Hartlepool (football club) 141
Hartson, John 49
Harvey, Colin 77–8, 89, 103, 209
Hauwe, Pat van den 88–9, 128, 149
Hawkins, Graham 66, 67, 68, 71, 72
Hawthorns 118, 148, 149, 150
   see also West Bromwich Albion
Hayes, Eddie 154
Hayward, Sir Jack 65
Hearts 12, 19, 177
Heath, Adrian 76, 84, 94, 103, 108–9, 110
Heaton, Mick 71–2, 77
Hegarty, Paul 7
Henderson, Willie 159
Henry, Thierry 31, 97
Hereford (football club) 140
Heysel Stadium, Brussels 59, 110, 162, 167
Hibbitt, Kenny 50, 54, 62, 66–7, 71, 86
Hibernian 3, 119, 122, 131, 159, 237
Higgins, Mark 79, 263
Highbury 52, 56, 83, 142, 147, 216–17
Highfield Road 127, 217
Hill, David 212, 215–16, 217–18
Hill, Gordon 259
Hill, Ricky 103
Hillsborough 33, 40, 59, 62, 94, 147, 162, 203–4
Hoddle, Glenn 62, 219–20, 239

Hoeness, Uli 101, 102–3
Holland (football team) 220
Holton, Jim 143
Holy City Zoo nightclub, Birmingham 44, 47
Hopkins, Robert 149–50
Horne, Nicky 261
Houllier, Gerard 206
Huddersfield Town 22, 63
Hughes, Emlyn 50, 54, 55, 56, 109, 126
Hughes, Mark 90, 128
Hunter, Norman 144–5
Hutchison, Don 229

Ibrox 93, 151, 159, 160–2, 163, 165, 166, 167, 170, 172, 174, 176, 179, 180, 204
Iceland 21
Iceland (football team) 127
Il Ciocco 167
Independent Television (ITV) 34, 119, 130, 183, 187, 189, 215, 247
Inter Bratislava 98
Iommi, Toni 44
Ipswich Town 124, 142, 149, 167
Isle of Heather Cup 158
Isle of Lewis 153, 156–9
Istanbul 256
Isthmian League 190
Italia 90 59
Italy 166–7
   Serie A 184, 228

Jacqui (Andy's partner) 239
James, Leighton 85
Jan (Andy's partner) 110, 111
Japan 134, 135
Jennings, Pat 239
John, Elton 119
Johnson, David 75
Johnson, Peter 238, 240, 242, 243, 244

INDEX

Johnston, Maurice (Mo) 85, 130, 163, 165, 166
Johnston, Willie 118
Johnstone, Derek ('Big Ba') 93, 118
Johnstone, Jimmy 12, 120, 121, 177
Jordan, Joe 23, 115, 118, 125, 126, 130, 159
Juventus 51, 110, 171, 261

Kamara, Chris 133
Kanoute, Freddie 117
Kartz, Harry 45
Keane, Roy 3, 37, 134–5, 150, 228
Keaton, Michael 175–6
Keegan, Kevin 23, 31, 119, 207, 229, 235–6, 254
Keizer, Jan 129
Kellock, Billy 66, 67
Kelly, Tony 150
Kendall, Howard 71–8, 80–2, 84–5, 87–9, 91, 101, 103, 104, 106–7, 109, 110–12, 127, 139, 209, 240, 243, 257
Kent 81
Kenwright, Bill 239, 240
Keown, Martin 50–1, 251, 252–3, 254
Keppel, Judith 188
Kettering (football club) 66
Keys, Richard 185–9, 207–8, 214, 216, 225, 232, 234–6, 249, 259–60
Kidd, Brian 209
Kilbowie Union 156
King, Andy 82
Kirk 157
Kirkcaldy 25
Kirkland, Chris 70
Klinsmann, Jurgen 237
Knox, Archie 7
Koeman, Ronald 220
Kogl, Ludwig 101, 102

Korea 134, 193
Korea (football team) 135
Krankl, Hans 104, 105

La Manga 239
Lancaster Gate 127
Larsson, Henrik 169
Latchford, Bob 57
Law, Denis 22, 23, 28, 35, 120, 177
Lawrenson, Mark 146
Lawton, Tommy 10, 79, 200
Le Tissier, Matthew 204–5
League Championship 63, 113
League Cup 7, 28, 30–1, 32, 33, 40, 41, 43, 52, 53, 54, 56, 59–60, 61, 62, 71, 73, 76, 78–9, 83, 85–6, 89, 94, 104, 106, 114, 121, 124, 131, 145, 183, 203, 205, 210
League of Ireland 168
League Managers Association 48
Lee, Francis 35, 100
Lee, Gordon 79, 89
Leeds United 10, 31, 59, 63, 76, 107, 115, 120, 122, 142, 144–5, 149, 207, 226, 235, 246
    see also Elland Road
Leicester City 59, 96, 111
Leighton, Jim 128, 130, 196
Leonard, Keith 26
Lerby, Soren 101, 102
Lewis, Lennox 225–6
Lineker, Gary 111, 112, 113
Little, Brian 31–2, 41, 45, 141, 201, 263
Liverpool 74
Liverpool (football club) 10, 23, 27, 31, 41, 50, 54, 57, 73, 78, 83, 89, 91, 95, 107, 109–10, 114, 143, 146, 164, 169, 170, 172, 206, 214–15, 229–30, 234, 235, 239, 251–2
    see also Anfield
Lloyd, Larry 146

Lochgoin Primary School, Glasgow
    14–15, 155
Lochs 158
Lorimer, Peter 120
Los Angeles 44
Love Street 179
Lulu (Andy's horse) 262
Luton 43
Luton Town 66, 92, 103–4
LWT 183, 189
Lynam, Des 186
Lyon 133

McAlman, Mrs 21
McAlpine, Hamish 7
McArthur, Mrs 14, 155
McAvennie, Frank 130
McCarthy, Mick 68, 134
McCoist, Ally 93, 152, 164, 173–7, 179,
    264
McDonald, Iain 7
Macdonald, Malcolm 40, 159–60
McFadden, James 132
McFarland, Roy 146
McGrain, Danny 155
McGrath, Paul 49, 106, 192–4
McLaren, Roy 6
McLean, Jim 10, 11–13, 17–20, 64, 152,
    172, 175, 185
    and Andy's auditions for Dundee
        United 2, 3
    BBC interview incident 19–20
    character 1, 4–5, 19–20
    clashes with Andy 24
    and Dundee United salaries 15
    resignation from Dundee United 19
    as Scotland manager 119, 121
    sells Andy to Aston Villa 25–6
    supports Andy's football career 4–6
McLean, Tommy 19
McLeish, Alex 128

McLeod, Ally 114, 118–19, 122
McLintock, Frank 219, 239
McMenemy, Lawrie 83
McNaught, Ken 33
McNeill, Billy 12–13, 146–8
McQueen, Gordon 119
Madden, John 184
Magaluf 69–70
Maine Road 35
Mallaig 156
Manchester Boys 164
Manchester City 26, 35, 48, 57, 59, 145,
    202, 226
Manchester United vi, 7, 13, 21, 28, 31,
    37–8, 52, 63, 64–5, 75, 76, 94, 101,
    105–6, 107–8, 109–10, 111, 112,
    119, 132, 135, 147–8, 149, 167,
    168, 192, 196–7, 203, 206, 219,
    220, 228–9, 235, 246, 248, 249–50,
    251, 252–3, 254–5, 260, 261
    see also Old Trafford
Manor Ground 76
Mariner, Paul 81
Marseille 133
Marshall, David 132
Marshall, Harry 63
Marwood, Brian 103
Mason, Don 115
Mason, Gary 225–6
Match of the Day (TV programme) 29
Matthaus, Lothar 101
Melvin, Andy 182, 183–4, 185, 187, 191,
    212, 215, 216, 218–19, 221, 222,
    224, 234, 248, 250
Mendieta, Gaizka 246
Meridian 189
Merseyside 73, 74, 78, 81, 84, 102, 185,
    238, 240
Merson, Paul 138
Mexico 130
Middle East 41–2

Middlesbrough 235

Middlesbrough (football club) 124, 246

Milan (football team) 22, 151, 168, 171, 220, 228, 259, 261

Miller, Alex 155

Miller, Joe 164

Miller, Paul 63, 97

Miller, Willie 128

Millwall (football club) 66

Milosevic, Savo 201

Molineux 47, 48, 52, 56, 57–8, 60, 62, 63, 65, 66, 71, 74, 75, 94, 143, 246

Monaco (football club) 220

Monday Night Football (TV programme) 207–8, 222–3, 225

Monroe, Marilyn 188

Montford, Arthur 182

Montgomerie, Colin 263

Montpellier 133

Moore, Bobby 219

Moore, Brian 189

Moores family 239

Moran, Kevin 106, 112

Morley, Tony 149

Mortimer, Dennis 31, 37, 41, 52, 250–1

Mortimer, Paul 195

Motherwell (football club) 16

Motson, John 189

Mountfield, Derek 79, 84, 98, 104, 108

Mourinho, Jose 206

Moyes, David 10

Muller, Gerd 8–9

Munich 101, 229

Murdoch, Bobby 263

Murdoch, Rupert 210

Murray, David 167

Murrays (Andy's maternal grandparents) 156–7, 159

Napoleon Bonaparte 174

Narey, Dave 7

National Football League (NFL) 184, 216

Needham, David 55

Neef, Gerry 21, 22

Neeskens, Johan 42

Netherlands 100

Neville, Gary 107–8

Newcastle United 2, 10, 31, 76, 91, 117, 159, 207, 229–30, 235

Nicholas, Charles 130

Nicholl, Chris 35

Nicklaus, Jack 14

Ninian Park, Cardiff 127–9

Nisbet, Scott 177

Nistelrooy, Ruud van 31, 36, 251

Noades, Ron 211

North Africa 200

North American Soccer League 22

Northern Ireland (football team) 124

Norway (football team) 121

Norwich City 11, 26, 66, 75, 176

Nottingham Forest 17, 22, 43, 48, 52, 53–6, 57, 71, 75, 84, 140, 143, 145, 146, 167, 170, 214–15, 235, 245

Notts County 82

Nunes 81

Okocha, Jay Jay 246

Old Firm 17, 161, 170–1

Old Trafford 7, 10, 28, 40, 58, 64, 75, 86, 123, 143, 148, 164, 168, 192–3, 196, 209, 220, 235, 248, 251, 252–3

O'Leary, David 142, 201, 202, 207

OnDigital 211

Ondrus, Anton v, 36, 114, 115–16

O'Neill, Martin 55–6, 170

Ormond, Willie 10, 114, 116, 119–20

Outer Hebrides 153, 156–9

Owen, Michael 3, 132

Oxford United 76

Ozzy (Andy's cat) 262

Paisley, Bob 164, 169, 207
Palmer, Carlton 149
Pandiani 228
Panenka, Antonin 104
Paris St Germain 168
Park Foods 238
Parkes, Phil 239
Parkhead 165, 170
Parkin, Derek 56
Parrott, John 93
Parry, Alan 132–3
Partick Thistle 25
Partridge, Pat 259
Paton, Brian 155
Pearce, Stuart 235
Pearson, Stephen 132
Pele 80, 92, 135
Peterborough (football club) 66
Pettigrew, Willie 16
Pfaff, Jean-Marie 102
Pflugler 102
Philadelphia Eagles 261
Phillips, David 129
Pittodrie 114, 178
Point 158
Pom (Andy's cat) 262
Port Vale (football club) 80
Portsmouth (football club) 26
Portugal 150
Portugal (football team) 121, 124, 126
Prague 36, 38, 115, 121
Premiership vi, 28, 31, 59, 110, 117, 160,
    170–1, 201, 207, 211, 212, 214–15,
    219, 227, 232, 233, 244, 245, 248,
    253, 254, 255, 261
Premiership Plus pay-per-view 233
Preston 71
Price, Paul 85
Professional Footballers' Association (PFA)
    16, 33–5, 39, 65, 84, 117
PSV Eindhoven 23, 62

Queens Park Rangers (QPR) 60, 89, 98
Question of Sport, A (TV programme)
    93–4, 175

Radio Five Live 134
Radio One 157
Raith Rovers 25, 164
Ranieri, Claudio 206
Ranson, Ray 202
Rapid Vienna 104–5
Ratcliffe, Kevin 11, 79, 80, 102, 108, 109,
    128
Raul 21
Real Madrid 13, 21, 151, 259, 261
Real Sociedad 204
Redknapp, Harry 132
Regis, Cyrille 148, 204
Reid, Mike 78
Reid, Peter ('Inchy') 60, 78–9, 84, 85, 87,
    93, 94, 97, 98, 102–3, 106, 108–9
Republic of Ireland (football team)
    134–5, 193
Revie, Don 1, 41, 57
Reykjavik 127
Reynolds Arena 58
Riazor Stadium 228
Rice, Pat 248, 249
Richards, John 50, 54, 56, 71
Richardson, Kevin 87, 195
Riley, George 85, 149
Rioch, Bruce 115
Roberts, Dave 133
Roberts, Graham 98, 171–2
Robertson, John 53, 125
Robson, Sir Bobby 63, 124, 237, 244
Robson, Bryan 148
Robson, John 41
Rocky (Andy's dog) 262
Roker Park 94
Rolland, Andy ('the Major') 9
Roma (football club) 18

Romania (football team) 115
Ronaldo 21
Rooney, Wayne 10, 16
Rossi, Paolo 51
Rotherham (football club) 66
Rotterdam 112
Rough, Alan 121, 128, 130
Rous Cup 126
Roxburgh, Andy 131
Royle, Joe 237
Rush, Ian 128

St Andrews 27, 46, 76, 139, 145–6, 149,
    150, 246
St James' Park 2, 90, 159–60
St John, Ian 78, 130, 183
St John's Wood 240
St Johnstone (football club) 25, 175
St Mirren (football club) 179
Saints (Southampton) 60, 83, 205, 208
    see also Southampton (football club)
Sampdoria (football club) 166–7
Santiago Bernabeu 21
Saunders, Ron 6, 25, 26–7, 28, 31, 50,
    138, 148, 250
    clashes with Andy 32–5, 36–7, 39, 40,
        41–3, 44–6, 47–8, 49, 52, 116–17,
        134
    controlling nature 35–6
    fear of flying 29–30
    on training 26–7
Schalke 21, 22–3, 24
Schmeichel, Peter 7, 70, 228
Scholes, Paul 132
Schumacher, Michael 232
Scolari, Felipe 135
Scotland (football team) 7, 10, 36, 52,
    100, 114–32, 182–3, 229
Scotland Schoolboys 155
Scotland U-23 side 16, 115
Scottish Amateur Youth 156

Scottish Cup 12–13, 163–4
Scottish Daily Express (newspaper) 10
Scottish First Division 17
Scottish Football Association (SFA) 132
Scottish Juveniles 156
Scottish League 7, 131, 154, 158, 168–71
Scottish League Cup 18
Scottish Premier League (SPL) 49, 166,
    168–71, 177
Scottish Professional Youth 2–3
Scottish Television (STV) 182
Seaman, David 70
Second Division 35, 63, 68, 138, 149
Seoul 135
Serie A (Italian football) 184, 228
Shamen 217
Shankly, Bill 27, 50, 58, 122, 207
Sharp, Graeme 78, 82–3, 85, 89–91, 94,
    95, 96, 98, 102, 105, 106, 109, 112,
    122–3, 126, 127, 130
Shaw, Gary 139–40, 263
Shawfield Stadium, Clyde 3
Shearer, Alan 2, 31, 97, 160
Sheedy, Kevin 5, 82–3, 87, 95, 103–4,
    105, 108, 109
Sheffield United 80, 243
Sheffield Wednesday 103, 110, 186, 203,
    204
Sheringham, Teddy 31, 215
Sherpa Van Trophy Final 189
Sherwood, Steve 85–6
Shilton, Peter 29, 54, 55, 60
Shizuoka 135
Shot at Glory (film) 175–6
Shreeves, Geoff 227
Shrewsbury (football club) 66, 82, 140
Simeone, Diego v, 116
Simpson, Neil 178
Skol Cup 176–7, 178–9
Sky v, vi, vii, 2, 38, 59, 132, 139, 160,
    168, 185, 187, 209–12, 214, 215,

INDEX

Sky (*cont.*)
218, 221–3, 225, 227, 229, 230, 233, 237–43, 247, 251–4, 259, 261, 262
see also British Sky Broadcasting (BSB); BSkyB
Sky News 254
Sky Sports 185, 215, 234, 254, 259
Sky Sports News 227
Sky Strikers cheerleaders 216
Small, Bryan 6–7
Smith, Alex 19
Smith, Dougie 7
Smith, Gordon 31
Smith, Tommy 50, 109
Smith, Walter 7–8, 132, 172
Solano, Noberto 117
Sonia 217
Souness, Graeme 9, 23, 108, 125, 129, 130, 151, 152–3, 163–5, 166–7, 168–9, 170, 171–4, 176–7, 178–9, 181
South Africa 92
Southall, Neville 79, 80–1, 82–4, 85, 97, 98, 108, 128, 129
Southampton (football club) 2, 60, 82, 83–4, 94, 143, 204, 207–8, 217
see also Dell, Southampton; Saints (Southampton)
Spackman, Nigel 176
Spain 126, 127, 228, 238, 239, 240
Spain (football team) 127, 135
Sparks (charity) 189
Speedie, David 51, 129
Spink, Nigel 139
Stainrod, Simon 89, 140
Stanley Park 89
Stein, Colin 8, 146, 159, 160
Stein, Jock 13, 121–4, 125, 126, 127, 128–30, 131, 165–6
Stelling, Jeff 227

Steven, Trevor 85–6, 87, 96, 98, 102, 105, 108, 170
Stevens, Gary 108, 109, 164, 168
Stewart, Ray 53
Stoke City 61, 64, 67, 76–7, 84
Stornoway 156, 158
Sturrock, Paul 7, 126
Stuttgart (football club) 260–1
Sun (newspaper) 37, 88
Sunderland (football club) 87, 95, 97, 145, 175, 206, 244
Super Sunday (TV programme) 232
SV Hamburg 23
Swain, Kenny 149
Sweden 66–7
Sweden (football team) 123–4, 126
Swift, Frank 200
Swindon (football team) 219–20
Switzerland (football team) 115

Talbot, Brian 149
Talksport 132–3, 225
Tannadice 1, 2, 5, 7, 9, 16, 20, 24, 26, 172, 174, 175
Tarrant, Chris 188
'Tartan XI' squad 131
Taylor, Graham 137–9, 148, 193, 201
Taylor, Jack 259
Taylor Report 59
Tayside 16
Teale, Shaun 195
Teddy (Andy's dog) 262
Telford (football club) 95, 96
Terry, Steve 85, 86
Third Division 141
Thomas, Bob 129
Thomas, Clive 258–9
Thomas, Dave 60, 62, 85
Thompson, Alan 169
Thompson, Garry 140
Tiffany's nightclub, Tayside 16–17

INDEX

Todd, Colin 146
Torino (football club) 22
Toronto 127
Toshack, John 31, 159
Tottenham Hotspurs 10, 49, 62–3, 94,
    97–8, 117, 171, 208, 216, 217, 237,
    247
Towner, Tony 66–7, 68
Tranmere Rovers 79, 239
Tunisia (football team) 133
Turf Moor side 85
Turkey (football team) 256
Turner, Graham 112, 140, 141–3, 146,
    147
Tyler, Martin (the Voice) 96, 139, 185,
    189–90, 191, 214, 223–5, 226, 228,
    233, 251–2
Tyne Tees TV 69

UEFA 170–1
UEFA Cup 52, 124, 138
    1974 21
    1978 42
    1987 18
University College Dublin 98
Upton Park 143
Ure, Ian 7

Valley 68, 227
Vassell, Darius 30
Venison, Barry 235
Vicarage Road 138
Victoria Ground 76
Vieira, Patrick 3
Vienna 119
Villa Park 24, 29, 30, 39, 42, 44, 45, 50,
    113, 116, 138, 139, 140, 143, 146,
    147, 150, 186, 194, 195, 199, 202,
    203, 213, 228, 243, 246, 248, 250–1
Villa, Ricardo 62
Vogts, Berti 132

Wakeling, Vic 217–18
Wales (football team) 124, 127–9
Walker, Jim 193–4
Walker, Murray 232
Wallace, Jock 152
Wallace, Rod 31
Walters, Mark 167, 176–8
Watford (football club) 26, 85–6, 119,
    138–9, 149
Watson, Dave 145, 237
Webb, David 143
Wembley 32, 53, 54, 80, 85, 105–6, 112,
    125, 206, 229
Wenger, Arsene 107, 141, 220, 248–9,
    252, 254–5
West Bromwich Albion vi, 118, 148–51,
    152, 173, 182, 194
    see also Hawthorns
West Ham (football club) 53, 227,
    249–51
Whaddon Road 195
White Hart Lane 97
White, Peter 42
Whiteside, Norman 106, 192–3
Who Wants to Be A Millionaire (TV
    programme) 187–9
Whyte, Chris 149
Wilkins, Ray 163–4, 167, 168
Wilkinson, Howard 57, 103, 244
Wilkinson, Paul 110
Willis, Peter 106
Wilson, Bob 126
Wimbledon (football club) 190
Wirral 238, 243
Wolverhampton Wanderers vi, 27, 34,
    47–58, 60–72, 74, 75, 76, 121, 124,
    125, 140, 143, 158–9, 164, 195,
    250–1
    financial crisis 57–8, 60, 63, 64–5, 68
    see also Molineux
Woods, Chris 167, 170, 204

INDEX

Woods, Tiger 14
Woosnam, Ian 262–3
World Cup v, 114, 115, 118, 119, 130,
132, 182–3, 258
1970 8, 215
1974 10, 119
1982 7, 124, 125, 126, 127, 189
2002 193
World Cup qualifiers, 1981 123
Wright, Billy 57
Wright, Ian 221–2

Wycombe Wanderers 141, 190
Wylie, Ron 146

Yashin, Lev 71
Yeovil (football club) 26
Yorke, Dwight 31, 172
Yorkshire TV 66
Young, Alex 79
Young, Willie 143

Zidane, Zinedine 8, 21, 245